FINANCIAL SECTOR OF THE AMERICAN ECONOMY

edited by

STUART BRUCHEY
UNIVERSITY OF MAINE

A GARLAND SERIES

CONTESTABLE MARKETS THEORY, COMPETITION, AND THE UNITED STATES COMMERCIAL BANKING INDUSTRY

ROSS N. DICKENS

Routledge
Taylor & Francis Group

LONDON AND NEW YORK

First published 1996 by Garland Publishing, Inc.

Published 2019 by Routledge
2 Park Square, Milton Park, Abingdon, Oxon OX14 4RN
52 Vanderbilt Avenue, New York, NY 10017

First issued in paperback 2019

Routledge is an imprint of the Taylor & Francis Group, an informa business

Library of Congress Cataloging-in-Publication Data

Dickens, Ross N., 1961–
  Contestable markets theory, competition, and the United
States commercial banking industry / Ross N. Dickens.
    p.   cm. — (Financial Sector of the American Economy)
  Includes bibliographical references and index.
  ISBN 0-8153-2390-5 (alk. paper)
  1. Banks and banking—Deregulation—United States.
  2. Competition. I. Title. II. Series.
HG2491.D53   1996
332.1'0973—dc20   95-52164

ISBN 13: 978-1-138-86382-8 (pbk)
ISBN 13: 978-0-8153-2390-7 (hbk)

This book is dedicated to

Robin Schrohenloher Dickens

October 16, 1961 - May 4, 1995

CONTENTS

LIST OF TABLES

LIST OF FIGURES

ACKNOWLEDGMENTS

I would like to thank Drs. George Philippatos, Harold Black, Jean Gauger, and James Wansley for their assistance and comments. Thanks also to the Louisiana Tech College of Administration and Business Research Division for technical support (especially to Annette Shows).

PREFACE

The focus of this work is to investigate the changing nature of competition in the United States' commercial banking industry from 1973-1988 by examining earnings from individual products. The industry underwent tremendous changes during this period. The most important changes arguably came with the passage of the Depository Institutions Deregulation and Monetary Control Act of 1980 (DIDMCA). Not only was the underlying cost structure from the preceding forty plus years completely altered by the phase out of the Federal Reserve's Regulation Q (which regulates the interest rate banks may pay on deposit accounts), but banks also had to contend with new competitors (S&Ls, mutual savings banks, and credit unions) in product areas that traditionally had been the province of banks (most notably checking accounts).

The "tool" used to investigate this issue is the Contestable Markets Theory (CMT) set forth by Baumol (1982) and Baumol, Panzar, and Willig (1982) which is discussed at length in Chapter 1.[1] Put simply, CMT's framework is used to explain how commercial bank's behavior (and profits) could change as other competitors are allowed to enter banks' traditional product areas. Much of the content of this work explains the complicating factors making measurement difficult and the methods to control for these factors (when possible).

The issues examined in this work are from the commercial banking industry of the 1980s, but are very applicable to 1995 and the future as Congress contemplates legislation that would overturn the Banking Act of 1933's (better known as Glass-Steagall) separation of commercial and investment banking. The same process of potential competition with thrifts' (S&Ls, mutual savings banks, and credits unions) entering traditional commercial banking product areas that existed in the 1980s would be repeated if commercial banks enter traditional investment banking markets areas.

---

[1] A current example of Contestable Markets Theory's use in the commercial banking field is Devaney, M. and B. Weber, "Local Characteristics, Contestability, and the Dynamic Structure of Rural Banking," *The Quarterly Review of Economics and Finance*, 271-287, Volume 35, 3 (Fall), 1995.

Congress is also considering, but is less likely to pass, legislation that would allow commercial banks greater inroads into the insurance industry. The passage of such legislation would create another situation similar to the environment in banking in the 1970s and 1980s.

However, the most concrete area of change since the end of this work's study period (1988) that relates to the usage of ideas expressed in this work is the adoption of the Riegle-Neal Interstate Banking and Branching Efficiency Act (signed by President Clinton in September, 1994). The act allows full interstate banking as of the end of September, 1995. As such, Bank Holding Companies (BHCs) will be able to buy a bank in any of the fifty states.

At first, banks in different states must be operated as separate institutions by the BHC. However, full interstate branching will be allowed in June, 1997 (unless individual states choose not to participate or "opt out" or they could "opt in" earlier). At that time, a BHC could combine all of its different banks into one bank and operate all locations as branches of one bank.

As such, one can expect a decrease in the number of banks that will exist in the U.S. over the next decade. In the traditional structure-conduct-performance (SCP) model of economics, the fewer the competitors, the higher the price charged for a given product. Hence, this legislation would be considered contrary to consumers' interests under the SCP model.

However, few analysts predict such economic profits for the envisioned banking environment. While the SCP model does not explain this expectation, CMT can. As long as there is one potential competitor that is a viable threat to enter a given banking market, CMT predicts that the existing firm(s) in the market will not earn economic profits.

Given the Justice Department's allowance of numerous bank mergers in the 1990s that arguably would not have occurred because of antitrust concerns in earlier periods (such as the Chemical Bank and Chase Manhattan merger of August,1995), it seems evident that the ideas underlying CMT are being used in the government's economic policies. As such, the implications of this study's argument—that potential entry can thwart excess profits—seem to be in use today.

Contestable Markets Theory, Competition, and the United States Banking Industry

I

Contestable Markets Theory and Commercial Banking

INTRODUCTION

The commercial banking industry has been one of the more heavily regulated in the United States. Yet, since 1980 the industry has been eased slowly, but effectively, into a less regulated environment. Hence, the welfare effects of this recent deregulation could provide evidence as to whether additional changes would be helpful to consumers.

One way to examine the beneficial market effects of deregulation is to utilize the Theory of Contestable Markets (CMT) as set forth in Baumol (1982) and Baumol, Panzar, and Willig (1982). Originally, CMT was developed as a way to explain why industry structures other than perfectly competitive may be optimal. The basis of the theory is that no industry can earn economic profits for an extended period unless other potential sellers, willing to charge lower prices, are blocked from entering the industry. To block new entries (or threats of such entries), the incumbent firms would need to price their products and services at a level that would discourage new competition.

CMT has received considerable attention in the economics literature. However, most of the attention has been devoted to non-empirical discussions of the assumptions [Baumol (1982), Baumol, Panzar, and Willig (1982)], the robustness [Schwartz and Reynolds (1983), Baumol and Willig (1986), and Schwartz (1986)], or the empirical plausibility of the theory [Dixit (1982), Bailey and Baumol (1984), Shepherd (1984), and Schwartz (1986)]. Most of the empirical work that has been published is centered on the airline industry [Bailey and Panzar (1981), Call and Keeler (1985), and Morrison and Winston

(1987)], as it was represented as an ideal candidate for testing CMT implications by Bailey and Baumol (1984). Baumol and Willig (1986) discuss how the theory may be used in examining the banking industry.[1]

Perfect contestability is the ideal benchmark of CMT. In this case, the incumbent's price, p, would be equal to the price found in a market with perfect competition, p_c. In an imperfectly contestable market, p_c < p < p_m. Where p_m is the monopoly price. Of course, p_c < p < p_m would also hold in an industry with more than one seller, but in which sellers were not atomistic. The disciplining force for CMT is the threat of entry and not the existence of current competitors. This expectational framework is another difference from the traditional structure-conduct-performance (SCP) model and will be discussed further below.

Hit-and-run entry is the focus of perfect contestability. The threat of a potential entrant to underprice the incumbent, obtain a large portion of the business, and exit before the incumbent can react leads the incumbent to set price at p = p_c.[2] Imperfect contestability can result if there were a lag in the exit period or if sunk costs were not completely recoverable. Both of these conditions make hit-and-run entry more difficult and, thus, provide some pricing power to the incumbents.

Another possibility is hit-and-stay entry in which the entrant would not be able to recover a sufficient amount of sunk costs on exit to make hit-and-run entry a better alternative. The cost of entry is justified when the entrant can underprice the incumbent and earn enough economic profit to cover the entry cost before the incumbent is able to react. After the incumbent reacts, the new entrant stays in the market at the new, lower price. If hit-and-stay entry were optimal, the incumbent's price would be in the range for an imperfectly contestable market. It is not anticipated that the commercial banking industry in the U.S. will be found to be perfectly contestable—before or after the deregulatory legislation of the 1980s as perfect contestability is an ideal condition which does not exist. Also, the test period (1973-1988) shows evidence of both threats of entry and actual entry into newly allowed product and geographic areas. Thus, evidence supporting imperfectly contestable markets as well as the traditional SCP model (the more competitors the closer p is to p_c) is expected. The tests presented later do not attempt to prove or disprove that CMT holds, but to provide empirical evidence to support or refute its predictions.

It is misguided to compare CMT and the traditional SCP model as if they were competing hypotheses. CMT is a more general theory that includes perfect competition as one of its specific forms. Perfect contestability depends on a rational expectations framework with information allocation efficiency—a before-the-event type knowledge. Perfect competition relies on asset allocation efficiency—a bookkeeping or after-the-fact type knowledge. Therefore, the interpretations of the results of this paper do not categorize results as supporting one theory as opposed to the other, but point out how they are in agreement with predictions of either or both forms of theory.

The major innovation of this paper is applying CMT to the U.S. banking industry at a level other than examining the entire firm. The assumptions of CMT, discussed below as they relate to banking, do not hold well at the firm level since entry and exit are severely circumscribed by regulation. It is possible to work around this problem by recognizing that "entry" and "exit" by means of altering prices can occur.

However, problems arise if a portfolio of products is examined. First, it would be difficult to define the appropriate portfolio. Second, once the portfolio is chosen, the question arises as to which competitors to include. Credit unions, savings and loans, mutual savings banks, and/or finance companies could all be included if certain portfolios were chosen.

Indeed, the possibility of examining levels other than entire product portfolios is raised by Berger, Hanweck, and Humphrey (1987). In examining economies of scope in banking, they note that a "multi-product banking firm is competitively viable if no other set of firms with different scales and/or product mixes could jointly produce the same mix at lower (scale-adjusted) cost" (p. 501).

This suggestion can be reduced to an even more elementary level concerning a single product. A product should only be offered if no other producer can offer it at a lower price. Bailey and Baumol (1984), in a similar manner, state that "even if exit from the industry as a whole is difficult, mobility of capital may permit easy and rapid entry into and exit from particular markets in that industry" (p. 114). Finally, Davies and Lee (1988) state that the entry of a single product into a specific market does not mean that the entrant is burdened by high fixed costs if that firm is a multiproduct producer. Therefore, the tests conducted in this study that are thought to be more likely to provide greater supporting evidence for CMT's predictions are those examining individual products and not those examining some subset portfolio or the entire banking firm.

If individual products and services were examined instead of the output of the firm as a whole, then banks have more competition for individual products, such as checkable deposits or automobile loans, than from just other banks. Competition comes from any other provider of that product. Considering each product or service individually allows an examination of the competition for customers in a setting conducive for the use of CMT which, at its most elementary form, is based on single product firms.

The financial product innovations and regulatory changes (the Depository Institutions Deregulation and Monetary Control Act of 1980 [DIDMCA] and the Garn-St Germain Act of 1982) of the late 1970s and early 1980s provide an excellent period of competitive change to apply CMT to commercial banking products in the U.S. That is, if commercial banks were earning economic profits because they held a virtual monopoly on a product such as demand deposits, then the economic profits should cease as other institutions are allowed to offer that product or similar products (e.g. checkable deposits).

Schwartz (1986) states that "perhaps the most direct test of whether the threat of entry affects price is to consider situations where potential entrants' costs are reduced by an exogenous structural change such as the removal of a tariff or the expiration of a patent. If incumbents' price is not affected by a change unless actual entry occurs, the inference is of noncontestability" (p. 50). Product innovations and regulatory change provide just such a new competitive arena. If commercial banks were earning economic profits based on barriers to entry (or were expected to earn such profits in the future), those (expected future) profits should decline as others were allowed to offer the same products. A decline before entry is consistent with contestable markets theory while a decline after entry is more in line with the traditional SCP model.[3]

APPLICATION OF CONTESTABLE MARKETS THEORY TO COMMERCIAL BANKING

This paper examines commercial banking products and services using CMT as set forth in Baumol (1982) and Baumol, Panzar, and Willig (1982). Bailey and Baumol (1984) state that "neither large size nor fewness of firms necessarily means that markets need function unsatisfactorily" (p. 111). To avoid new entrants, the incumbent firms would need to price their products and services at levels that would discourage new competition.

The assumptions for a single product firm are applicable to the banking industry under special conditions.

1- Entry into and exit from the industry are free.[4] (This ease of entry and exit does not mean costless movement.)
2- There are no sunk costs (or any fixed costs are recoverable on exit from the industry—except in the case of hit-and-stay entry as discussed above).
3- New entrants enjoy the same cost structure as incumbents because they both have access to the same technology and efficiency levels, meaning that there is no cost disadvantage to potential entrants.
4- Output is homogeneous in nature.
5- There is a contracting period such that incumbent firms have a lag in their response to market changes.
6- Consumers react more quickly to market changes than incumbent firms.

While the assumptions of CMT do not hold completely for the establishment of a bank or even a branch office, they are satisfied fairly well when individual products and services are considered.

Each assumption will be discussed below as it relates to the United States commercial banking industry. However, first, a brief discussion follows as to the necessity of each assumption. As CMT was presented by Baumol, Panzar, and Willig (1982), the only assumptions included were the second and third which led to the freedom of entry and exit (the first) assumption. Brock (1983) includes the fifth and sixth assumptions in his review article. Bailey and Baumol (1984) reacted that the fifth and sixth assumptions were not needed, but do facilitate the use of the theory. The homogenous output assumption is required such that two products can be truly competitive or product differentiation could allow different optimal market prices for the two goods.

CMT is far from being universally accepted as an improvement over the traditional SCP model. Shepherd (1984), in a very critical work, states that CMT allows internal conditions (degree of competition and any monopoly powers of firms already in the market) to be outweighed by external conditions (potential new entrants). Brock (1983) holds that costlessly reversible entry requires incumbents to be sluggish to react to price changes from new entrants when the incumbents livelihood depends on quick reactions. He labels this situation as implausible unless some force restrains the incumbents. Davies and Lee (1988) relate that entry as market discipline dates back at least to J.B. Clark (1912) and has had other more recent supporters as well. They also report that another large problem with CMT is that as the requirements for perfect contestability are violated, there is no continuous function to predict the degree of deviation caused by the violation. Even Baumol and Willig (1986) report that studies of the airline industry have not shown CMT holding as well as expected.

However, CMT does add to the body of knowledge by developing arguments as to why market structures other than perfectly competitive ones may be optimal when the perfect competition assumption of producer size is violated. The first problem in using this theory to examine the U.S. commercial banking industry is to identify the proper competitive level and product set for which the assumptions hold well enough to justify its use. The framework for the study could be commercial banks or commercial banks along with other deposit taking financial institutions.[5] Each product could be examined separately or in the context of a portfolio. If it were deemed proper to examine the products in a portfolio context, the question arises as to which product combination would constitute the appropriate portfolio. The answer to these issues would determine what entry and exit situations need to be addressed. The following possible categories will be addressed below: 1) the entire portfolio of products and services of commercial banks, 2) some portfolio that is a subset of all products and services, and 3) individual products and services.

Entire Portfolio

Nathan's (1988) study on the Canadian commercial banking industry provides support for the possibility of using the entire portfolio. However, the regulatory environment is basically different in Canada such that the application of CMT may differ greatly in the two countries.[6] Hanweck and Rhoades (1984) point out that the commercial banking industry in the U.S. has firms that are relatively homogeneous in that they offer the same basic services, are subject to similar cost conditions, and are subject to the same general demand and supply conditions. These conditions will satisfy some of the basic assumptions of CMT. Another possible support for using CMT on the entire portfolio comes from the results of Smirlock (1985). He reports that there is no relationship between concentration measures and profits, if market share is considered. CMT would generally predict such a result. If the industry classification for this study is to be the entire portfolio of products of U.S. commercial banks, then entry into and exit from commercial banking are severely circumscribed by regulation.

Entry at the Banking Level. Entry at the banking level is possible through three venues: 1) a new bank charter (*de novo* entry); 2) a new branch (*de novo* branching); or 3) the purchase of an existing office or charter (via branch acquisition or merger with another bank).

The United States has a dual chartering system for new banks. Therefore, for *de novo* entry, the prospective managers must choose between a national or state charter. To obtain a national charter, the approval of the Office of the Comptroller of the Currency (OCC) must be received. State charters are granted by the corresponding state regulatory agency in all fifty states. In addition, national banks must be approved by the Federal Deposit Insurance Corporation (FDIC), and most state chartered banks are required to obtain FDIC certification as well.

De novo entry provides another problem in that the number of new entrants allowed has varied greatly over time. Rose (1986) relates that the number of new entrants varied from 79 in 1968, to 360 in 1974, down to 145 in 1978, and up to 202 in 1980. Accounting for such differences would be difficult.[7]

De novo branching also requires the approval of state authorities along with the possibility of approval from the OCC and FDIC. However, the United States does not have a uniform bank branching law. Instead, each state has its own laws concerning the abilities of banks to branch within its geographic borders. There are three main divisions of branch banking: unit, limited, and statewide. Unit banking states do not allow banks to operate more than one office in their states.[8] Limited branching states allow some branching, but the number of branches or the geographic area is circumscribed. The usual geographic boundary is a county, however, the laws can vary greatly from state to state. Statewide branching states allow banks to open branches anywhere throughout the state. As of 1988, twenty-seven states had statewide branching, nineteen had limited branching, and four were unit banking states (FDIC *Banks & Branches Data Book* 1989).

Each one of these classification systems has important effects on the level of competition. In general, the greater the restriction on branching, the less the level of competition (if only commercial banks are being considered). Under economic market structure theory (fewer competitors mean less efficient resource use), banks in unit banking states should earn economic profits while those banks in heavily branched areas should earn lower or no economic profits. However, a classification such as: "banks in unit banking states should earn more than banks in limited branching which should earn more than banks in statewide branching states" is not possible. The laws of limited branching states vary so much that some of them are almost unit banking states while others are almost unlimited branching states. The differences in the laws further complicates the comparison of the three.

Entry via the purchase of an existing branch from another institution or the purchase of another institution also involves regulatory approval. Approval may be needed from the state banking authority, the OCC, FDIC, and the Justice Department. The Security and Exchange Commission (SEC) will also be involved if the purchase involves the issue of new securities or the buying of the stock of the acquired bank.

Exit at the Banking Level. Exit at the banking level could come from failure or selling the firm. However, neither of these two forms of exit is particularly easy in banking given the underlying regulatory system. Banks that could fail are closely monitored by regulators. While some of this attention could come from a desire by the regulators to prevent the failure of one bank from harming others, most of the attention derives from the existence of deposit insurance. The FDIC (the usual insuring agency) closely monitors possible failing banks to minimize its potential costs from having to pay off the insured deposits of failed banks. Such monitoring may eliminate some bank failures.

Exit via selling is also difficult given the need for the parties involved to obtain the approval of the regulatory authorities. A bank's management can not decide that banking is no longer as profitable as expected and proceed to sell to the highest bidder in a short period of time. Their decision will first have to generate offers and the appropriate filings for regulatory approval. Such delays may discourage management from selling at times that they otherwise would consider appropriate.

Portfolio Examination

The most complete manner to investigate commercial banking products would be in terms of the portfolio of products offered. Such a description opens up the possible competitors to include nonchartered firms as well as other depository and financial institutions. Murray and White (1983) find economies of scope in Canadian credit unions (which have balance sheets similar to U.S. savings and loans' balance sheets) and provide indirect evidence that banks would also benefit from such cost complementarities. This finding suggests that the portfolio of products should be considered.

However, many problems arise if a portfolio approach were taken such that a portfolio of products were examined. First, it would be difficult to define the products to place in the portfolio. For example, all deposit accounts could be included or just transactions accounts. All loans could be considered or just personal loans. Second, once the choice of the products is made, then the problem becomes what companies should be included in the study. Money center, regional, and rural banks could be included in the same study if certain portfolios of products were deemed appropriate given that these banks have very different portfolios as a general rule. Credit unions, savings and loans

(S&Ls), mutual savings banks, and/or finance companies could also be included in the study, if certain types of portfolios were chosen. Given that all depository institutions could be included if a particular portfolio were chosen, it would seem that an argument could be made for including all depository institutions. However, it is difficult to consider seriously the entry of a small credit union having an effect on the price of a product offered by a money center bank.[9] A third difficulty using a portfolio is the existence of loss-leader products. These products are often used to gain market share which would bring erosion of earnings for strategic reasons. This study assumes that the goal of the firm is to maximize profits in the current period and so does not attempt to explain behavior that leads to less than maximum profits.

Individual Products

The possibility of examining levels other than entire product portfolios is raised by Berger, Hanweck, and Humphrey (1987) and, along with the statements of Bailey and Baumol (1984) and Davies and Lee (1988) presented above, supports the idea that CMT can be used to study a single product entry process. As such, the first portion of this study examines individual products and not a portfolio or subset portfolio of the entire banking firm.

If individual products and services were examined instead of the output of the firm as a whole, then banks have more competition for individual products, such as demand deposits or automobile loans, than just other banks. Depending on the product, competition comes from S&Ls, credit unions, finance companies, money market mutual funds, major retailers, and/or the commercial paper market. Considering each product or service individually allows an examination of the competition for customers in a setting conducive for the use of CMT which, at its most elementary form, is based on single product firms.[10]

A very real concern is that a depository institution could not truly compete unless it had a complete range of financial products and services to offer. However, the focal point of this discussion is that it is possible for a firm's pricing to be such that another firm with the same cost structure can underprice the incumbent firm if entrance to the market were gained. This point is true even if the new firm were a one product firm. Elliehausen and Wolken's (1986) results support the idea that competition is found in some, but not all products on an interinstitutional basis. They find that commercial banks, S&Ls, and credit unions are substitutable sources for residential mortgages; commercial banks, S&Ls, and finance companies are substitutable sources for personal loans; and that commercial banks and S&Ls are substitutable sources for automobile loans.

Nonchartered firms and Bank Holding Companies. Possible competitors for portions of the portfolio or for individual products of a commercial bank are nonchartered firms and companies that are owned by bank holding companies. (For instance, a finance company owned by a bank.) Their actions can be examined in the same way as the allowance of new products by regulated firms. However, to predict their effects on market variables, their actions would need to be identified. Their existence should not greatly alter the examination of individual products.

DISCUSSION OF THEORY ASSUMPTIONS FOR INDIVIDUAL PRODUCTS

While the assumptions of CMT do not hold perfectly for the establishment of a bank or even a branch office, they are satisfied fairly well when individual products and services are considered.

Entry and Exit

It is possible to enter and exit quickly from areas such as automobile loans, credit cards, and deposit accounts. For example, increasing the quantity of credit cards outstanding generally requires a mass mailing with pre-approved credit limits. Any financial services firm could enter the credit card lending business if it had a current mailing list of potential customers or it could even buy such a mailing list. Exit has also been manifested by banks selling their portfolios as shown by the examples listed in Table 1.1.

Table 1.1: Credit Card Account Sales from 1984-1990*

Seller (Buyer)	Outstanding Balances (in millions)	Date
Continental Bank (Chemical Bank)	$824	April 1984
Texas American Bancshares (Republic Bank)	$50	December 1986
Beneficial National Bank (First Chicago)	$1,100	December 1986
National Bancshares Texas (Lomas & Nettleton)	$41	February 1987
Louisiana Bancshares (Lomas & Nettleton)	$157	April 1987
Avco National Bank (Household Bank)	$322	May 1987
Bank of Mid-America (Lomas & Nettleton)	$120	July 1987
Colonial National Bank (Household Bank)	$317	July 1987
First RepublicBank Delaware (Citicorp)	$623	September 1988
Equibank (CoreStates Bank)	$100	November 1988

* Source: Ausebel, L.M. The Failure of Competition in the Credit Card Market. *The American Economic Review* March 1991, pp. 50-81.

Table 1.1: (cont.)

Seller (Buyer)	Outstanding Balances (in millions)	Date
Meritor Financial Group (Chase Manhattan)	$85	February 1989
Society for Savings Bancorp (First Chicago)	$230	March 1989
Michigan National Bank (Chase Manhattan)	$1,100	May 1989
Empire of America (Citicorp)	$650	May 1989
Colonial National Bank (Household Bank)	$98	June 1989
Leader Federal Savings (Chase Manhattan)	$36	July 1989
California Federal Bank (Chase Manhattan)	$125	August 1989
Chevy Chase Savings (CoreStates Bank)	$200	September 1989
Imperial Savings & Loan (Wells Fargo Bank)	$280	September 1989
Dreyfus Corp. (Bank of New York)	$790	September 1989
First City Bancorporation (Bank of New York)	$552	October 1989

Source: Ausebel, March 1991.

Table 1.1: (cont.)

Seller (Buyer)	Outstanding Balances (in millions)	Date
BankSouth (Society National)	$41	December 1989
Bank of Boston (Chase Manhattan)	$625	December 1989
Investors Savings Bank (Chase Manhattan)	$24	December 1989
Bank of New England (Citicorp)	$652	January 1990
Colonial National Bank (Household Bank)	$50	February 1990
Fleet/Norstar (Norwest)	$200	April 1990

Source: Ausebel, March 1991.

Problems are encountered if one were to consider the only potential competition for a bank as a new bank. First, the banking industry does not have freedom of entry and exit (especially given the regulatory process for entry and exit discussed earlier), and the cost to enter differs by state. The fact that states have different branching laws is *prima facia* evidence that entry and exit are not the same for all banking competitors. Even if all "monetary" entrance and exit costs were ignored, the "reputation capital" needed for entry is difficult to obtain and could be hurt badly by exit from the industry. Regulators might not approve further entries and exits if management had undertaken such actions in the past.[11] Thus, CMT's assumptions are more closely followed when examining individual products rather than the banking firm's portfolio of products as a whole.

However, scaling back operations could suffice for exit if reputational capital would be harmed by complete exit from the industry. A firm could "exit" the industry by charging higher than market clearing prices for its services. The higher cost will decrease the quantity demanded for its product and reduce its presence in that market. The firm could prevent the harming of its reputation with regulators, but no longer be as deeply involved in the industry. "Re-entry" could then be obtained simply by pricing the product at or below current market levels.

Sunk Costs

While entering any one of the products or services would involve a great deal of sunk costs if the new competitor were starting from scratch, a potential competitor (such as an S&L or credit union) with brick and mortar, employees, and processing equipment in place would have very little additional physical sunk costs if it were to offer a new product. This situation would make entry almost costless once regulatory approval for the product or service was received (as is the case after the deregulatory acts in 1980 and 1982).

Cost Structure

S&Ls, credit unions, and other potential competitors have access to equal quality computer equipment, buildings, and employees as banks. With the Depository Institutions Deregulation and Monetary Control Act (DIDMCA) of 1980, they were also able to gain access to the same clearing system operated by the Federal Reserve System. At that time, these institutions were brought into the reserve system of the Federal Reserve on virtually the same basis as banks.[12] [13] All these developments mean that banks, S&Ls, credit unions, and mutual savings banks should face approximately the same cost structure and technology levels (tax structures temporarily ignored). Kane (1984) points out that these firms have the same economies of scope from added products and the same subsidization through deposit insurance. Benston (1972) states that "commercial banks and savings and loans have just about the same cost structure with respect to size of operations" (p. 313) for trust services, safe deposit boxes, and deposits.[14]

S&Ls and credit unions do have certain tax benefits over banking firms which calls into question the issue of equal-cost structures.[15] However, banks have traditionally offset their disadvantage with the use of industrial revenue bonds that allowed them to make tax-free interest loans to commercial interests.[16] Overall, the assumption of equal cost for potential competitors is assumed to hold given technological similarities, the reduction of tax breaks set forth above, and the data source used for this study when comparing individual products which is discussed in Chapter 3 below.

Homogeneous Output

The products produced are certainly homogeneous in nature. All depository institutions provide two intermediary services: time intermediation and denomination intermediation. Time intermediation allows depositors to delay consumption until the future while allowing borrowers to consume more now than they otherwise would be able. Denomination intermediation is the process in which the depository institutions take in deposits denominated in small units and lend them to others in larger units. A deposit at any of these institutions provides these same basic services and the proceeds from loans are equally spendable by the borrower no matter where the funds are borrowed.

Contracting Period

A contracting period for the incumbent is present in certain areas given revolving credit agreements, lines of credit, and terms of account use. A new entrant could, therefore, enter the market and force the incumbent to react to the new, lower pricing structure it has introduced given that consumers could react more quickly than the incumbent.

Customer Reaction

The speed of consumer reaction is based on the level of price sensitivity for each product. Some products, such as a basic savings account, may be fairly price insensitive while others, such as automobile loans, may be much more price sensitive. The more price sensitive the product, the more likely that new competition will be successful in drawing away customers.

Contestability versus Competition

As mentioned above CMT and the traditional SCP model should not be considered competing hypotheses since CMT includes perfect competition as one of its forms. CMT should be viewed in an expectational framework. As expectations are always changing, tests results in exact agreement with CMT predictions would more likely mean an error in the testing procedures or data source than finding a situation in complete agreement with CMT.

Bailey and Baumol (1984) state that evidence to date suggests that the contestability benchmark does not hold fully in the first years after deregulation. However, as pointed out in Schwartz (1986) and Shepherd (1984), contestability does not hold unless pricing changes before entry are actually implemented. Schwartz also states that "while perfect contestability seems impossible to prove, imperfect contestability seems impossible to thoroughly disprove" (p. 48). Hence, the tests of this paper do not attempt to prove or disprove that CMT holds, but to provide empirical evidence to support or refute its predictions.

Products Examined

Applying CMT to banking units is more involved than just examining banks since other financial institutions also compete for the customers in the financial service markets in question. For instance, Boczar (1978) states that commercial banks and finance companies have overlapping customer bases for personal finance loans such that they are in direct competition with each other. The level of competition has increased over the last ten to fifteen years as the financial services industry has been deregulated (or re-regulated), as evidenced by the increase in product offerings allowed. These difficulties make it much more interesting to examine the effects of all competition on bank pricing and not just focus on the difference between branching laws. The difference in branching laws could then be used as another variable in the examination of pricing competition.

Possible tests could be made on any of the liabilities (deposits), assets (loans), or products (trust services) of banks. Tests could also be made as to the charge or payment for loans or deposits for the firms that participate in each area.

An examination of any type of deposit, loan, or service is possible. The most likely candidates would be:

> Deposits: checkable, savings, and time (non-negotiable CDs);
> Loans: installment (automobile), credit card, real estate, and commercial.

Checkable Deposits. The change in the area of checkable deposits is one of the most intriguing. Before 1972, only commercial banks were allowed to offer checkable deposits (in the form of demand deposits). This restriction, along with the necessity of the check clearing system, meant that banks did not have to worry greatly about possible competitors to this service. The barriers to entry, along with the existence of Regulation Q, should have made it possible for the banks to earn economic profits on the accounts.[17] However, based on CMT, changes in the banks' pricing behavior should be found with the innovation of NOW (Negotiable Order of Withdrawal) accounts. In

1972, savings banks in New Hampshire and Massachusetts were given permission to issue NOW accounts which paid explicit interest on demand deposit-like accounts. CMT would have commercial banks (the incumbent firms) reacting to this development by increasing the amount of implicit interest paid on checkable deposits to stem any further future competition. The spread of NOW accounts to all of New England in 1976, the ability of credit unions to offer share drafts since 1977 with approval from the National Credit Union Administration (NCUA), the passage of DIDMCA of 1980, which allowed financial institutions in the U.S. to issue NOW accounts, and the passage of the Garn-St Germain Act of 1982 which allowed Money Market Demand Accounts (MMDAs) are further actions taken by the regulatory agencies that should spur changes in banks' pricing behavior.

The result is that banks, S&Ls, and credit unions are now competing for checkable deposit accounts. This competition also includes brokerage houses offering money market mutual funds (MMMF).[18] These accounts were first offered in October 1972 and there were only four in existence by the end of 1973. They were originally set up to circumvent regulatory restrictions that raised the minimum Treasury bill noncompetitive bid from $1,000 to $10,000. They more closely resembled demand deposit accounts after limited check writing and credit card privileges were offered with the accounts. MMMFs grew slowly until 1977 at which point they grew from $3.9 billion to $230 billion by 1982. In response to banks' demands for a competitive account, the Garn-St Germain Act of 1982 allowed banks to issue MMDAs.[19]

Savings Deposits. Under Regulation Q, banks and S&Ls were limited in the amount of interest they could pay for regular savings deposits. Credit unions were not restricted by Regulation Q (officially credit unions pay dividends not interest on regular share accounts), but the rate that credit unions were allowed to pay was regulated by the NCUA. The rates allowed varied over time, but S&Ls were allowed to pay .25% more than banks. At the time of DIDMCA, banks paid 5.25%, S&Ls paid 5.5%, and credit unions paid 6%. However, with the phased removal of Regulation Q in the early and mid-eighties, all three institutions may now pay any rate desired. If market interest rates were high enough (as in the 1970s and early 1980s), it would be expected that each type of institution would be paying its maximum rate of explicit interest.[20] Only implicit interest payments could be used to equate the rates paid by each competitor if the Regulation Q limit had been reached. Brewer (1988) allows that S&Ls paid higher implicit rates above the explicit limit for savings accounts than they would if higher explicit rates were allowed.

Time Deposits. Financial institutions are, and have been, allowed to pay market rates for jumbo ($100,000 or more) certificates of deposit (CDs). In highly competitive markets, it would be expected that each institution would pay the current market rate that would approximate the appropriate maturity U.S. Treasury certificate. Because negotiable CDs are money market instruments that are bought and sold in an efficient national market, they are likely to have only slight differences in the rates paid between institutions.[21] Non-negotiable CDs, however, are much more likely to be affected by regional or local competition for funds.

Installment Loans. The specific type of installment loans to be considered will be automobile loans. Banks compete with finance companies (such as GMAC, Ford Motor Credit, and Chrysler Credit Corporation), credit unions, and S&Ls for this type loan. The pricing of these loans by banks should vary as S&Ls obtained the ability to make such loans and as finance companies change their positions.[22] In general, automobile loans could prove a good instrument for CMT since competitors "enter and exit" quite quickly by lowering and raising the interest rates they charge as compared to the other competitors. However, a complication is raised since finance companies often "enter" the market to help the manufacturing parent and not to take advantage of economic profits being reaped by the current participants. The major interest for this study is the allowance of S&Ls to make consumer loans with the passage of DIDMCA.

Credit Cards. Banks, S&Ls, and credit unions all compete for credit card customers.[23] DIDMCA allowed S&Ls to join this competition. The confounding of any test from the presence of nonfinancial institutions would make this category of loans difficult to interpret with CMT.

Real Estate Loans. The market for real estate loans (especially home mortgages) virtually belonged to S&Ls and mutual savings banks (see Table 1.2) prior to DIDMCA. The revisions allowed thrifts to de-emphasize mortgage lending (somewhat) and allowed banks to compete in a more competitive market. The pricing of home mortgage loans should reflect banks' position as the potential entrant as opposed to the normal position as the industry incumbent. However, it is doubted that much movement took place in this market until later in the test period given the percentages in Table 1.2. Banks did not rush in to compete in this area and thrifts' balance sheets are still dominated by mortgages. However, the banking institutions have recently (June 1989) originated more mortgage loans for 1-4 family dwellings than even S&Ls, and have held a greater volume of these loans in their portfolios ($689 billion versus $682 billion) since the first quarter of 1989.[24]

Mortgage bankers are also competitors in the home mortgage market, but generally via the securitized loans of the secondary market as well as the traditional route of construction loans, but not the long-term loan originations common to thrifts as shown in Table 1.2. Mortgage bankers have a higher percentage of originations to the commercial mortgage market than the home mortgage market.

Commercial Loans. Prior to deregulation, banks competed with finance companies for the intermediary commercial loan market. The finance companies tended to specialize in areas in which many banks did not participate such as accounts receivable factoring.[25] In many ways, banks were competing with direct financing (stocks, bonds, and, especially, commercial paper) for commercial loan business. Over time, banks have seen many more of their largest commercial customers' needs being filled by the commercial paper market. S&Ls are allowed to supply more loans to businesses and have targeted the smaller businesses that now make up a larger portion of banks' commercial loan portfolios. CMT would predict that banks would react to this new competition by lowering the rates charged on their loans. However, since S&Ls are limited in the percentage of assets that they can have

Table 1.2: Percent of 1-4 Family Mortgages Held by Selected Financial
Institutions

Year	Commercial Banks	Thrifts	Other[1]
1973	16.3%	44.9%	12.3%
1974	16.6%	44.7%	11.9%
1975	15.7%	45.6%	11.5%
1976	15.5%	46.9%	11.3%
1977	16.0%	47.3%	11.0%
1978	16.7%	46.7%	10.8%
1979	16.8%	44.3%	12.4%
1980	16.2%	42.5%	14.0%
1981	16.0%	40.7%	15.7%
1982	15.7%	35.6%	16.7%
1983	14.2%	30.4%	14.5%
1984	14.9%	32.0%	11.5%
1985	14.3%	37.3%	10.9%
1986	13.9%	32.9%	10.4%
1987	14.1%	30.8%	12.4%
1988	14.5%	30.7%	11.8%

[1] The "Other" category includes mortgage bankers, but primarily consists of individuals such that the percentage of 1-4 family mortgages held by mortgage bankers is quite small relative to thrifts and commercial banks.

Source: *Federal Reserve Bulletin* published by the Federal Reserve System for years 1975-1988.

as commercial loans, the new entry may not be as strong as in other areas and any decrease in rates by banks could be more difficult to detect.[26] The finding of Slovin and Sushka (1984) that commercial banks have monopoly power in the pricing of commercial loans is a further condition that may preclude discovering differences in loan pricing over time.

NOTES

1. Chapter 2 contains a discussion of the existing literature covering Contestable Markets Theory.

2. Given CMT's expectational framework, it is possible that an incumbent is currently pricing at p_c and new entry still occurs. In this case, the entrant must expect that the incumbent will price at a level greater than the p_c that should exist in the future period. Thus entry into an industry does not necessarily prove that $p > p_c$ at the present time.

3. It must be noted here (and will be discussed in greater detail in Chapter 3) that many potential reasons are available to explain a decrease in earnings for banking products during the 1973-1988 test period. Not only was there an increased threat of entry and increased entry, but also the phase out of Regulation Q (potentially raising the cost of acquiring funds), increases in operating expenses from the development of ATM systems, et cetera, and increases in loan losses from oil and LDC loans to name the obvious other major

4. Baumol (1982) states that "free" entry and exit are in the sense of the entrant not suffering any disadvantages in terms of production or perceived product quality as compared to the incumbent. Free entry is not necessarily costless or easy.

5. Rhoades (1979) finds that the presence of S&Ls, credit unions, and mutual savings banks does have a pro-competitive effect on banks. This result provides support for a firm level approach.

6. For example, in 1980 Canada had national branching and 12 chartered banks versus no uniform branching law and more than 14,000 banks in the U.S. At the end of this study period, Canada had 8 domestic banks and 59 foreign banks versus approximately 12,000 U.S. banks.

7. Further difficulties arise if the number of new banks varies greatly from year to year for each state. The changes in the number of new entrants make comparisons within a given state more difficult over time.

8. Some states do allow other offices, but they do not offer the full services of the main office.

9. It is true that the introduction of a new competitor such as a credit union would have a theoretical effect on the pricing of a product, but the effect would likely be too small to measure.

10. However, Hanweck and Rhoades (1984) point out that the traditional SCP model holds that a large firm is unlikely to be bothered greatly by aggressive tactics of a small competitor. CMT holds that the threat of aggressive tactics will affect the bigger firm.

11. One possible source of competition is from banks that already exist within the market. However, it will be assumed that the threat of greater competition from already existing banks is of lesser concern than new entrants.

12. 12. See Smith (1982).

13. While it is true that non-bank financial institutions were given the ability to use Federal Reserve Services, they still are not on equal basis with banks. The non-bank institutions can not own stock in the Federal Reserve and access to the Fed's discount window is available only after the traditional borrowing sources have refused credit.

14. It could be argued that the offering of a new product would provide more potential economies of scope to S&Ls and credit unions since they have traditionally been much less diversified than commercial banks. However, that position is based on the portfolio of products approach which is not being considered given the difficulties of defining the proper portfolio as discussed above.

15. Credit unions pay no taxes since they are not-for-profit organizations.

16. Further, Cook and D'Antonio (1984) offer an argument that credit unions would be even more competitive if they faced taxes. Their position is that the credit unions, if taxed, would have incentives to raise the interest rates (dividends) they pay on deposits and lower rates they charge on loans and could actually obtain more of an advantage if taxed (however, their results imply that credit unions have some monopoly powers).

17. Pyle (1974) examines the effect on saving deposit earnings of savers in S&Ls with the passage of the Interest Rate Adjustment Act of 1966 which placed S&Ls under Regulation Q. He uses a recursive, rate-adjustment model to predict what rates would have been paid by the S&Ls had they not been under Regulation Q. His general finding is that savers lost over five billion dollars during the three year period, 1968-1970, compared to what they would have earned. This lost income was a savings or economic profit for the S&L industry. It is believed that the same type savings was

18. A legitimate point to be raised is that MMMFs do not share the same cost structures as true depository institutions since they operate with no depository insurance and generally have $500 minimum withdrawal limits. It is argued that the monopoly rents being earned by commercial banks were so high and the ability to obtain low-risk, high interest investments was so great that MMMFs could outbid commercial banks for DDA deposits given the existence of Regulation Q.

19. Gauger and Schroeter (1990) find that the introduction of MMDAs led to the shifting of funds from savings accounts to MMMFs and MMDAs which were grouped together for testing purposes. They find that NOWs are close substitutes for MMMFs and MMDAs, but not DDAs, savings accounts, or small time deposits.

20. However, some local markets could still be paying below Regulation Q rates if competitors colluded or if there were only one local provider of savings deposits.

21. The rates on the negotiable CDs would differ if the risk of the issuer were perceived as being greater or less than the average issuer of negotiable CDs.

22. Since many finance companies are subsidiaries that make loans to purchase the product of the parent corporation, their pricing of loans is tied to the performance of the parent company. Aggressive pricing is often used to increase the quantity of demand of the parent's product.

23. Petroleum companies also offer credit cards, but they are not universally accepted at retail outlets other than service stations. The Discover Card offered by Sear's financial group is issued via a savings bank, although it is often considered a non-traditional credit card option.

24. It is believed that the recent innovations in the securitization of mortgages may have aided this development.

25. Factoring is the selling of a firm's accounts receivables to the "lending" agency. The receivables are bought at a discount that depends on the probability of collection and the level of interest rates as well as other firm specific criteria.

26. Especially if the quality of borrowers is declining as smaller firms replace larger firms. In this case, it would appear that the average rate charged by banks for their commercial loans was increasing instead of decreasing.

II

Literature Review

The literature directly applicable to contestable markets in the banking industry is rather sparse even if one considers economies of scale/scope papers as direct CMT studies. However, a fairly rich literature exists in exploring the assumptions of Contestable Markets Theory as well as in exploring competition in banking based on market structure. This review principally surveys the major papers setting forth CMT's foundations and the banking competition papers that are related even tangentially to this subject.

CMT's major assumptions and its relation to the traditional SCP model are set forth in Baumol (1982) and Baumol, Panzar, and Willig (1982). The theory was developed as a way to explain why industry structures ranging from one with the atomistic competitors of perfect competition to one with the limited number of competitors of an oligopoly or even a monopoly may be optimal, as opposed to the traditional case of monopoly being the least optimal compared to perfect competition as the ideal. Optimality in CMT does not depend monotonically on the number of competitors. As the number of competitors increases (decreases), optimality is not necessarily increased (decreased). The originators of the theory admit that perfect contestability is not a description of reality, but instead an ideal benchmark—just as perfect competition is.

While the traditional SCP model, especially oligopoly situations, depends on the actions or assumed motivations of the incumbent firm, CMT focuses on the pressures of potential competition and its effects on the incumbent. The basis of the theory is that no industry can earn economic profits for an extended period unless other potential sellers, willing to charge lower prices, are blocked from entering the industry by the incumbents' offering their product at a price too low to allow profitable underpricing.

Baumol (1982) states that "a contestable market is one into which entry is absolutely free, and exit is absolutely costless" (p. 3). The freedom of entry does not mean costless or even easy entry, but that the new competitor would not have any disadvantages in product quality (real or perceived) or production. In comparing contestable and perfectly competitive markets, he states that contestable market firms "need not be small or numerous or independent in their decision making or produce homogeneous products" (p. 4). As such, while a perfectly competitive market would be perfectly contestable, a perfectly contestable market would not necessarily be perfectly competitive.

Baumol lists the welfare effects of a contestable market as: 1) economic profit must be zero or negative, 2) production must be absent of inefficiencies, and 3) in the long-run, no product can be sold below or above p_{mc}, the marginal cost. The absence of any of the three results would lead to the entry of new competitors. If economic profit could be made, then the industry would be ripe for hit-and-run or hit-and-stay entry as discussed in the previous chapter. Production inefficiencies would allow a new competitor with an efficient production technique to produce at a lower cost and either earn an economic profit at the pre-entry price or price its product below the incumbent's. A price, p, above p_{mc} would lead to economic profits and/or the entry of another competitor willing to charge a price between p and p_{mc}. This process would be repeated until the price was lowered to p_{mc}. Charging a price below p_{mc} in the long-run is not possible because no company can sustain production in the long-run below p_{mc}.[1]

A very large portion of the Baumol and the Baumol, Panzar, and Willig papers consists of the development of the conditions needed for a contestable market in an oligopoly. The focus is on the production range under which contestability will hold. As such, the works point out the need to determine economies of scale and/or scope empirically to assure that contestability may be used in the given study area. Emphasis is given to the fact that long-run equilibrium can not be found if economies of scale and/or scope were limitless or if producers were not operating at the most efficient level to gain the maximum of economies of scale and/or scope. For this reason, studies on economies or scale and/or scope for banking will be discussed below after a discussion of CMT's assumptions.[2]

The assumptions needed for CMT have received considerable attention in the economics literature. In addition to the pathbreaking works by Baumol (1982), and Baumol, Panzar, and Willig (1982), many other articles have appeared examining the theory's assumptions or offering empirical evidence.

As CMT was presented by Baumol, Panzar, and Willig, the only assumptions included were the second and third (in the list below) which led to the freedom of entry and exit (the first) assumption. These assumptions, first presented in Chapter 1, are again listed below.

1- Entry into and exit from the industry are free. (This ease of entry and exit does not mean costless movement.)
2- There are no sunk costs (or any fixed costs are recoverable on exit from the industry—except in the case of hit-and-stay entry).
3- New entrants enjoy the same cost structure as incumbents because they both have access to the same technology and efficiency levels, meaning that there is no cost disadvantage to potential entrants.

It must be noted that the focus on entry as a market discipline goes back at least to J.B. Clark (1912), and has been updated by Bain (1956) to consider specifically barriers to entry and by Caves and Porter (1977) to include firm mobility.

In reference to the first three assumptions of CMT, Spence (1983) states "I do not mean to suggest that there are no cases in which capital or resources or both are sufficiently reversibly mobile to make the model descriptively useful. In some of the service industries, the conditions may be met. If capital can be rented and has multiple uses, one can see the potential applicability of the model. It is useful to remember that the theory does not predict a great deal of actual entry and exit. It is the potential entry that constrains structure and price" (p. 987). This statement leads one to believe that CMT can be a useful model for financial service products.

The sufficiency of the first three assumptions listed above is raised by Brock (1983) in his review. He states that "as we have seen, costlessly reversible entry needs incumbents to be sluggish relative to challengers and consumers must be quicker to respond to price changes than the incumbents whose very livelihood depends on rapid reaction. This seems implausible unless regulators or some other force restrains the reaction time of incumbents" (p. 1065). In the same manner, Dixit

(1982) states that for contestability to hold there must be in addition to the first three assumptions the conditions that incumbents can change prices only with a nonzero time lag and the consumer must respond to a price difference with a shorter lag. Bailey and Baumol (1984) have suggested that the arguments of Brock (1983) and Dixit (1982) are not needed if entrants can write firm contracts with consumers for delivery over some fixed period, but the added assumptions do facilitate the use of the theory. Hence, these two assumptions (the fifth and sixth from the preceding chapter) are included as part of those necessary for contestable markets:

5- There is a contracting period such that incumbent firms have a lag in their response to market changes.
6- Consumers react more quickly to market changes than incumbent firms.

Shepherd (1984) expresses the assumptions presented above in a slightly different manner. He states: 1) Entry is free and without limit. As such a new entrant is not limited to a foothold, but is theoretically capable of replacing the incumbent. 2) Entry is absolute. The entrant is able to establish itself before the incumbent can react. 3) Entry is perfectly reversible. He further states that if there were any departures from these pure conditions, the analysis of Baumol, Panzar, and Willig is speculative (p. 573).

The last assumption to be added by Shepherd is that:

4- Output is homogeneous in nature.

When Baumol (1982) stated specifically that firms in contestable markets did not have to produce homogeneous products, he was addressing the case of a multiproduct producer. However, in the case of single product firms it is necessary that products be homogeneous. Otherwise, product differentiation could allow different optimal market prices for two similar goods. Therefore, it is necessary that products be homogeneous or optimal pricing policy could possibly be other that $p = p_{mc}$.

AGGREGATE EMPIRICAL RESEARCH IN CMT

Non-banking Markets

Most of the empirical work using CMT centers on the transportation industry—airlines in particular. Selected works examining airlines include Bailey and Panzar (1981), Call and Keeler (1985), Morris and Winston (1987), and Butler and Houston (1989). Bailey and Baumol (1984) reported the airline industry as an ideal candidate for testing CMT implications, although much of the results to that point suggested behavior explained by standard oligopoly theory. In discussing the results since the reduction of regulations in the airline industry, they state that the existing evidence suggests that "the contestability benchmark does not fully hold sway in the first years after deregulation" (p. 130).

Support for CMT comes from two of the above studies while the other two are generally unsupportive. Bailey and Panzar (1981) examined the airline industry and found that the presence of potential competition from trunk carriers effectively kept the pricing of local service carriers below their regulated prices, as CMT would expect. Morrison and Winston (1987) include in their study a regression to explain consumer surplus that uses not only a variable for the actual number of competitors in a market, but one for the number of potential competitors as well. They find that both variables are significant (with the variable for actual competitors four times as large) which they state is evidence of imperfect contestability for airlines.

Call and Keeler (1985) find that established firms do not reduce airfares until after new entry occurs, contrary to CMT's implications of price reductions from the threat of new entry. Finally, Butler and Houston (1989) also find little support for CMT. They look at entry into airline markets on four different levels: 1) a new flight to a city already being serviced; 2) small scale entry (one or two flights) into a new city; 3) large scale entry (three or more flights) into a new city; and 4) creating a new hub city. They find that sunk costs increase as one moves from the first to the fourth option and, therefore, CMT has less applicability as well. They also state that since incumbents are able to change prices quickly using the computer reservation systems (a violation of the fifth and sixth assumptions of the theory), few airline markets are truly contestable.

Two other studies from the transportation industry are those of Bailey and Friedlaender (1982) and Davies (1986). Bailey and Friedlaender provide a survey of the studies completed to that point on the trucking and railroad industries and state that the general findings are of scope economies in network configurations. Davies examines the ocean liner shipping industry in Canada and finds contestability to be the best explanation of its pricing behavior.

An additional, non-transportation industry study is by Teece (1980). He examines the petroleum industry and states that as long as economies of scope derive from proprietary information (such as is needed in producing a set mix of petroleum products from a given type crude oil) a multiproduct enterprise is most efficient and contestability concerns need to be addressed.

Financial Institutions

A direct examination of contestability in the banking industry is contained in Nathan (1988). She uses a CMT framework to examine the Canadian banking system. Canada's 1980 Bank Act allowed greater entry by foreign banks into its banking system. Prior to its passage, there were only twelve chartered banks in Canada. In 1988, there were eight domestic banks as well as fifty-nine banks closely held by foreign banks. Entry into the banking system had been affected on a relatively large scale during the eight year period. Given the ability to enter more freely after 1980 and the nationwide branching allowed in Canada, Nathan examines contestability at the firm level using a log-linear revenue function for the sixty-seven banks operating in Canada during 1983-1988. She then calculates the Rosse-Panzar χ statistic (the sum of revenue elasticities with respect to factor prices) to test for the degree of competition. The results show the Canadian system to be best described as monopolistically competitive and Nathan suggests that CMT is a useful theory to describe the industry.

Kane (1984) provides a non-empirical discussion of changes in the financial services industry that is based on possible scope economies and the possibility of regulatory avoidance. He contends "that contemporary adaptations exploit scope economies rooted in technological change" (p. 759). Kane "depicts the fusion of financial-services competition as confirming the contestability model of multimarket competition" (p. 760). It is his belief that regulatory interference imposes entry restrictions (and leads to added regulatory avoidance costs) that slows the rate of adaptation to a market that eliminates high-cost producers in favor of low-cost ones. The deregulatory acts of 1980 and 1982 led to a reduction in some of these interferences, thus making some direct competition possible and some avoidance costs less. Kane models this process using: $C(X_1,X_2) + C_{a,r}$ versus $C_1(X_1) + C_2(X_2)$, where $C_{a,r}$ is the cost of regulatory avoidance.[3] The issue is whether the cost of the regulatory avoidance is greater or less than the savings from the economies of scope. The reduction of $C_{a,r}$ leads to more opportunities to combine production (thus blurring past interinstitutional product segmentations)—a process that Kane terms "structural arbitrage."[4]

The empirical works generally related to CMT in the financial services industry are studies of economies of scale and/or scope. Baumol and Willig (1986) discuss the results of some of the early studies listed below and suggest banking and other financial institutions as an up to then largely unexplored area for application of CMT. Studies examining economies of scale and/or scope include Mullineaux (1978), Benston, Hanweck, and Humphrey (1982), Gilligan, Smirlock, and Marshall (1984), Gilligan and Smirlock (1984), Hunter and Timme (1986), Berger, Hanweck, and Humphrey (1987), Noulas, Ray, and Miller (1989), Lawrence (1989), Hunter, Timme, and Yang (1990), and Cebenoyan (1990).

Mullineaux (1978) examines FCA data from 1971-1972 using a translog cost function. The use of the translog cost function (replacing the normal Cobb-Douglas or CES forms) allows one to estimate a U-shaped average cost curve as well as to account for size and branching economies. Mullineaux finds greater economies of scale for banking organizations than is found with the same data using Cobb-Douglas and CES cost functions. He generally finds the efficient operating range to be between $50 million and $100 million in deposits. Benston, Hanweck, and Humphrey (1982) use FCA data for the years 1975-1978 and find that unit banks with over $50 million in deposits suffer diseconomies and that optimal economies are gained between $10 million and $25 million. This finding contrasts with Mullineaux's. Gilligan, Smirlock, and Marshall (1984), and Gilligan and Smirlock (1984) find economies of scope "across the balance sheet" for banking firms when dividing output into loans and deposits. Scale economies are found to dissipate as deposit size reaches $100 million or more—a result similar to Mullineaux's.

Hunter and Timme (1986) examine economies of scale while allowing for technical change using a specialized form of the translog cost function model. According to Hunter and Timme "technical change is said to result when the maximum or efficient output that can be produced from any given set of inputs increases over time due to such factors as experience, increased knowledge, new innovations, and better production techniques" (p. 153). They collected data over 1972-1982 for 91 banks from *Bank Compustat* and find that technical change has allowed increasing economies of scale over the test period.

Berger, Hanweck, and Humphrey (1987) use measures to examine expansion-path scale economies and expansion-path subadditivity that capture changing scale and product mix at the same time on FCA data from 1983. Their measures try to overcome some of the problems of estimating a translog function around zero production points and no substantial evidence of scope economies is found for the banks in their study. As related earlier, their insight into the possible competitive viability of a multi-product firm helped lead to the possibility of examining banking on a single product level.

Noulas, Ray, and Miller (1989) examine economies of scale and scope for 330 banks in 1986 with over $1 billion in assets using a translog variable cost function.[5] They find economies of scale/scope are exhausted as banks grow past the $3 billion to $6 billion range which is much higher than earlier studies.

Hunter, Timme, and Yang (1990) use 1986 data from the Federal Reserve System's end-of-year Call Reports and Report of Income and Dividends for 311 non-unit banks using a second order translog cost function with deposits as outputs and another with deposits as inputs. They find "no measurable cost complementarities in multiproduct production" (p. 524). Such a result means non-subadditivity in production or no economies of scope. They do state that their approach does not take into account possible complementarities from risk reduction.

Cebenoyan (1990) uses the hybrid Box-Cox transformation of a translog cost function to examine 1983 FCA data to test if banks have economies of scope. He states that past studies using translog cost functions have either had to estimate scope economies with approximations or have estimated subadditivity directly, which requires the presence of scope economies as a necessary condition. His results for a model with five outputs (demand deposits, time deposits, installment loans, commercial loans, and real estate loans) does not find economies of scope. His finding would allow specialization by financial competitors and supports the examination of CMT on a single product basis, if it is not necessary to compete on a multiproduct level.

Lawrence (1989) uses FCA data from 1979-1982 to examine the many forms of the functional cost models being used to examine economies of scale and/or scope. He finds that the Cobb-Douglas specification is not adequate while more complicated functional forms such as Box-Cox transformations are also rejected by the data. The best fit of the data used is produced by a translog equation. This result brings the findings of Cebenoyan into question. Overall, the results from the various studies put the optimal level of operation either around $100 million or between $3 billion and $6 billion depending on the data and methodology used.

Economies of scale and/or scope tests have also been conducted on nonbank financial institutions. Dowling, Philippatos, and Choi (1983) examine economies of scale for merging savings and loan companies using the translog cost function over the 1977-1981 period. Their results show $500 million to $750 million as the range over which economies of scale are maximized. These results provide evidence that one of the reasons for S&L mergers was to obtain these economies. However, Mester (1985), in a study of California savings and loans, finds constant returns to scale and no economies of scope. Dowling and Philippatos (1989) use the Semi-Annual Financial Reports from the Federal Home Loan Bank Board for the 1973-1983 period to estimate a translog cost model. Their basic result is that economies are exhausted once an S&L's asset size grows above $2 billion.

Further support for economies of scope in S&Ls comes from Murray and White (1983). Using a translog cost function for data from 1976-1977, they find economies of scope between mortgages and consumer lending for credit unions in British Columbia (institutions whose balance sheets resemble traditional U.S. savings and loans associations').

Other works in financial institutions that are not directly related to CMT or even economies of scale and/or scope, but do provide some insight for a contestability study in banking are discussed next. To provide some framework to the discussion, tests examining operations at the firm level are related first followed by tests concerning assets, liabilities, and, finally, other related studies.

OTHER EMPIRICAL RESEARCH IN CMT

Firm Level Studies

Hannan (1983) examines bank profitability and the threat of entry using data from banks operating in Pennsylvania in 1970. His test is based on the exact knowledge of those firms that are threatening entry. He finds that large banks that are potential entrants into a market impact negatively the profitability of incumbent firms. Non-potential entrants are found to have no profitability impact on the incumbents. These results are consistent with CMT expectations. Marlow (1983) also examines performance (as measured by effective interest rates charged for home mortgages) and entry into banking markets. He models mortgage rates for commercial banks and savings and loans based on loan characteristics (term to maturity, et cetera) as well as new entry into a SMSA market via main offices or branches. He finds that, ceteris paribus, new entry (via new firms or branching) decreases mortgage rates. Unfortunately, Marlow's study can not answer directly any questions concerning potential as opposed to actual entry.

Thomas and Rivard (1990) examine new bank entry in the Florida market for the periods 1977-1979, when only countywide branching was allowed, and 1982-1984, when statewide branching was allowed. (The 1980-1981 period allowed greater than countywide, but less than statewide branching.) They examine eighteen markets during that time and note that there were seventy-two new bank entries in the latter period versus only nineteen in the former. They also modeled the number of entries as a function of general market information such as the profit of the incumbent firms, expected growth in population, market size, and personal income. They find that the model does not explain the number of entries as well for the second period and conclude that more competition (measured by number of firms) is associated with less restrictive branching laws.

Smirlock (1985) examines the relationship between concentration in a market and profitability. He finds that once one accounts for market share, there is no relationship between concentration and profitability. The general findings of his paper are in agreement with CMT. No significant relationship is found in markets with fewer competitors to greater profits—as the traditional SCP model would hold. Smirlock believes that those competitors that are the most efficient have garnered the highest market share and earned the greatest profit. It would, therefore, be possible for a spurious relationship to be found between profitability and concentration. Smirlock estimates a cross-sectional regression that has profit (return on equity, capital, or assets are proxies) as its dependent variable and includes variables for market share (a bank's total deposits divided by the relevant market's total deposits—the market being an SMSA or non-SMSA county), concentration (three-bank deposit concentration), and an interaction variable between the two as well as various control variables. His data are for the years 1973-1978 and consist of financial statement information for over 2,700 unit banks operating in the jurisdiction of the Federal Reserve Bank of Kansas City. When he estimates his full regression model, the market share variable is significantly positive (.01 level) while the concentration ratio is never significant and the interaction term between the two is significantly negative (.10 level) for all profitability proxies. It must be noted, however, that his R^2s are never greater than .06.

An introduction to past works is provided in Gilbert (1984). He presents a survey of the studies examining bank market structure and competition that updates the works of Heggestad (1979), Rhoades (1977), and Benston (1972).[6] He notes the disturbing lack of consistent results as is also later noted in Smirlock (1985). Of the forty-four studies in Gilbert's survey, thirty-two find significant association between market structure and bank performance. However, seven of the thirty-two find significance only for a very limited number of the tests conducted in each of those studies. Gilbert draws three conclusions from the past studies: 1) concentration in the local market area (SMSA or non-SMSA county) is the relevant measure of market structure; 2) average interest rates and service charge rates are poor measures for bank performance; and 3) bank profit rate is an appropriate measure of bank performance.

Heggestad (1984) and Schmidt (1984) both disagree with the first conclusion, but for different reasons. Heggestad responds that "many different types of firms produce either identical products or very close substitutes. There is now very little reason to conclude that changes in concentration of local bank deposits will have the same effect as found in studies of the early 1970s. Future empirical studies must redefine the line of commerce. In all likelihood, it will be necessary to reject the commercial banking line of commerce concept in favor of distinct and separate markets for each financial product" (p. 649).[7] Schmidt states that "banks face rather direct competition from nonbank financial institutions, and markets for some banking services are statewide or even national, rather than local" (p. 657). Both arguments can be used to support using CMT to examine banking products.

One study not included in Gilbert is that of Hanweck and Rhoades (1984). They model performance measures (rate of return and three proxies for the prices of services) for 1969-1977 to test if dominant firms are able to use predatory pricing (a characteristic not consistent with CMT). They modeled the performance measures as dependent on the sum of the market share of all "dominant" firms in 147 SMSA and 112 non-SMSA county markets, as well as a binary (dummy) variable that was set to one if a dominant firm was present; zero if not. They also included a three-firm concentration ratio, market deposit growth, market deposit size, dummy variables for state branching laws, total loans/total assets, and time deposits/time and savings deposits. They find that prices and non-interest expenses are higher in markets with dominant firms present, but also find that dominant firms have no effect on profit performance.

Asset Studies

Boczar (1978) examines competition between banks and finance companies for personal loans. The study is based on personal surveys from those obtaining personal loans. A multivariate probit model is used to estimate the probability that a loan was obtained at a commercial bank based on characteristics often used in credit scoring models (income, age, homeowner, et cetera). The results show that the borrowing profiles of customers differ between the two institutions, but not on the basis of the risk proxy used in the study. Finance company borrowers were nine times more likely to be misclassified than bank borrowers by the model. Boczar suggests that the model's predictive problems are evidence that banks and finance companies do compete for the same customers.[8]

Marlow (1982) examines bank structure and mortgage rates. The data are from a survey for providers of single-family, nonfarm, conventional mortgages in 1975. Respondents include S&Ls, mortgage bankers, commercial banks, and mutual savings banks. The relevant market is defined as a SMSA. The methodology is a general regression model that controls for population, number of firms, number of branches, deposit concentration ratios, loan characteristics, and a dummy variable for unit versus branch banking. He finds that the larger the number of competing firms and the lower the concentration of deposits in a given market, the lower the interest rate on home mortgages, all else held equal. He also finds that rates are lower in unit banking states than in states with branching. These findings point to greater competition arising from the number of firms and not from the number of branches. They are also not in line with CMT, since greater potential threat of entry is to be found in states with branching.

Curry and Rose (1984) respond to Marlow's study by pointing out that he should have used concentration ratios from all competitors and not just from the commercial banks. Even if banks were the largest deposit holders in a given market (thus leaving the numerator of the concentration ratio unchanged), ignoring the other competitors will affect the denominator of the ratio and bias the measures to being more concentrated than is true. However, their results are only a slight improvement over Marlow's, as measured by the R^2, and a slightly more significant result on the concentration ratio variables (both studies use three- and five-firm concentration ratios).

Slovin and Sushka (1984) examine the determinants of commercial loan rates using cross sectional bank survey data. Forty-five different variables are used in estimating loan rates and these rates are then divided into five areas (with examples of each variable type in parenthesis): environment (Herfindahl index), bank customer relationship (other services used, amount previously borrowed), bank portfolio and liquidity (total loans/total assets, total bank assets), borrower characteristics (borrower's total assets, borrower's net profit), and loan characteristics (size of loan, maturity). Some of the variables in each category were statistically significant, but most importantly for implications to a CMT study is the finding that all variables included in the environment category are found to be significant. The authors suggest that this result implies that there are differences in loan rates across the banking industry which can not be explained by credit risk. Therefore, the banking firm should not be assumed to be a price taker—meaning that it has some monopoly power in the commercial loan market. Thus an additional reason of the expectation of non-contestability in the commercial loan market in the data used in this study.

Elliehausen and Wolken (1986, 1990) examine prices charged on first mortgage, automobile, and personal loans for commercial banks, savings institutions, credit unions, and finance companies in the Boston, Massachusetts market. The data were collected for each month from December 1978 through August 1983. Their results show that there is interinstitutional competition for the same type of loans.[9] They found three distinct product markets: 1) automobile loans at commercial banks and savings institutions; 2) personal loans between commercial banks, savings institutions, and finance companies; and 3) mortgage loans between commercial banks, savings institutions, and credit unions.

Ausubel (1991) finds that competition in the credit card market has failed to decrease returns. The study uses data from two sources. The primary data come from a survey conducted by the author in 1986 with a follow-up in 1988 that generated responses from twenty-one of the sixty largest card issuers in the U.S. for the 1983-1988 period. He finds that although there are more than 4,000 credit card issuers and regulatory barriers to entry are relatively low, prices on credit cards have been sticky (average rate near 18%) over the six year period and that banks earned three to five times their ordinary returns during the period. The second data source is from the FCA program. This source confirms the author's original findings for the much larger issuers. The author conjectures that the major reason behind the lack of competition is that consumers do not expect to have to pay interest, but do so. If banks lower their rates, then they would most likely attract the customers that do expect to pay interest, which generally have higher credit risk. Therefore, the banks do not aggressively underprice competitors.

Liability Studies

Bundt and Schweitzer (1989) examine the cost of bank funds for the 100 largest U.S. banks for each year 1978-1985 using annual balance sheet and expenditure records obtained from annual Reports of Income and Condition published by the Federal Reserve System. They find that the cost of retail deposits (retail deposits being demand, savings, NOW, and ATS) has increased relative to wholesale deposit's cost (wholesale deposits being federal funds, money market CDs, and money market time deposits). More surprising than this result is the source of the relative increase in retail deposit cost. The authors find the cost increase is from greater processing costs (actually greater non-interest expense which is a proxy for processing cost) and not from relatively higher interest rates paid. They argue that the increase is from a one time increase in the difficulty of processing the new accounts that were created during this period. 1985 data supported this idea since processing costs were found to be decreasing relative to past measures.

Cooperman, Lee, and Lesage (1990) examine competition for retail CDs with six-month maturities between banks and thrifts (predominantly S&Ls). Their data consist of the weekly six-month CD interest rates offered by the five largest banks and five largest S&Ls in six major U.S. cities over the period 1983-1985. Using a vector autoregressive model, they find that "commercial bank institutions exert a unidirectional influence on thrift rates" (p. 43). If this same relationship held for other type deposits and loans, then traditional oligopoly theory rather than CMT would best describe pricing behavior. A very important fact to note is that the sample in this study consists of institutions with multiple billions of dollars in deposits versus the small (almost all under $1 billion in deposits) size of the institutions in FCA data. Rate competition in smaller cities could vary from the findings of this study.

Related Studies

Wolken and Derrick (1986) examine non-price competition in commercial banking by using the advertising expense information provided in the Federal Reserve's FCA data for the year 1978. They find advertising expenditures are best explained by changes in the number of competitors with expenditures increasing with new entrants. This result is consistent with a banking firm trying to use non-price measures to maintain and/or attract customers during a period when interest rates on deposits were under Regulation Q. They go on to state that they find no support that branching, market power, or market structure affect advertising.

Rose (1989) discusses the risk reduction possible for banks when entering non-bank areas such as insurance and data processing. He examines the changes in cash flows associated with systematic variables such as the level of interest rates or economic activity and finds that many nonbank financial and nonfinancial firms have lower systematic risk than banking firms as seen by lower fluctuation in cash flows from changes in general economic variables.

Overall, the literature has not tested directly for CMT in banking except for the Nathan (1988) study. The existing work also raises questions as to whether economies of scope truly exist in financial service firms. These facts along with the confounding nature of banking regulation allow for a wide open testing of commercial bank products for the attributes of CMT, but raise questions as to the likelihood of finding clear, if any, results supporting CMT.

NOTES

1. It is interesting to note that since the long-run price can not be below p_{mc}, predatory or loss leader pricing is not possible as a tool to limit competition, as noted in Bailey and Baumol (1984).

2. "Economies of scope" was coined by Panzar and Willig (1981) to describe the savings from producing products together (scope) as opposed to just those from producing more of the same product (scale). A multiproduct cost function exhibits economies of scope whenever the costs of producing two goods are subadditive. Subadditivity means that it costs less to produce the goods together than to produce them separately: $C(X_1,X_2) < C_1(X_1) + C_2(X_2)$. $C(X_1,X_2)$ represents the cost function of producing two goods together in the same production run while $C_1(X_1)$ and $C_2(X_2)$ represent the cost function of producing two goods, but in separate production runs.

3. See endnote 2 for a short discussion of the economies of scope represented by the rest of the equation.

4. Kidwell (1984), in his discussion of Kane's work, states that he believes it is the computer innovations of the 1970s that have led more to the decrease in $C_{a,r}$ and not as much the deregulatory acts of 1980 and 1982.

5. Most studies done to that point had used FCA data which has few banks with over $1 billion in assets included.

6. It should be noted here that Benston's work is focused on economies of scale in commercial banks and savings and loans and not on market structure in particular.

7. Although Heggestad (1984) disagrees with Gilbert's conclusion, one of his own works [Heggestad and Mingo (1977)] states that "the local nature of banking markets severely limits the choices available to consumers. The existence of competition within local markets is therefore very important" (p. 649). The study then goes on to define local markets as SMSAs.

8. One difficulty with Boczar's study is that it does not include specifically those customers that were denied loans at one institution, but were granted such loans at another.

9. This inference is based on the manner in which rates charged on loans react to changes by other potential competitor actions.

III

Methodology

Six methodological techniques to test CMT in the U.S. commercial banking industry are presented below along with a discussion of the data used for the tests conducted. The tests range from purely market measurements to societal measurements and are presented in the order in which they are conducted and reported in the results section. Those tests that are to be left for future research or are thought to be theoretically correct, but impractical are reported last.

PROFITABILITY MEASUREMENT

An ideal test for CMT is to determine the rate of implicit (pre-1980) and explicit (post-1980) interest paid on deposits by banks or the interest charged on loans over the entire test period. The rates can then be compared with those paid or charged by the banks for previous years. The method of comparison would be the standard t-test:

$$t = \frac{\bar{X}_1 - \bar{X}_2}{(s^2(1/n_1 + 1/n_2))^{.5}}$$

Where
- X_g is the average for the first ($g = 1$) and second ($g = 2$) time periods being compared,
- n_g is the number of observations in each group, and
- s^2 is the variance of the observations (assumed to be equal for the two sub-groups).

The rates paid should be such that no other competitor could economically afford to pay more for the accounts over the long run and earn economic profits. Financial comparisons can be made between loan and deposit types that are assumed to be more competitive versus those thought to be less competitive.[1]

Given the difficulty of estimating the value of implicit interest paid or charged, this study does not test the rates charged or paid directly and/or indirectly, but uses "Net Earnings" from Functional Cost Analysis (FCA) data for the years 1973-1988 (the FCA program will be discussed more fully below). Data are given for the annual net earnings for checkable deposits (interest, commercial, personal, and average), time deposits (savings, time, certificates of deposit under $100,000, money market funds, and average), and loans (installment, real estate, and commercial).

The net earnings percentage for the various deposit and loan types are not based on net earnings after taxes. Therefore, the difficulties that would arise if banks with different tax structures were examined are not evident. The accounting procedure used to make the calculations is also set in place by the Federal Reserve System, and the method used to calculate net earnings did not change during the test period such that values are comparable from year to year. The basic format to calculate net earnings is set forth below for deposits and loans.

Deposits: Service Charge Income + Penalty Income + Portfolio Income - Interest Expense (if applicable) - Account Maintenance and Clearing Expenses = Net Earnings.

Loans: Interest Income + Other Income—Overhead Expenses - Losses from Nonperforming Loans - Cost of Money = Net Earnings.

It is important to note that Net Earnings are given in percentage and not dollar terms. A lower dollar profit could be found if a producer raised prices with new competition and earned higher profit per unit, but lower total dollar profits from a decrease in units sold. However, net earnings are roughly equivalent to the more familiar net interest margin used by bank managers. Hence a reduction in net earnings is considered to be equivalent to a reduction in market power leading to a lowering of prices in traditional economic terms. Given the highly volatile interest rate swings during the study period, examining prices (interest rates paid or received) is deemed less satisfactory to examine CMT implications than examining earnings spread. Since banks have little control over the general level of interest rates in the economy, the percentages used from Portfolio Income and Cost of Money are assumed to be market determined. Because banking product prices are generally interest sensitive, net earnings are used to perform this direct test instead of prices. If banking were perfectly contestable, all expected price reductions from the allowance of new competitors brought about by regulatory changes would be reflected before actual entry occurs. The discussion of Bailey and Baumol (1984) leads to an expectation of results consistent with imperfectly contestable markets. Hence, t-tests are used to determine when net earnings change and if they change in the manner predicted by CMT.

Basic t-statistics are calculated for each variable to compare:
- pre-1980 averages with post-1980 averages and
- each year's average with the prior year's (1973 with 1974; et cetera.)

The FCA program is conducted by the Federal Reserve and participation by reporting banks is strictly voluntary. This fact leads to three problems with the data that can be seen by examining Table 3.1. First, the majority of participating banks are extremely small in deposit size—less than $50 million. Also, few banks with deposits of $1 billion or more have participated. Therefore, generalizing results from tests using these data to larger banks should not be done. Second, there is the possibility that there is a self-selection bias in the data for banks worrying more than the "average" bank does about costs. However, since this study is concerned with efficient pricing, this possible bias is not thought to be too worrisome. Third, the number of participating banks has been decreasing over the test period; possibly due to mergers, failures, or the belief that the FCA program is not beneficial enough to warrant the banks' participation.

The reports are divided into three bank deposit size categories shown in Table 3.1: less than $50 million, between $50 million and $200 million, and greater than $200 million. The data used in this methodology are in aggregated form. This fact means that tests must be conducted using the three size categories given by the Federal Reserve. It also means that it is not possible to separate the data by state to compare firms in different regulatory environments. Ideally, disaggregated data should be used. Disaggregated data, which are compiled quarterly, are kept by the Federal Reserve. Unfortunately, a change in the administration of the FCA program renders that data unavailable at present such that annual, aggregated data must be used for this study.

Table 3.1 presents the total number of participating banks for each year and for each deposit size category by year. Table 3.2 lists the variables used in the tests that follow as well as a description of each variable. The net earnings for non-checkable deposits, checkable deposits, and loans by size group are reported in Table 3.3, Table 3.4, and Table 3.5, respectively. In general, earnings were better for almost every product during the 1980-1981 period regardless of the size grouping or product.

Given the general turbulence of the period examined, the t-test results are expected to provide evidence for both imperfectly contestable and competitive markets. Not only does this period have increasing threats of entry and increased entry; it also saw the phase out of Regulation Q, the increasing costs of installing more computers (e.g. ATM systems), and the increase in problem loans to oil concerns and lesser developed countries (LDC loans). To improve interpretation of the t-test results, investigation of the determinants of net earnings during the test period is conducted with the following general regression equation:

$$\text{Earnings}_i = \alpha_i + \beta_1(I_i) + \beta_2(\text{GNP}_i) + \beta_3(\text{PC}_i) + \beta_4(\text{SC}_i) + e_i$$

where: α is the intercept term,
β_i's are regression coefficients,
I is a variable for the general level of interest rates,
GNP is a variable for the general level of economic activity (used only for loans),
PC is a variable for the processing costs of issuing and maintaining deposit and loan accounts, and
SC is a variable for service charge income (used only for checkable deposits).
$_i$ is a general designation for group size and/or year.

Ideally, for CMT to be the possible explanatory factor, the explanatory variables of the fit regression should not be statistically significant. That is, the changes in earnings from year to year should

Table 3.1: Descriptive Statistics for Functional Cost Analysis Data

	Number of Participants by Deposit Size Group (deposit size in millions)		
Year	Less Than $50	$50 to $200	More Than $200
1973	473	291	98
1974	525	281	99
1975	557	289	96
1976	443	317	109
1977	412	332	102
1978	379	316	85
1979	358	313	80
1980	284	295	61
1981	264	285	65
1982	214	308	86
1983	169	292	92
1984	145	280	84
1985	162	260	81
1986	154	262	74
1987	129	247	58
1988	108	217	56
Mean	299	287	83

Table 3.2: Key to Functional Cost Analysis Variables

Variable	Description
DEPOSITS	
ATDNE	Average time deposit net earnings. This category includes SDNE, TDNE, CDNE, and MCDNE.
SDNE	Savings deposit net earnings. These deposits are the traditional passbook-type savings deposits used by individuals.
TDNE	Time deposit net earnings. Includes club accounts, time open accounts, special notice savings accounts, bank savings bonds, and other time deposits.
CDNE	Certificate of deposit net earnings. Includes only those CDs with less than $100,000.
MCDNE	Money market fund net earnings. Includes CDs with $100,000 or more as well as Federal Funds purchased and other money market funds.
ADDNE	Average checkable deposit net earnings. Includes IDDNE, PDDNE, and CDDNE.
IDDNE	Interest-bearing checkable deposit net earnings. Includes NOWs, Super NOWs, and MMDAs as they are offered for both individuals and other organizations able to hold this type account.
PDDNE	Personal checkable deposit net earnings. A subset of IDDNE in which only those accounts owned by individuals are considered.
CDDNE	Commercial demand deposit net earnings. True, non-interest bearing demand deposits.

Table 3.2: (cont.)

Variable	Description
LOANS	
RENE	Real estate loan net earnings. Consists of both commercial and personal real estate loans.
ILNE	Installment loan net earnings. Consists of personal (automobile) installment loans.
CCNE	Credit card loan net earnings. Includes merchant fees as well as personal accounts.
CLNE	Commercial loan net earnings.

Table 3.3: Average Net Earnings for Non-checkable Deposits

Year	ATDNE	SDNE	TDNE	CDNE	MCDNE
Small Banks (Under $50 million in deposits)					
1973	0.78%	1.13%	0.95%	0.46%	.
1974	0.68%	1.20%	0.83%	0.25%	.
1975	0.82%	1.04%	0.89%	0.63%	.
1976	0.91%	1.22%	1.10%	0.60%	.
1977	0.96%	1.26%	1.26%	0.62%	.
1978	1.19%	1.55%	1.50%	0.71%	.
1979	1.23%	1.86%	1.65%	0.69%	8.47%
1980	0.90%	2.33%	1.74%	-0.07%	11.47%
1981	0.68%	3.60%	2.71%	-0.87%	13.96%
1982	0.53%	3.36%	1.55%	-0.64%	12.34%
1983	0.70%	1.84%	1.71%	0.13%	9.48%
1984	0.47%	1.55%	1.33%	0.07%	3.22%
1985	0.75%	0.95%	1.92%	0.50%	2.66%
1986	0.77%	0.33%	2.28%	0.53%	2.02%
1987	1.06%	0.45%	1.94%	1.13%	1.79%
1988	0.96%	0.71%	-1.52%	0.96%	2.50%

Key to Variables

ATDNE - average time deposits net earnings
SDNE - savings deposits net earnings
TDNE - time deposits net earnings
CDNE - certificates < $100,000 net earnings
MCDNE - money market funds net earnings

Table 3.3: (cont.)

Year	ATDNE	SDNE	TDNE	CDNE	MCDNE

Medium Banks ($50 million to $200 million in deposits)

Year	ATDNE	SDNE	TDNE	CDNE	MCDNE
1973	0.78%	1.22%	0.94%	0.38%	.
1974	0.63%	1.57%	0.86%	-0.24%	.
1975	0.71%	1.11%	0.86%	0.26%	.
1976	0.93%	1.24%	0.95%	0.61%	.
1977	1.00%	1.31%	1.10%	0.63%	.
1978	1.16%	1.61%	1.00%	0.47%	.
1979	1.47%	2.19%	1.57%	0.66%	9.37%
1980	1.05%	2.69%	2.15%	-0.29%	11.76%
1981	1.01%	4.12%	2.52%	-0.70%	14.85%
1982	0.33%	3.37%	1.74%	-0.96%	12.56%
1983	0.64%	1.93%	1.69%	-0.12%	9.14%
1984	0.71%	2.08%	1.55%	0.12%	2.82%
1985	0.96%	1.49%	2.17%	0.44%	2.90%
1986	1.01%	0.81%	2.41%	0.66%	3.11%
1987	1.16%	0.63%	2.32%	0.99%	2.91%
1988	1.20%	1.31%	1.51%	1.06%	2.86%

Key to Variables

> ATDNE - average time deposits net earnings
> SDNE - savings deposits net earnings
> TDNE - time deposits net earnings
> CDNE - certificates < $100,000 net earnings
> MCDNE - money market funds net earnings

Table 3.3: (cont.)

Year	ATDNE	SDNE	TDNE	CDNE	MCDNE
Large Banks (Over $200 million in deposits)					
1973	0.53%	1.12%	0.67%	.	.
1974	0.42%	2.18%	1.32%	-1.22%	.
1975	0.59%	1.45%	0.81%	-0.26%	.
1976	0.57%	0.94%	0.25%	0.32%	.
1977	0.76%	1.06%	0.54%	0.51%	.
1978	1.28%	1.71%	1.02%	0.41%	.
1979	1.86%	2.44%	2.33%	0.70%	10.28%
1980	1.25%	3.00%	1.50%	-0.24%	10.87%
1981	1.32%	4.38%	2.22%	-0.72%	14.73%
1982	0.63%	3.55%	0.91%	-0.99%	12.35%
1983	0.78%	1.99%	1.19%	0.01%	8.86%
1984	0.79%	2.11%	1.40%	-0.02%	2.44%
1985	1.09%	1.60%	2.17%	0.41%	3.08%
1986	1.13%	0.63%	2.36%	0.58%	1.98%
1987	1.34%	0.62%	2.61%	0.98%	2.88%
1988	1.21%	1.11%	2.61%	0.86%	2.63%

Key to Variables

> ATDNE - average time deposits net earnings
> SDNE - savings deposits net earnings
> TDNE - time deposits net earnings
> CDNE - certificates < $100,000 net earnings
> MCDNE - money market funds net earnings

Table 3.4: Average Net Earnings for Checkable Deposits

Year	ADDNE	IDDNE	CDDNE	PDDNE
Small Banks (Under $50 million in deposits)				
1973	3.61%	.	4.65%	2.08%
1974	3.75%	.	4.64%	1.82%
1975	3.50%	.	4.25%	2.66%
1976	3.54	-0.58%	4.86%	1.72%
1977	3.53%	-0.07%	4.48%	2.03%
1978	3.71%	0.22%	5.44%	1.92%
1979	4.42%	0.49%	5.17%	3.08%
1980	5.31%	1.69%	6.21%	3.56%
1981	6.25%	3.63%	7.57%	4.25%
1982	5.89%	3.54%	7.25%	4.05%
1983	4.12%	1.66%	5.48%	1.87%
1984	4.29%	1.85%	7.85%	2.05%
1985	3.91%	1.51%	6.71%	1.64%
1986	2.97%	1.20%	5.67%	-2.66%
1987	2.17%	0.94%	.	.
1988	2.45%	1.19%	.	.

Key to Variables

ADDNE - average checkable deposits net earnings
IDDNE - interest-bearing checkable deposits net earnings
CDDNE - commercial demand deposits net earnings
PDDNE - personal checkable deposits net earnings

Table 3.4: (cont.)

Year	ADDNE	IDDNE	CDDNE	PDDNE

Medium Banks ($50 million to $200 million in deposits)

Year	ADDNE	IDDNE	CDDNE	PDDNE
1973	3.44%	.	4.54%	1.70%
1974	3.80%	.	4.53%	1.71%
1975	3.38%	.	3.91%	1.62%
1976	3.29%	0.05%	4.17%	0.57%
1977	3.41%	0.02%	4.34%	-0.21%
1978	3.42%	0.26%	4.69%	1.97%
1979	4.20%	0.53%	5.19%	2.35%
1980	4.98%	1.78%	6.23%	2.67%
1981	5.28%	2.36%	7.18%	2.22%
1982	5.28%	2.72%	7.15%	1.64%
1983	3.69%	1.26%	6.27%	1.07%
1984	4.25%	1.75%	7.05%	2.16%
1985	3.68%	1.69%	6.51%	1.70%
1986	3.07%	1.45%	5.75%	1.26%
1987	2.19%	0.90%	4.54%	0.91%
1988	2.31%	1.13%	4.94%	0.68%

Key to Variables

ADDNE - average checkable deposits net earnings
IDDNE - interest-bearing checkable deposits net earnings
CDDNE - commercial demand deposits net earnings
PDDNE - personal checkable deposits net earnings

Table 3.4: (cont.)

Year	ADDNE	IDDNE	CDDNE	PDDNE
Large Banks (Over $200 million in deposits)				
1973	2.71%	.	3.98%	0.49%
1974	3.49%	.	5.23%	0.11%
1975	2.89%	.	3.69%	0.77%
1976	2.61%	0.04%	3.78%	-0.49%
1977	2.52%	.	3.60%	-0.24%
1978	3.17%	.	4.24%	0.46%
1979	3.79%	-0.13%	4.95%	1.46%
1980	4.41%	1.99%	.	.
1981	4.61%	1.48%	.	.
1982	4.34%	1.94%	5.24%	2.44%
1983	2.94%	0.08%	6.11%	0.42%
1984	3.81%	1.00%	6.83%	-0.41%
1985	3.24%	0.71%	6.59%	-1.07%
1986	2.97%	0.62%	6.19%	0.64%
1987	2.11%	0.59%	5.11%	0.14%
1988	2.19%	0.64%	5.23%	0.09%

Key to Variables

ADDNE - average checkable deposits net earnings
IDDNE - interest-bearing checkable deposits net earnings
CDDNE - commercial demand deposits net earnings
PDDNE - personal checkable deposits net earnings

Table 3.5: Average Net Earnings for Loans

Year	RENE	ILNE	CLNE	CCNE
Small Banks (Under $50 million in deposits)				
1973	2.42%	2.79%	2.34%	-1.23%
1974	2.17%	2.63%	2.53%	-2.56%
1975	2.42%	3.05%	2.19%	-13.54%
1976	2.64%	2.92%	1.99%	-1.60%
1977	2.71%	3.00%	2.00%	-0.33%
1978	2.81%	3.24%	2.29%	-0.97%
1979	2.48%	3.04%	3.02%	-1.91%
1980	1.93%	2.56%	4.14%	-2.20%
1981	1.16%	2.52%	5.07%	-3.53%
1982	1.59%	3.22%	3.72%	-2.13%
1983	2.31%	3.26%	1.93%	.
1984	2.25%	2.52%	1.94%	.
1985	2.61%	2.38%	1.48%	.
1986	2.77%	1.75%	-0.09%	.
1987	2.60%	1.77%	0.26%	-5.95%
1988	2.65%	1.64%	1.26%	-3.32%

Key to Variables
    RENE - real estate loans net earnings
    ILNE - installment loans net earnings
    CLNE - commercial loans net earnings
    CCNE - credit card loans net earnings

Table 3.5: (cont.)

Year	RENE	ILNE	CLNE	CCNE
Medium Banks ($50 million to $200 million in deposits)				
1973	2.53%	2.74%	2.65%	1.18%
1974	2.18%	2.36%	3.28%	-0.08%
1975	2.53%	2.74%	2.45%	-5.80%
1976	2.76%	2.92%	2.12%	1.49%
1977	2.93%	3.08%	2.12%	1.62%
1978	2.77%	2.92%	2.64%	0.56%
1979	2.33%	2.72%	3.78%	0.33%
1980	1.65%	2.47%	4.51%	-0.27%
1981	0.46%	1.72%	5.48%	-1.07%
1982	1.05%	2.56%	3.40%	-0.73%
1983	2.29%	2.99%	1.63%	1.95%
1984	2.33%	2.67%	1.89%	2.11%
1985	2.84%	2.59%	0.94%	3.82%
1986	3.18%	2.48%	0.06%	3.28%
1987	2.99%	1.89%	0.69%	2.26%
1988	2.84%	1.89%	1.40%	-0.94%

Key to Variables
    RENE - real estate loans net earnings
    ILNE - installment loans net earnings
    CLNE - commercial loans net earnings
    CCNE - credit card loans net earnings

Table 3.5: (cont.)

Year	RENE	ILNE	CLNE	CCNE
Large Banks (Over $200 million in deposits)				
1973	2.80%	2.24%	2.60%	1.71%
1974	2.22%	1.35%	3.54%	0.97%
1975	2.73%	2.03%	2.59%	5.82%
1976	2.88%	2.31%	1.80%	2.98%
1977	3.25%	2.67%	1.83%	3.32%
1978	2.68%	2.77%	2.92%	2.87%
1979	1.98%	2.20%	4.10%	1.80%
1980	1.63%	1.34%	4.61%	-1.78%
1981	0.76%	1.63%	5.38%	1.33%
1982	0.84%	2.83%	3.21%	2.98%
1983	2.11%	3.20%	1.43%	2.46%
1984	2.02%	2.85%	1.97%	3.74%
1985	2.89%	2.74%	1.53%	3.99%
1986	2.21%	2.62%	1.18%	3.28%
1987	3.11%	2.40%	1.51%	4.85%
1988	2.66%	2.30%	2.08%	3.28%

Key to Variables
    RENE - real estate loans net earnings
    ILNE - installment loans net earnings
    CLNE - commercial loans net earnings
    CCNE - credit card loans net earnings

not be from general economic variables, but from possible changes in competition. However, the period after deregulation involved both the threat of entry and actual entry as well as the other confounding events mentioned above. Hence, the expected results are likely to be more difficult to interpret than those in less eventful market conditions. Proxies for the interest rate variable are the average six and three month U.S. Treasury Bill rates, the average federal funds rate, and the portfolio credit or expense from the FCA data. It is expected that all of the four interest proxies will yield the same general results. Proxies for GNP include the real gross national product for each of 1973-1988, GNP lagged one year to test if general economic conditions take time to be reflected in product earnings, and the unemployment rate.[2] It is expected that real GNP and the unemployment rate will have the same general significance, but opposite in sign. It is also expected that the lagged GNP variable will be less significant than the non-lagged GNP variable for consumer loans (real estate, installment, and credit cards) given the relatively long lag period of a year.

A potential problem for the checkable deposit regressions exists since both PC and SC variables are used. These variables are believed to be highly correlated. A simple Pearson's correlation is calculated between the processing cost and service charge for each type of checkable deposit. The Pearson correlation and the probability that it is truly zero follow the tested categories: average (-0.1747, 0.2378), interest-bearing (-0.3832, 0.0192), commercial (0.7970, 0.0001) and personal (0.0223, 0.8857). This potential multicollinearity problem is not considered too damaging given the stability of the results for these net earnings categories presented in Chapter 4.

Assuming that banks learn to be more adaptable after each economic assault from new competitors, it is expected that the level of significance in the differences between net earnings levels would decline with each sub-period. CMT does not make direct predictions concerning the appropriate length of time for an incumbent to react to new entry. Therefore, the interpretation of the results will keep that consideration in mind.

The net earnings from savings are not expected to change significantly over the test period from a contestability standpoint. The competitors are not new to this product, which is believed to be mature. It must be noted, however, that savings deposits have been a major source of the funds that have been shifted to NOWs and MMDAs with their introductions, as found in Gauger and Schroeter

Table 3.6: General Economic Data

Year	Treasury Bill Rate[1] 3 months	6 months	Federal Funds Rate[2]	Unemployment Rate	GNP[3]
1973	7.041%	7.178%	8.73%	4.8%	$2,746
1974	7.886%	7.926%	10.50%	5.5%	$2,727
1975	5.838%	6.122%	5.82%	8.3%	$2,696
1976	4.989%	5.266%	5.04%	7.6%	$2,825
1977	5.265%	5.510%	5.54%	6.9%	$2,958
1978	7.221%	7.572%	7.93%	6.0%	$3,116
1979	10.041%	10.017%	11.19%	5.8%	$3,191
1980	11.506%	11.374%	13.36%	7.0%	$3,188
1981	14.029%	13.776%	16.38%	7.5%	$3,248
1982	10.686%	11.084%	12.26%	9.5%	$3,166
1983	8.630%	8.750%	9.09%	9.5%	$3,278
1984	9.580%	9.800%	10.23%	7.4%	$3,503
1985	7.480%	7.660%	8.10%	7.1%	$3,620
1986	5.980%	6.030%	6.81%	6.9%	$3,719
1987	5.820%	6.050%	6.66%	6.1%	$3,854
1988	6.690%	6.920%	7.57%	5.4%	$4,024

1   Rate on new issues within period, bank-discount basis.
2   Since July 19, 1975 the daily effective rate is an average of the rates on a given day weighted by the volume of transactions at these rates. Prior to that date, the daily effective rate was the rate considered most representative of the day's transactions, usually the one at which most transactions occurred.
3   All GNP figures are in billions of 1982 dollars.

Source: *Economic Report of the President* (1989). U.S. Government Printing Office, Washington D.C.

(1990). Therefore, it is likely that total dollar earnings from savings deposits has decreased, but it is not expected that any net earnings percentage changes are brought about by increased competitive threats during the deregulatory period. It is expected that the phaseout of Regulation Q will lead to decreased net earnings, but if that belief is correct, the interest proxy in the regression should become less positive (or more negative) as Regulation Q is phased out.

Non-negotiable CD rates should not vary significantly between competitors within local markets. Depositors are known to shop for competitive rates for these funds. No increased threat of entry is expected here, therefore, only the phaseout of Regulation Q should possibly decrease the net earnings for this product. If so, the interest proxy should show a lower positive (or more negative) coefficient.

If CMT holds, banks should pay relatively higher and higher rates (implicit and/or explicit) for checkable deposits as greater competitive threats are perceived. It is expected that greater threats of new competition will be found in the accounts aimed at individuals: personal and interest-bearing checkable accounts. Explicit interest payments were not allowed for commercial banks until after the passage of DIDMCA. It is expected that the net earnings will decrease and that the rate paid on checkable deposit dollars relative to the Treasury bill rate would increase from 1973 to 1988. The elimination of Regulation Q should improve the likelihood of interest proxies being significant. Hence, the tests are biased against finding the expected CMT effects. Therefore, CMT conditions are potentially stronger than results may indicate.

No real difference is expected for commercial loans. Banks have had competition in this area before S&Ls were allowed to compete, and it is not expected that these new competitors will be able to underprice the incumbent firms. The increases in loan losses from oil concerns and LDC loans would yield a decrease in net earnings over the test period. These conditions are expected to be partly controlled for by the economic proxy in the regression estimation.

It is expected that S&Ls will be a viable new competitor for installment loans, but the prior existence of finance companies in this market may decrease the impact of the S&L's entry. The reaction to net earnings may also be delayed since past installment loans in the portfolio would take time to be paid off, and until that time the portfolio would consist of more than just loans made under the new competitive era.

It is also expected that the ability of banks to make more mortgage loans will have little initial effect on S&L rates simply because banks did not make a large push to enter the mortgage lending market as shown in Table 1.2. Table 3.7 provides a summary of the a priori effects predicted by CMT for each product.

The a priori expectation that a break in the net earnings of the various products occurred with the changes in 1980 is examined with a series of tests: the Farley-Hinich, the Gujarati, Quandt's log likelihood ratio method, and the Chow.

The Farley-Hinich test, discussed in Farley-Hinich (1970a), Farley-Hinich (1970b) and Farley, Hinich, and McGuire (1975), is conducted to examine if there were a structural break in the slope(s) of each of the regression equations during the period examined. This test is useful if the exact location of a suspected shift is not known (as is assumed when using the standard Chow test). The discussion of the test here follows that of Farley, Hinich, and McGuire (1975). Each of the coefficients which is suspected of instability is modeled as a linear function of time: $\beta_i = \beta_i + \delta_i t$, where $t = 1/n, 2/n, \ldots, T/n$ ($T = n = 16$, the number of years in the study, when all data are available). The augmented model is still linear, but with a term $\delta_i x_{it}$ for every term $\beta_i x_{it}$. The coefficients on the δ_i's are then jointly tested for significance from zero. This procedure approximates a discrete shift in the slope at an unknown point by a linear continuous shift. A univariate model of the form: $y_t = \beta_0 + \beta_1 x_t + \epsilon_t$ would be tested using: $y_t = \beta_0 + (\beta_1 + \delta t) x_t + \epsilon_t$. For the multivariate case, the model would become: $Y = XB + H\delta + \epsilon$ where H is an n x p matrix whose t,ith element is tx_{it} (n is the number of observations and p is the number of estimated parameters). The general formulation for the regressions considered here is:

$$\text{Earnings}_i = \alpha_i + (\beta_1 + \delta t) \, I_i + (\beta_2 + \delta t) \, GNP_i + (\beta_3 + \delta t) \, PC_i + (\beta_4 + \delta t) \, SC_i + e_i$$

Where the variables are as described above.

Let SSE_0 be the sum of the squared residuals from the non-augmented model ($\delta = 0$) and SSE be the sum of the squared residuals from the augmented model, then the null hypothesis that the two procedures are equal is rejected if $R_n = (SSE_0 - SSE)/SSE$ is significantly different from zero. The test statistic, $R_n[(n-2p)/p]$, has approximately a $F_{p,n-2p}$ distribution when n is large. The results of the

Table 3.7: Contestability Expectations

Deposit or Loan Type	Contestability Expected?
Average Time Deposit	No
Savings Deposit	No
Time Deposit	No
Certificates of Deposit (< $100,000)	No
Money Market Funds	No
Average Checkable Deposits	?
Personal Checkable Deposits	Yes
Interest-Bearing Checkable Deposits	Yes
Commercial Demand Deposits	No
Real Estate Loans	?
Installment Loans	Yes
Credit Card Loans	Yes
Commercial Loans	?

Average Time Deposits consists of savings, time and certificates of deposits (< $100,000).

Average Checkable Deposits consists of personal and interest-bearing checkable deposits and commercial demand deposits.

tests conducted here must be regarded as suspect given that n is never greater than sixteen.

The Gujarati test is used to locate possible shifts in both the slope(s) and intercept of each regression. The test is discussed in Gujarati (1970) and the discussion here follows that presentation. Given two linear regressions: $y_{1t} = \alpha_1 + \beta_1 x_{1t} + \epsilon_{1t}$ and $y_{2t} = \alpha_1 + \beta_2 x_{2t} + \epsilon_{2t}$ where the subscripts 1 and 2 refer to two sets of observations and ϵ_{it}'s are assumed to be equal then it is possible to have the following coefficient characteristics.

1. The intercept and slope coefficients are the same ($\alpha_1 = \alpha_2$ and $\beta_1 = \beta_2$).
2. Only the intercepts differ ($\alpha_1 \neq \alpha_2$ and $\beta_1 = \beta_2$).
3. Only the slope coefficients differ ($\alpha_1 = \alpha_2$ and $\beta_1 \neq \beta_2$).
4. Both the intercept and slope coefficients differ ($\alpha_1 \neq \alpha_2$ and $\beta_1 \neq \beta_2$).

The Chow test is general in nature in that it only discloses if the regressions are different, but not the nature of that difference. The Gujarati (or Dummy Variable Approach as it is called by its originator) uses the following linear regression: $y_t = \beta_0 + \beta_1 D + \beta_2 x_t + \beta_3 (DX_t) + \epsilon_t$ for $t = 1, 2, \ldots, (N_1 + N_2)$ where $D = 1$ if the observation lies in the first set of observations $(1, \ldots, N1)$ and $= 0$ if the observation lies in the second set of observations $(N1 + 1, \ldots, N2)$. This formulation means that β_0 is the intercept of the second set and $\beta_0 + \beta_1$ is the intercept of the second group (and is different from the first set if β_1 is statistically significant). β_2 is the slope of the second set and $\beta_2 + \beta_3$ is the slope of the second group (and is different from the first set if β_3 is statistically significant). The formulation for the general regression to be tested is then:

$$\text{Earnings}_i = \alpha_i + \beta_1 D + \beta_2(I_i) + \beta_3(DI_i) + \beta_4(GNP_i) + \beta_5(DGNP_i) + \beta_6(PC_i) + \beta_7(DPC_i) + \beta_8(SC_i) + \beta_9(DSC_i) + e_i$$

where $D = 1$ if year is between 1973 and 1979 (inclusive) and $= 0$ if year is between 1980 and 1988 (inclusive). It is now possible to discern if changes occur in the intercept and/or the slope(s) of the regression if a change is found during the time period.

Quandt's log likelihood ratio method described in Quandt (1958, 1960) is employed to determine the year of the shift (if any) for the various regressions. The discussion of the test here follows Brown, Durbin, and Evans (1975). The test is appropriate when it is believed that a regression relationship may have changed at an unknown point in time $t = r$ from one constant relationship specified by B_1, σ_{12} to another specified by B_2, σ_{22}. For each r from $r = k + 1$ to $r = T-k-1$ where k is the number of parameters being estimated and T is the total number of observations, the log likelihood ratio is calculated. That ratio follows:

$$\lambda_r = \ln \left[\frac{\text{(maximum likelihood of the observations given } H_0)}{\text{(maximum likelihood of the observations given } H_1)} \right]$$

where H_0 is the hypothesis that the observations in the time segments $(1, \ldots, r)$ and $(r + 1, \ldots, T)$ come from the same regression. It can be shown that $\lambda_r = .5r\ln\sigma_1^2 + .5(T-r)\ln\sigma_2^2 - .5T\ln\sigma^2$ where σ_1^2, σ_2^2, and σ^2 are the ratios of the residual sums of squares to number of observations when the regression is fitted to the first r observations, the remaining $T-r$ observations, and the whole set of T observations, respectively. The minimum λ_r is the estimated point at which the switch from one relationship to another has occurred. The calculations can be used to discern if a shift was abrupt or gradual over time.

The Chow test presented in Chow (1960) is conducted to test specifically if there were a change between the pre- and post-1980 periods. The general equation:

Earnings$_i$ = α_i + $\beta_1(I_i)$ + $\beta_2(GNP_i)$ + $\beta_3(PC_i)$ + $\beta_4(SC_i)$ + e_i is calculated for all observations to obtain SSE (with $N_1 + N_2-k$ degrees of freedom where k = number of estimated parameters), for the first N_1 observations (1973-1979) to obtain SSE$_1$ (with N_1-k degrees of freedom), and for the last N_2 observations (1981-1988) to obtain SSE$_2$ (with N_2-k degrees of freedom). A standard F test is now employed with F calculated as:

$$F = \{[SSE-(SSE_1 + SSE_2)]/k\} / \{SSE_3)$$
$$\text{where } SSE_3 = \{(SSE_1 + SSE_2)/(N_1 + N_2-2k)\}$$

which has k and $N_1 + N_2-2k$ degrees of freedom.

All four tests are used to provide added information regarding the timing and/or source of changes during the test period for the net earnings factor. The information generated should aide in the interpretation of the basic t-tests on the changes in net earnings in determining whether CMT predictions are being met or not.

ONE FACTOR MODEL

A one factor model is used to examine the effects of pre- and post-product entry on commercial bank's stock returns. The basic model was developed by Sharpe (1963, 1964), but the model's foundations and extensions are owed to numerous other researchers as well. The emphasis on the model used here is not on announcement affects as is standard in event studies, but on the changes in the intercept and slope terms in the model given below:

$$R_{jt} = \alpha_j + \beta_j(R_{mt}) + e_{jt}$$

where R_{jt} is the actual rate of return on stock j and day t,
           R_{mt} is the return on the market portfolio for day t,
           α is the intercept term,
           β is the slope (measuring systematic risk sensitivity),
and e_{jt} is the unsystematic component of firm j's return for
                      day t (the usual ordinary least squares assumptions
                      are assumed to hold).

This method is not a direct test for contestability, given that it would be examining the entire banking firm (or, in most cases, a bank holding company) for which the assumptions of contestability are not well-satisfied (as discussed earlier), but can provide evidence to support or refute the theory. The reactions of the individual products to increased competition should be reflected in earnings and, therefore, the firm's stock price and its sensitivity to systematic risk. CMT would hold that the β of the stocks would increase as greater competition is threatened.[3]

The estimation is made for all banks or bank holding companies for which there are sufficient data on the CRSP NYSE/AMEX and OTC tapes for any year during the 1973-1988 test period. A company is discarded if it has twenty or more missing returns over the yearly periods estimated. Table 3.8, Table 3.9, and Table 3.10 provide a

Table 3.8: Observations Used To Calculate Beta by One-state or
Multistate Operation

Year	All	(O/N)[1]	One-State	(O/N)	Multi-State	(O/N)
1973	191	(159/32)	140	(121/19)	51	(38/13)
1974	201	(164/37)	147	(123/24)	54	(41/13)
1975	206	(168/38)	153	(128/25)	53	(40/13)
1976	210	(172/38)	157	(132/25)	53	(40/13)
1977	221	(177/44)	166	(136/30)	55	(41/14)
1978	237	(191/46)	181	(149/32)	56	(42/14)
1979	242	(196/46)	186	(154/32)	56	(42/14)
1980	249	(199/50)	192	(157/35)	57	(42/15)
1981	250	(199/51)	197	(161/36)	53	(38/15)
1982	255	(200/55)	197	(158/39)	58	(42/16)
1983	244	(190/54)	189	(151/38)	55	(39/16)
1984	248	(196/52)	190	(156/34)	58	(40/18)
1985	239	(193/46)	180	(154/26)	59	(39/20)
1986	242	(202/40)	184	(160/24)	58	(42/16)
1987	231	(185/46)	168	(143/25)	63	(42/21)
1988	200	(157/43)	146	(125/21)	54	(32/22)

1   Numbers listed are for stocks traded on the NASDAQ OTC market
and the NYSE or AMEX exchanges.

Table 3.9: Observations Used To Calculate Beta by Organizational
Form

Year	All Banks	(O/N)[1]	OBHCs[2]	(O/N)	MBHCs	(O/N)
1973	191	8	(8/0)	47	(41/6)	136	(110/26)
1974	201	7	(7/0)	48	(40/8)	146	(117/29)
1975	206	7	(7/0)	49	(41/8)	150	(120/30)
1976	210	7	(7/0)	50	(42/8)	153	(123/30)
1977	221	7	(7/0)	52	(43/9)	162	(127/35)
1978	237	7	(7/0)	58	(48/10)	172	(136/36)
1979	242	7	(7/0)	57	(47/10)	178	(142/36)
1980	249	4	(4/0)	64	(54/10)	181	(141/40)
1981	250	4	(4/0)	65	(55/10)	181	(140/41)
1982	255	2	(2/0)	67	(57/10)	186	(141/45)
1983	244	1	(1/0)	60	(51/9)	183	(138/45)
1984	248	1	(1/0)	61	(53/8)	186	(142/44)
1985	239	2	(2/0)	54	(49/5)	183	(142/41)
1986	242	4	(4/0)	63	(58/5)	175	(140/35)
1987	231	4	(4/0)	59	(51/8)	168	(130/38)
1988	200	3	(3/0)	50	(42/8)	147	(112/35)

1   Numbers listed are for stocks traded on the NASDAQ OTC market
    and the NYSE or AMEX exchanges.
2   Includes banking firms that are OBHCs and those for which it was
    not possible to discern if MBHCs or OBHCs.

Table 3.10: Observations Used To Calculate Beta by Branching Ability

Year	All	Unit Banking	(O/N)[1]	Limited Branching	(O/N)	Statewide Branching	(O/N)
1973	191	26	(24/2)	112	(91/21)	53	(44/9)
1974	201	31	(26/5)	116	(94/22)	54	(44/10)
1975	206	33	(27/6)	118	(97/21)	55	(44/11)
1976	210	31	(25/6)	106	(95/11)	73	(52/21)
1977	221	35	(25/10)	111	(99/12)	75	(53/22)
1978	237	37	(27/10)	123	(109/14)	77	(55/22)
1979	242	37	(27/10)	130	(116/14)	75	(53/22)
1980	249	39	(28/11)	128	(113/15)	82	(58/24)
1981	250	38	(27/11)	119	(104/15)	93	(68/25)
1982	255	34	(25/9)	109	(93/16)	112	(82/30)
1983	244	27	(17/10)	109	(93/16)	108	(80/28)
1984	248	26	(17/9)	109	(94/15)	113	(85/28)
1985	239	17	(10/7)	117	(103/14)	105	(80/25)
1986	242	6	(5/1)	130	(109/21)	106	(88/18)
1987	231	3	(3/0)	115	(97/18)	113	(85/28)
1988	200	5	(5/0)	91	(76/15)	104	(76/28)

1 Numbers listed are for stocks traded on the NASDAQ OTC market and the NYSE or AMEX exchanges.

breakdown of the number of observations for each year (and are broken
down into various subgroups to be discussed below). The parameters
α and β are estimated for each firm for a given year using the value
weighted index of all stocks listed on the CRSP tapes as the proxy for
the market portfolio. An average β (equally weighted) is calculated for
all stocks for a given year (presented in Table 3.11, Table 3.12, and
Table 3.13) and these yearly averages are compared using the standard
t-test given below:

$$t = (\overline{X} - X) / [s(1/N_1 + 1/N_2)]^{.5}$$

where

$$s = \{[(N_1-1)s_1^2 + (N_2-1)s_2^2] / [N_1 + N_2-2]\}^{.5}$$

and N_i and s_i^2 are the number of observations and standard deviation
for the first and second sample, respectively.

The result could provide evidence to support or refute the
predictions of contestability. If the banks were more (less) sensitive to
systematic risk with the entry of new competitors, contestable markets
theory would be supported (not supported). No significant reaction
could be a result of all individual product changes being insignificant
or from significant positive and negative changes offsetting each other.
A major benefit from examining this data would be the ability to
examine disaggregated data as well as industry averages. Differences
between various banking firms based on operation level (bank, BHC or
OBHC, and MBHC), branching status (unit, limited, or statewide), and
number of states (one-state vs multistate) are examined (these are the
subgroups in Table 3.6). The "bank" category contains all observations
which are commercial banks and are not operated under bank holding
companies. The "BHC or OBHC" category includes bank holding
companies that are specifically designated as operating one bank
(OBHCs) as well as bank holding companies that are not specifically
designated as owning one bank, but for which only one bank is found
under its ownership (BHCs). The "MBHC" category includes banks
holding companies owning more than one bank.

Satisfaction of CMT's assumptions holds that the greater the
opportunity to compete against the incumbent, the greater the β as
discussed above. As such statewide branching, and multistate operations
are predicted to have increases in β during the test period. On the other

Table 3.11: Mean Betas by One-State or Multistate Operations

Year	Combined Data			One-State Banking			Multistate Banking		
	All	OTC	NY/AM	All	OTC	NT/AM	All	OTC	NY/AM
1973	0.37	0.35	0.48	0.33	0.32	0.40	0.50	0.47	0.59
1974	0.52	0.49	0.67	0.43	0.40	0.59	0.77	0.76	0.81
1975	0.47	0.42	0.68	0.39	0.35	0.58	0.70	0.65	0.85
1976	0.40	0.36	0.59	0.34	0.30	0.52	0.58	0.54	0.70
1977	0.34	0.30	0.51	0.30	0.26	0.45	0.49	0.44	0.62
1978	0.42	0.39	0.56	0.38	0.35	0.54	0.56	0.54	0.62
1979	0.48	0.44	0.63	0.44	0.41	0.57	0.60	0.55	0.77
1980	0.40	0.38	0.48	0.37	0.35	0.43	0.51	0.48	0.60
1981	0.37	0.33	0.52	0.34	0.31	0.46	0.50	0.43	0.68
1982	0.43	0.38	0.60	0.39	0.35	0.55	0.57	0.52	0.71
1983	0.32	0.24	0.59	0.28	0.22	0.52	0.45	0.33	0.76
1984	0.33	0.24	0.65	0.28	0.22	0.55	0.50	0.34	0.84
1985	0.44	0.37	0.74	0.38	0.33	0.66	0.64	0.54	0.85
1986	0.54	0.50	0.75	0.49	0.46	0.72	0.69	0.65	0.79
1987	0.57	0.51	0.82	0.52	0.48	0.79	0.71	0.64	0.86
1988	0.47	0.42	0.62	0.41	0.39	0.51	0.62	0.55	0.72

Table 3.12: Mean Betas by Organizational Form

Year	Bank			OBHC[1]			MBHC		
	All	OTC	NY/AM	All	OTC	NY/AM	All	OTC	NY/AM
1973	0.07	0.07	.	0.30	0.27	0.57	0.42	0.41	0.46
1974	0.19	0.19	.	0.43	0.36	0.78	0.57	0.55	0.63
1975	0.25	0.25	.	0.43	0.35	0.85	0.49	0.45	0.63
1976	-0.17	-0.17	.	0.38	0.30	0.77	0.43	0.41	0.54
1977	0.25	0.25	.	0.30	0.22	0.67	0.36	0.34	0.47
1978	0.29	0.29	.	0.41	0.34	0.75	0.43	0.41	0.51
1979	0.36	0.36	.	0.48	0.42	0.74	0.48	0.45	0.60
1980	0.21	0.21	.	0.35	0.32	0.51	0.42	0.40	0.48
1981	0.28	0.28	.	0.32	0.29	0.51	0.39	0.36	0.53
1982	0.15	0.15	.	0.38	0.32	0.70	0.45	0.41	0.57
1983	0.03	0.03	.	0.25	0.19	0.56	0.34	0.26	0.59
1984	0.00	0.00	.	0.26	0.20	0.68	0.35	0.26	0.65
1985	0.03	0.03	.	0.36	0.30	0.86	0.47	0.40	0.73
1986	0.24	0.24	.	0.45	0.45	0.39	0.58	0.52	0.80
1987	0.18	0.18	.	0.51	0.49	0.65	0.61	0.53	0.86
1988	0.18	0.18	.	0.37	0.33	0.54	0.50	0.46	0.64

1   Includes banking firms that are OBHCs and those for which it is not possible to discern if MBHCs or OBHCs.

Table 3.13: Mean Betas by Branching Ability

Year	Unit Banking			Limited			Statewide		
	All	OTC	NY/AM	All	OTC	NY/AM	All	OTC	NY/AM
1973	0.34	0.34	0.29	0.42	0.39	0.51	0.30	0.28	0.43
1974	0.44	0.41	0.61	0.57	0.54	0.70	0.46	0.43	0.62
1975	0.42	0.36	0.72	0.51	0.46	0.73	0.40	0.37	0.54
1976	0.29	0.26	0.43	0.39	0.37	0.57	0.46	0.39	0.64
1977	0.25	0.16	0.50	0.36	0.36	0.36	0.36	0.27	0.59
1978	0.36	0.30	0.54	0.42	0.41	0.45	0.47	0.39	0.65
1979	0.39	0.33	0.58	0.46	0.45	0.55	0.54	0.47	0.71
1980	0.32	0.29	0.41	0.43	0.42	0.50	0.39	0.35	0.50
1981	0.35	0.27	0.55	0.35	0.34	0.43	0.41	0.35	0.57
1982	0.43	0.38	0.56	0.40	0.38	0.57	0.46	0.39	0.62
1983	0.33	0.22	0.52	0.30	0.25	0.63	0.33	0.24	0.59
1984	0.30	0.20	0.49	0.28	0.23	0.61	0.38	0.27	0.73
1985	0.42	0.29	0.60	0.38	0.35	0.65	0.52	0.42	0.83
1986	0.56	0.61	0.32	0.52	0.48	0.77	0.55	0.51	0.75
1987	0.75	0.75	.	0.53	0.48	0.78	0.62	0.54	0.84
1988	0.61	0.61	.	0.45	0.43	0.54	0.47	0.40	0.66

hand, those operations would have the greatest opportunity to take on other investments and possibly decrease β. The argument is not as clear for the operation level categories. If a MBHC owns multiple banks in various states, it is believed to be open to greater potential competition. However, if the MBHC is set up inside a single state and is used to circumvent anti-branching regulations, it could be in a lesser competitive environment. Discussion of the results from this category will keep these considerations in mind. It is believed that at the firm level of measurement, CMT's predictions will be less likely to hold than the market opportunity argument.

EXCESS MARKET VALUE

The excess market valuation (EMV) method is used in Hirschey (1985) and can provide evidence, but not direct proof, of conditions satisfactory for CMT to hold. Excess market value as measured by Hirschey is:

$$\frac{EMV}{Sales} = \frac{Market\ Value - Book\ Value}{Sales}$$

CMT would predict that EMV would decrease as the threat of entry becomes greater. If EMV does not decrease until after new entry, then CMT is not supported.

The general EMV model was developed by Thomadakis (1977) and the discussion here follows Hirschey (1985). In general, the market value of a firm can be viewed as the present value of the future cash flows from tangible assets and from intangible assets:

$$MV(F) = MV(T) + MV(I)$$

where   MV(F) is the market value of the firm,

             MV(T) is the market value of tangible assets,

and   MV(I) is the market value of intangible assets.

The subcomponents of MV(F) are not observable, although MV(T) can be approximated using the accounting measure of book value and/or replacement cost values.

MV(I), which is due to intangible assets such as market power, patents, goodwill, and brand loyalty, can then be estimated. Excess market valuation is one approach to consider the market value of the intangible assets. Sales are used to normalize the expression. When EMV is positive, market value reflects valuable intangible assets not reflected in book value data.[4]

Market value consists of the market value of equity and debt. Market value of common stock is taken from the CRSP tapes. For the banking firms of this study, all deposits are assumed to have a market value of 1:1 with book value. Market value of any long term debt and/or preferred stock is proxied by book values instead given the difficulty of obtaining market values for them. Using these proxies will bias the test against finding EMV. Since "sales" is not easily defined for a banking firm, another normalizing variable is necessary. Three different normalizing variables are used: gross income from normal operations, gross income less investment income, and loans. The general model for this study is:

$$\frac{EMV}{NV} = \frac{Market\ Value\ -\ Book\ Value}{NV}$$

where Market Value equals the market value of common stock plus the book value of preferred stock plus the book value of liabilities, book value is equal to total assets which is taken from balance sheet information provided in Moody's *Bank & Finance Manual*, and NV is the given normalizing variable used. The various normalizing variables are used because it is thought that some firms could emphasize investment income over traditional loan income. Therefore, gross income less investment income would be a way to account for that possibility versus the use of gross income from normal operations or loans. CMT holds that EMV should decrease as new threats of entry are found. As with the prior two test, potential confounding effects are present that bias the tests from finding the expected decrease in EMV. First, the test period saw a general decrease in interest levels by 1988 from their 1973 and 1974 levels. Basic time value of money calculations show that greater market values will result from lower interest rates, all else held equal. Second, the stock market rose during this time, and assuming that bank stock values are positively correlated to the general market's, a rise in market value of bank stocks is expected. Third, the economy sustained one of the longest expansionary periods during the later part of the study period. Assuming an expanding economy gives banks the ability to make more loans and have fewer default problems from borrowers, a rise in market value is expected. Fourth, banks that had made oil and/or LDC loans were required during the test period to write off large portions of those loans—thus decreasing their book values which leads to a higher EMV expectation. All four of these confounding factors bias the results to higher EMVs. Interpretation of the results will keep these factors in mind.

Again, it will be possible to examine the data on a disaggregated basis. A firm was included in the sample for a given year if it had the appropriate data available from Moody's and could be matched on the CRSP data set. Average EMVs are calculated for each year, each group, and for pre- and post-1980 periods. Table 3.14 presents EMVs for the aggregated data. Table 3.15 presents EMVs for one-state and multi-state operations. Table 3.16 presents EMVs by ownership organizational form and Table 3.17 presents EMVs by branching ability. Finally, Table 3.18 presents EMVs for sub-period groupings. The average EMVs are compared using t-tests of the form given in the one factor model section above. Each year is compared with the subsequent one (1973 with 1974, et cetera) and the various levels of operations are compared: banks, BHCs and OBHCS, and MBHCs; unit banking, limited branching, and statewide branching; and one-state and multistate. CMT predicts that EMV will be less for those firms facing the greatest potential competition (holding company, statewide branching, and multistate operations) while the fact that they have greater market opportunities as well leads to a prediction of greater market value.

TOBIN'S q APPROXIMATION

A similar measure to EMV used in Hirschey is a Tobin's q approximation.[5] The ratio is calculated as:

Table 3.14: Excess Market Value Descriptive Data for Aggregated Data

Year	GI_II		GI		Loans	
	N	Mean	N	Mean	N	Mean
1973	203	-0.093	207	-0.036	209	-0.009
1974	208	-0.377	211	-0.257	212	-0.036
1975	216	-0.303	218	-0.206	219	-0.028
1976	223	-0.274	225	-0.183	228	-0.024
1977	235	-0.282	235	-0.195	240	-0.026
1978	248	-0.308	249	-0.206	256	-0.030
1979	251	-0.255	252	-0.183	258	-0.042
1980	258	-0.195	259	-0.138	266	-0.029
1981	264	-0.158	267	-0.103	273	-0.022
1982	258	-0.067	260	-0.047	267	-0.007
1983	265	0.024	268	0.055	271	0.012
1984	258	0.201	259	0.129	262	0.029
1985	254	0.387	256	0.272	264	0.053
1986	245	0.215	247	0.143	252	0.028
1987	232	0.624	232	0.434	235	0.059
1988	203	0.227	205	0.145	208	0.017

GI_II calculates Excess Market Value using gross income less investment income as the normalizing variable.

GI uses gross income as the normalizing variable.

Loans uses total loans as the normalizing variable.

Table 3.15: Excess Market Value Descriptive Data for One-state and
Multistate Operations

Operation Level	Year	GI_II		GI		Loans	
		N	Mean	N	Mean	N	Mean
One-State	1973	149	-0.243	153	-0.135	155	-0.020
	1974	154	-0.420	157	-0.288	158	-0.041
	1975	162	-0.365	164	-0.248	165	-0.034
	1976	168	-0.342	170	-0.229	173	-0.030
	1977	179	-0.335	179	-0.232	184	-0.030
	1978	190	-0.313	191	-0.220	198	-0.032
	1979	193	-0.278	194	-0.198	200	-0.029
	1980	201	-0.195	202	-0.138	208	-0.030
	1981	206	-0.140	209	-0.097	215	-0.018
	1982	199	-0.052	201	-0.038	208	-0.004
	1983	204	0.047	206	0.029	210	0.017
	1984	197	0.233	198	0.151	201	0.034
	1985	191	0.436	193	0.309	201	0.062
	1986	179	0.271	181	0.185	186	0.037
	1987	168	0.793	167	0.559	170	0.077
	1988	146	0.294	148	0.201	151	0.021

GI_II calculates Excess Market Value using gross income less
investment income as the normalizing variable.
GI uses gross income as the normalizing variable.
Loans uses total loans as the normalizing variable.

Table 3.15: (cont.)

Operation Level	Year	GI_II		GI		Loans	
		N	Mean	N	Mean	N	Mean
Multistate	1973	54	0.320	54	0.244	54	0.023
	1974	54	-0.254	54	-0.169	54	-0.023
	1975	54	-0.117	54	-0.076	54	-0.009
	1976	55	-0.066	55	-0.041	55	-0.005
	1977	56	-0.113	56	-0.078	56	-0.011
	1978	58	-0.294	58	-0.160	58	-0.021
	1979	58	-0.181	58	-0.132	58	-0.085
	1980	57	-0.196	57	-0.138	58	-0.027
	1981	58	-0.219	58	-0.126	58	-0.036
	1982	59	-0.115	59	-0.076	59	-0.018
	1983	61	-0.054	61	-0.040	61	-0.007
	1984	61	0.098	61	0.058	61	0.011
	1985	63	0.239	63	0.157	63	0.024
	1986	66	0.062	66	0.026	66	0.005
	1987	64	0.181	65	0.111	65	0.013
	1988	57	0.056	57	-0.001	57	0.004

GI_II calculates Excess Market Value using gross income less investment income as the normalizing variable.

GI uses gross income as the normalizing variable.

Loans uses total loans as the normalizing variable.

Table 3.16: Excess Market Value Descriptive Data by Organization
Form

Operation Level	Year	GI_II		GI		Loans	
		N	Mean	N	Mean	N	Mean
Banking	1973	8	0.179	8	0.149	10	0.019
Company	1974	8	0.209	8	0.134	8	0.020
	1975	10	0.124	10	0.054	10	-0.056
	1976	9	-0.209	9	-0.144	10	0.006
	1977	6	-0.154	6	-0.112	8	0.020
	1978	5	-0.233	5	-0.163	8	0.011
	1979	3	-0.291	3	-0.231	6	0.022
	1980	5	-0.277	5	-0.205	6	0.019
	1981	2	-0.174	2	-0.113	4	0.064
	1982	0	.	0	.	2	0.292
	1983	0	.	0	.	1	0.502
	1984	2	-0.464	2	-0.326	3	0.224
	1985	2	-0.038	3	-0.020	6	0.337
	1986	2	1.026	2	0.810	4	0.292
	1987	3	0.306	3	0.233	4	0.293
	1988	3	0.040	3	0.047	3	0.003

GI_II calculates Excess Market Value using gross income less
    investment income as the normalizing variable.
GI uses gross income as the normalizing variable.
Loans uses total loans as the normalizing variable.

Table 3.16: (cont.)

Operation Level	Year	GI_II		GI		Loans	
		N	Mean	N	Mean	N	Mean
One Bank	1973	47	-0.211	50	-0.148	50	-0.024
Holding	1974	46	-0.444	48	-0.296	49	-0.044
Company[1]	1975	49	-0.332	50	-0.216	51	-0.032
	1976	52	-0.317	52	-0.207	54	-0.028
	1977	55	-0.296	55	-0.208	58	-0.028
	1978	59	-0.270	60	-0.182	62	-0.028
	1979	61	-0.251	62	-0.181	63	-0.023
	1980	62	-0.237	63	-0.163	67	-0.033
	1981	69	-0.129	69	-0.088	73	-0.018
	1982	68	-0.007	68	-0.011	70	0.002
	1983	66	0.041	67	0.029	68	0.029
	1984	65	0.550	65	0.355	66	0.071
	1985	59	0.693	59	0.471	63	0.081
	1986	63	0.369	63	0.235	65	0.038
	1987	59	0.333	59	0.241	59	0.035
	1988	51	0.316	52	0.219	53	0.034

1 Includes banking firms that are OBHCs and those for which it is not possible to discern if MBHCs or OBHCs.

GI_II calculates Excess Market Value using gross income less investment income as the normalizing variable.

GI uses gross income as the normalizing variable.

Loans uses total loans as the normalizing variable.

Table 3.16: (cont.)

Operation Level	Year	GI_II		GI		Loans	
		N	Mean	N	Mean	N	Mean
Multibank	1973	148	-0.071	149	-0.008	149	-0.006
Holding	1974	154	-0.387	155	-0.265	155	-0.037
Company	1975	157	-0.322	158	-0.219	158	-0.025
	1976	162	-0.264	164	-0.178	164	-0.024
	1977	174	-0.283	174	-0.194	174	-0.027
	1978	184	-0.323	184	-0.215	186	-0.032
	1979	187	-0.256	187	-0.183	189	-0.050
	1980	191	-0.179	191	-0.128	193	-0.029
	1981	193	-0.168	196	-0.109	196	-0.025
	1982	190	-0.088	192	-0.059	195	-0.013
	1983	199	0.018	201	0.064	202	0.003
	1984	191	0.089	192	0.058	193	0.012
	1985	193	0.298	194	0.215	195	0.035
	1986	180	0.152	182	0.103	183	0.019
	1987	170	0.731	170	0.504	172	0.062
	1988	149	0.201	150	0.121	152	0.011

GI_II calculates Excess Market Value using gross income less investment income as the normalizing variable.
GI uses gross income as the normalizing variable.
Loans uses total loans as the normalizing variable.

Table 3.17: Excess Market Value Descriptive Data by Branching
Ability

Branching Level	Year	GI_II		GI		Loans	
		N	Mean	N	Mean	N	Mean
Unit	1973	31	-0.132	31	-0.094	31	-0.015
Banking	1974	33	-0.368	33	-0.253	33	-0.036
	1975	35	-0.238	35	-0.175	35	-0.001
	1976	36	-0.261	36	-0.167	36	-0.023
	1977	37	-0.262	37	-0.185	37	-0.024
	1978	38	-0.253	38	-0.183	38	-0.028
	1979	39	-0.148	39	-0.105	39	-0.018
	1980	42	-0.067	42	-0.048	42	-0.014
	1981	42	-0.023	42	-0.017	42	-0.002
	1982	36	-0.070	36	-0.052	36	-0.008
	1983	31	0.185	31	0.130	31	0.019
	1984	26	-0.044	26	-0.031	26	-0.004
	1985	16	-0.221	17	-0.174	17	-0.032
	1986	5	-0.223	6	-0.206	6	-0.028
	1987	4	-0.302	4	-0.226	4	-0.033
	1988	5	-0.442	5	-0.325	5	-0.040

GI_II calculates Excess Market Value using gross income less
investment income as the normalizing variable.
GI uses gross income as the normalizing variable.
Loans uses total loans as the normalizing variable.

Table 3.17: (cont.)

Branching Level	Year	GI_II		GI		Loans	
		N	Mean	N	Mean	N	Mean
Limited	1973	119	-0.020	121	0.037	123	-0.001
Branching	1974	123	-0.365	124	-0.248	124	-0.035
	1975	127	-0.314	128	-0.211	128	-0.035
	1976	111	-0.281	113	-0.187	113	-0.027
	1977	123	-0.280	123	-0.190	124	-0.027
	1978	133	-0.283	134	-0.198	136	-0.030
	1979	132	-0.270	133	-0.193	136	-0.060
	1980	134	-0.250	135	-0.172	137	-0.039
	1981	125	-0.207	128	-0.129	129	-0.030
	1982	109	-0.148	112	-0.098	112	-0.021
	1983	122	-0.067	125	0.044	124	0.006
	1984	119	0.207	119	0.130	118	0.027
	1985	130	0.380	130	0.262	131	0.045
	1986	130	0.123	130	0.076	131	0.013
	1987	114	1.043	115	0.722	116	0.089
	1988	89	0.363	90	0.229	91	0.019

GI_II calculates Excess Market Value using gross income less investment income as the normalizing variable.
GI uses gross income as the normalizing variable.
Loans uses total loans as the normalizing variable.

Table 3.17: (cont.)

Branching Level	Year	GI_II		GI		Loans	
		N	Mean	N	Mean	N	Mean
Limited	1973	53	-0.235	55	-0.163	55	-0.023
Branching	1974	52	-0.411	54	-0.281	55	-0.039
	1975	54	-0.321	55	-0.213	56	-0.030
	1976	76	-0.270	76	-0.185	79	-0.019
	1977	75	-0.296	75	-0.210	79	-0.024
	1978	77	-0.380	77	-0.230	82	-0.030
	1979	80	-0.284	80	-0.204	83	-0.024
	1980	82	-0.171	82	-0.127	87	-0.022
	1981	97	-0.152	97	-0.107	102	-0.020
	1982	113	0.013	112	0.006	119	0.006
	1983	112	0.078	112	0.047	116	0.016
	1984	113	0.251	114	0.165	118	0.038
	1985	108	0.486	109	0.352	116	0.075
	1986	110	0.343	111	0.240	115	0.048
	1987	114	0.238	113	0.163	115	0.032
	1988	109	0.147	110	0.097	112	0.017

GI_II calculates Excess Market Value using gross income less investment income as the normalizing variable.
GI uses gross income as the normalizing variable.
Loans uses total loans as the normalizing variable.

Table 3.18: Excess Market Value Means Comparison Over Time

Data Class	Period	GI_II	GI	Loans
All Data	1973-1979	-0.272	-0.182	-0.028
	1981-1988	0.172	0.117	0.020
	1983-1988	0.275	0.193	0.033
One-State	1973-1979	-0.327	-0.221	-0.031
Operation	1981-1988	0.218	0.149	0.027
	1983-1988	0.335	0.231	0.041
Multi-State	1973-1979	-0.103	-0.061	-0.019
Operation	1981-1988	0.035	0.017	0.000
	1983-1988	0.099	0.053	0.008
Banking	1973-1979	-0.010	-0.014	0.004
	1981-1988	0.124	0.102	0.237
	1983-1988	0.174	0.135	0.264
One Bank	1973-1979	0.381	0.255	0.048
Holding	1981-1988	0.258	0.172	0.033
Company[1]	1983-1988	-0.300	-0.204	-0.029
Multibank	1973-1979	-0.274	-0.182	-0.029
Holding	1981-1988	0.144	0.098	0.012
Company	1983-1988	0.240	0.173	0.023
Unit Banking	1973-1979	-0.237	-0.166	-0.021
	1981-1988	-0.042	-0.036	-0.006
	1983-1988	-0.040	-0.039	-0.007
Limited	1973-1979	-0.260	-0.171	-0.031
Branching	1981-1988	0.204	0.137	0.018
	1983-1988	0.331	0.238	0.033
Statewide	1973-1979	-0.312	-0.211	-0.026
	1981-1988	0.179	0.124	0.027
	1983-1988	0.256	0.177	0.038

1 Includes banking firms that are OBHCs and those for which it is not possible to discern if MBHCs or OBHCs.
GI_II calculates Excess Market Value using gross income less investment income as the normalizing variable.
GI uses gross income as the normalizing variable.
Loans uses total loans as the normalizing variable.

$$\hat{q} = \frac{\text{Market Value}}{\text{Book Value}}$$

where market value and book value are as defined for the excess market valuation procedure and the results are, therefore, expected to be similar to those of the EMV test. The ratio measures the value of replacing assets in place. The greater the value, the greater the value of being in a given industry as compared to outsiders. Again, only some indirect evidence and not a proof of contestability is possible, but CMT would hold that new entrance would bring a decrease in the q approximation value before new entry. As for excess market value, the ability to examine data on a disaggregated basis is an advantage of this test. Data sources are the same as for the excess market value ratio and the calculated q approximations are provided in Table 3.19 for one-state and multistate operations, Table 3.20 for branching ability, Table 3.21 for ownership organization, and Table 3.22 for sub-period comparisons.

Lindenberg and Ross (1981) point out that a firm with a stock of nonproductive assets such as excess cash or a securities position will tend to have a q biased toward 1.0. A banking organization exists almost entirely of such nonproductive assets. This fact will bias the test to finding the expected result for contestability that there is no advantage to being an industry insider. However, if the measure is greater than one before regulation is changed and a significant movement toward one is found with the change in regulation (before actual entry), CMT would be supported. If the q measure moves toward 1.0 after entry, then perfect contestability is not supported. The same four confounding factors that led to expected higher EMVs lead to higher expected q approximations. Therefore, the interpretation of results from this test will keep these confounding factors in mind.

Comparisons are made between years and groups as was done in the excess market valuation procedure above and the general predictions as to movement in the estimated q value are the same as the changes in EMV.

The following two evaluation methods are additional methods to evaluate CMT predictions, but are not conducted in the current study. A third area for future study based on obtaining disaggregated FCA data is also discussed briefly.

Table 3.19: Tobin's q Approximation Descriptive Statistics for One-
state and Multistate Operations

	All Data		One-state Operation		Multistate Operation	
Year	N	Mean	N	Mean	N	Mean
1973	209	0.995	155	0.989	54	1.015
1974	212	0.981	158	0.978	54	0.988
1975	219	0.985	165	0.982	54	0.996
1976	228	0.988	173	0.985	55	0.998
1977	240	0.987	184	0.984	56	0.994
1978	256	0.984	198	0.983	58	0.989
1979	258	0.985	200	0.984	58	0.989
1980	266	0.986	208	0.985	58	0.986
1981	273	0.989	215	0.990	58	0.984
1982	268	0.995	209	0.997	59	0.990
1983	272	1.010	211	1.014	61	0.996
1984	263	1.014	202	1.017	61	1.005
1985	264	1.029	201	1.034	63	1.013
1986	252	1.018	186	1.023	66	1.001
1987	235	1.036	170	1.047	65	1.007
1988	209	1.010	151	1.013	58	1.003

Table 3.20: Tobin's q Approximation Descriptive Statistics for
Ownership Organization

	Banking Organization		OBHC[1]		MBHC	
Year	N	Mean	N	Mean	N	Mean
1973	10	1.008	50	0.988	149	0.997
1974	8	1.006	49	0.977	155	0.980
1975	10	0.965	51	0.984	158	0.987
1976	10	0.999	54	0.986	164	0.988
1977	8	1.006	58	0.985	174	0.986
1978	8	1.001	62	0.985	186	0.983
1979	6	1.007	63	0.987	189	0.984
1980	6	1.004	67	0.982	193	0.986
1981	4	1.020	73	0.990	196	0.988
1982	2	1.094	70	0.999	196	0.993
1983	1	1.149	68	1.014	203	1.007
1984	3	1.059	66	1.035	194	1.006
1985	6	1.122	63	1.045	195	1.021
1986	4	1.124	65	1.023	183	1.013
1987	4	1.112	59	1.022	172	1.039
1988	3	1.005	53	1.020	153	1.007

1   Includes banking firms that are OBHCs and those for which it is
not possible to discern if MBHCs or OBHCs.

Table 3.21: Tobin's q Approximation Descriptive Statistics by
          Branching Ability

	Unit Banking		Limited Branching		Statewide Branching	
Year	N	Mean	N	Mean	N	Mean
1973	31	0.992	123	1.000	55	0.987
1974	33	0.982	124	0.981	55	0.978
1975	35	0.997	128	0.982	56	0.984
1976	36	0.989	113	0.987	79	0.989
1977	37	0.988	124	0.987	79	0.986
1978	38	0.985	136	0.984	82	0.983
1979	39	0.991	136	0.983	83	0.986
1980	42	0.993	137	0.982	87	0.988
1981	42	0.998	129	0.986	102	0.989
1982	36	0.995	113	0.989	119	1.001
1983	31	1.013	125	1.011	116	1.007
1984	26	0.997	119	1.014	118	1.018
1985	17	0.981	131	1.025	116	1.040
1986	6	0.984	131	1.012	115	1.026
1987	4	0.981	116	1.056	115	1.017
1988	5	0.976	92	1.013	112	1.010

Table 3.22: Tobin's q Approximation Descriptive Statistics for
 Comparison Over Time

Classification	1973-1988	1981-1988	1983-1988
All Data	0.986	1.012	1.019
One-State Operation	0.983	1.016	1.024
Multistate Operation	0.995	1.000	1.004
Banking Organization	0.998	1.085	1.096
OBHC[1]	0.985	1.018	1.026
MBHC	1.015	1.009	1.015
Unit Banking	0.989	0.997	0.997
Limited Branching	0.986	1.013	1.022
Statewide Branching	0.985	1.014	1.020

1 Includes banking firms that are OBHCs and those for which it is
 not possible to discern if MBHCs or OBHCs.

COMPENSATING DEVIATION MEASUREMENT

A direct measurement for CMT that has been used by Morrison and Winston (1987) is the compensating deviation measurement. It has been applied to the airline industry based on a discrete choice model proposed by Small and Rosen (1981). The model provides measurements of society's gain or loss from possible new competition. The discrete choice in this case would be if an account or loan is taken from a commercial bank or another provider. This measurement is left as a topic for possible future research.

CASH FLOW EVALUATION

Fundamental finance provides this measure to examine CMT. Theoretically, the net incremental after tax cash flows associated with entry into and exit from the various product markets for the new competitors as well as the changes for the incumbents could be calculated and then subjected to net present value analysis. The firms would desire to take all positive NPV projects—or to enter all product areas in which they can earn a return greater than their cost of capital for a project of the given level of risk. CMT would predict that firms would not earn positive NPV from investments unless no other firm had a cost of capital for that project that was greater than the incumbents. If outsiders could obtain positive NPV from investing in the incumbent's area, then the incumbent would be required to reduce earnings or face the increased competition. Unfortunately, no data are readily available to test this methodology at this time.

DISAGGREGATED FCA DATA

The basic net earnings test can be expanded to test the relationship between profitability and potential non-bank competition. Unfortunately, current changes in the management of the FCA program at the Federal Reserve renders the disaggregated data unavailable until 1993.

The Structure-Conduct Performance (SCP) model does not explain why two markets with the same concentrations have different degrees of profitability.[6] If similar markets have different net earnings after disaggregated FCA data are obtained, it should be possible to test if those markets have differing numbers of potential non-bank competitors. It is hypothesized that the greater the number of the non-bank competitors in the incumbent banking firms' market, the more likely the predicted outcomes of CMT will be found. CMT would also predict that lower net earnings would be found in states with greater branching abilities. Table 3.23 lists the changes in state branching laws from 1973-1988 for all fifty states and the District of Columbia. This information is used in evaluating excess market value and Tobin's q approximation as possible, but must wait to be used in examining the disaggregated FCA data.

Table 3.23: State Branching Laws for Each Year 1973-1988

STATE	Unit Banking	Limited Branching	Statewide Branching
ALABAMA		1973-1982	1983-1988
ALASKA			1973-1988
ARIZONA			1973-1988
ARKANSAS		1973-1988	
CALIFORNIA			1973-1988
COLORADO	1973-1988		
CONNECTICUT			1973-1988
DELAWARE			1973-1988
DISTRICT OF COLUMBIA			1973-1988
FLORIDA		1973-1979	1980-1988
GEORGIA		1973-1988	
HAWAII			1973-1988
IDAHO			1973-1988
ILLINOIS	1973-1981	1982-1988	
INDIANA		1973-1988	
IOWA		1973-1988	
KANSAS	1973-1986	1987-1988	
KENTUCKY		1973-1988	
LOUISIANA		1973-1988	
MAINE		1973-1974	1975-1988
MARYLAND			1973-1988
MASSACHUSETTS		1973-1983	1984-1988
MICHIGAN		1973-1986	1987-1988
MINNESOTA		1973-1988	
MISSISSIPPI		1973-1988	
MISSOURI	1973-1984	1985-1988	
MONTANA	1973-1988		

Sources: FDIC *Banks & Branches Data Book*. (1981-1988)

Amel, D.F. and D.G. Keane. State Laws Affecting Commercial Bank Branching, Multibank Holding Company Expansion, and Interstate Banking. *Issues in Bank Regulation* Autumn 1986, pp. 30-40.

Table 3.23: (cont.)

STATE	Unit Banking	Limited Branching	Statewide Branching
NEBRASKA	1973-1983	1984-1988	
NEVADA			1973-1988
NEW HAMPSHIRE		1973-1987	1988
NEW JERSEY			1973-1988
NEW MEXICO		1973-1988	
NEW YORK		1973-1975	1976-1988
NORTH CAROLINA			1973-1988
NORTH DAKOTA	1973-1988		
OHIO	1973-1979	1980-1988	
OKLAHOMA	1973-1982	1983-1988	
OREGON		1973-1980	1981-1988
PENNSYLVANIA		1973-1988	
RHODE ISLAND			1973-1988
SOUTH CAROLINA			1973-1988
SOUTH DAKOTA			1973-1988
TENNESSEE		1973-1988	
TEXAS	1973-1985	1986-1988	
UTAH		1973-1980	1981-1988
VERMONT			1973-1988
VIRGINIA		1973-1987	1988
WASHINGTON		1973-1980	1981-1988
WEST VIRGINIA	1973-1981	1982-1987	1988
WISCONSIN		1973-1988	
WYOMING	1973-1988		

Sources: FDIC *Banks & Branches Data Book.* (1981-1988)

Amel and Keane, Autumn 1986.

NOTES

1. A more complete discussion is presented below.
2. The data for the average six and three month U.S. Treasury Bill rates, the average federal funds rate, GNP, and the unemployment rate are gathered from the *Economic Report of the President* and are presented in Table 3.6.
3. To expand further the explanation of an expected greater β for a more contestable market, assume that an industry exists in a monopoly. This industry will have greater control over its earnings over time than the same industry if monopoly powers were reduced. Since earnings vary less over time, the monopoly's reaction to systemic conditions should also be less. Hence, the monopoly would have lower systematic risk and a lower β. In reverse, a more contestable market (meaning less monopoly power) will have less earnings stability (meaning a higher systematic risk) and a greater β. However, it can not be said that an industry that is contestable will have a higher β than an industry's that is not contestable. It can only be said that a contestable industry will have a greater β than if it were less contestable.
4. Hirschey relates that this measurement can be viewed as an analogue to the Lerner index of economic profits which is measured as: $L = (P-MC)/P$, where P is price and MC is the marginal cost. Under pure competition $L = 0$.
5. Tobin's q was developed by Tobin (1977) and interpreted in the current manner by Lindenberg and Ross (1981).
6. Smirlock [1985] finds that there is no relationship between market concentration and profitability once market share is taken into consideration.

IV

Results

This chapter reports and discusses the results of the empirical tests set out in Chapter 3 and is organized as follows. First, the results of the profitability measurement tests are reported along with the findings from the general regression equation used to explain those results. The discussion of the regression findings include the results from the Farley-Hinich, Gujarati, log likelihood ratio, and Chow tests. Second, the results of the one factor model are discussed followed by the discussion of the results from the excess market value method. Finally, the results from the Tobin's q approximation method are reported.

PROFITABILITY MEASUREMENT TESTS

The profitability measurement tests are performed using Functional Cost Analysis (FCA) data for the years 1973-1988. As discussed in Chapter 3, the FCA reports are divided into three bank deposit size categories: less than $50 million, between $50 million and $200 million, and greater than $200 million. Data are given for the annual net earnings for checkable deposits (interest, commercial, personal, and average), time deposits (savings, time, certificates of deposit under $100,000, money market funds, and average), and loans (installment, real estate, and commercial). Descriptive results were presented in Tables 3.1 through 3.3.

Basic t-tests are conducted to determine if net earnings (as defined in Chapter 3) change over the time period examined and if they change in the manner predicted by CMT. The earlier discussion leads to an expectation of results consistent with imperfectly contestable and competitive markets.

Basic t-statistics are calculated for each variable to compare:

- pre-1980 averages with post-1980 averages and
- each year's average with the prior year's (1973 with 1974; 1974 with 1975, et cetera.)

Table 4.1 provides a comparison of the pre- and post-DIDMCA costs and net earnings for non-checkable deposits and all loan types.[1] Significantly lower net earnings (at the .01 level) are found in the post-1980 data for all product categories except for money market funds. Lower net earnings are possibly caused by the major changes of the test period: the threatened new entry, the new entry, the phase out of Regulation Q, the initial increase in general operating costs associated with automation, and the increase in loan defaults. Savings deposits earned significantly less in the post-1980 period for the two largest deposit categories, but significantly greater for the smallest deposit group. Money market funds (consisting mostly of CDs of $100,000 and more) are found to earn significantly more after 1980 for all deposit categories. Credit card net earnings are found to be greater in the post-1980 period for the two smaller deposit categories (and significantly so for the smallest group). However, the largest asset category earned significantly less on credit card operations after 1980. Commercial loans earned less after 1980, but with differing significance. The middle and large deposit groups' net earnings are significantly different at the .01 and .10 levels, respectively, while the small group's earnings change is not significant. Given that new competition from S&Ls would be most expected for installment and credit card loans and the least for commercial loans, the results are generally as CMT would predict for those loan types.[2][3] However, the results for the loans and the deposits are also consistent with more competition from new entries as well. This result, of course, would be expected in a period when actual entries and threats of potential entry occurred contemporaneously.

Table 4.2 presents the same pre- and post-1980 test for average, commercial, and personal checkable deposits.[4] It would be expected that banks would earn significantly less for personal checkable deposits after 1980, since S&L and credit union operations are traditionally

Table 4.1: t-Tests Comparing Pre- and Post-DIDMCA Commercial
Bank Deposit and Loan Net Earnings

Variable Tested	Bank Deposits < $50 million	Bank Deposits $50-$200 million	Bank Deposits > $200 million
SDNE	-5.82 [1]	6.02 [1]	4.05 [1]
TDNE	5.34 [1]	9.89 [1]	8.90 [1]
CDNE	42.58 [1]	36.71 [1]	8.16 [1]
MCDNE	-30.13 [1]	-23.70 [1]	-12.47 [1]
RENE	82.85 [1]	105.32 [1]	59.26 [1]
ILNE	92.68 [1]	116.73 [1]	40.10 [1]
CCNE	-24.11 [1]	-0.48	9.97 [1]
CLNE	0.94	2.58 [1]	1.57 [2]

1   Significant at the .01 level.
2   Significant at the .10 level.

t statistic > (<) 0 means pre-1980 net earnings greater (less) than
post-1980.

Key to Variables (all are net earnings)
SDNE - savings deposits, TDNE - time deposits,
CDNE - certificates < $100K, MCDNE - money market funds,
RENE - real estate loans, ILNE - installment loans,
CCNE - credit card loans, and CLNE - commercial loans.

Table 4.2: t-Tests Comparing Pre- and Post-DIDMCA Commercial
Bank Checkable Deposit Net Earnings

Bank Deposit	Variable Tested			
Size (millions)	ADDNE	CDDNE	PDDNE	IDDNE
< $50	32.23 [1]	37.61 [1]	10.64 [1]	NA
$50 - $200	54.24 [1]	47.24 [1]	16.82 [1]	NA
> $200	25.85 [1]	NA	NA	NA

1   Significant at the .01 level.

t statistic > 0 means pre-1980 net earnings greater than post-1980.

Key to Variables
ADDNE - average checkable deposits,
CDDNE - commercial checkable deposits,
PDDNE - personal checkable deposits, and
IDDNE - interest-bearing checkable deposits.

targeted to individuals. Commercial demand deposit net earnings are not expected to change. Personal checkable deposits are found to earn significantly less in the post-1980 period as predicted for the two smaller groups, while commercial demand deposit net earnings are found to be significantly lower in the post-1980 period as well.[5] The average checkable deposits are found to earn significantly less as would be expected from a combination of the two prior categories.

One problem with the previous tests is that the large time period used may obscure changes in shorter time frames. More importantly for CMT, such tests limit the finding of changes in the time period just prior to new entry when the threat should provoke changes in pricing strategies. Therefore, t-tests are calculated to compare each year's net earnings with the prior year's. Table 4.3 presents these results for all non-checkable deposit categories. Although the exhibit provides the tests for 1973-1974 through 1987-1988, the more important tests are from 1978-1979 through 1982-1983 which should show the more immediate before and after affects of the regulatory changes in 1980 and 1982. Average time deposits are found to have earned significantly more in 1979, but less in 1980, 1981, and 1982 with the passage of DIDMCA, before generally earning more each of the subsequent years. A breakdown of the different variables contained in average time deposits is given below.

Savings deposits are expected to earn more each year prior to the phase out of Regulation Q. The general interest rate levels were increasing from 1973, but Regulation Q limited how much could be paid on savings deposits.[6] As expected, savings deposits earned significantly more for 1978, 1979, 1980, and 1981, but then earned significantly less in 1982, 1983, 1985, and 1986. The result is consistent with a decreasing pattern of interest rate levels during the later time period along with the gradual phase out of Regulation Q. It is expected that the net earnings will be explained well by the regression such that CMT is not a possible explanation for the decrease in net earnings.

Time deposits constitute a compiled category that includes club accounts and other miscellaneous time deposits. The test results follow the pattern for savings deposits for 1978 through 1982, but time deposits are found to earn significantly more in 1983, 1985, and 1986. Little interpretation is possible, though, since most of these type deposits have been curtailed since 1980.[7] For example, using FCA data, the average number of club accounts held at the largest deposit

Table 4.3: t-Tests Comparing Year by Year Commercial Bank
Non-Checkable Deposit Net Earnings

Years Compared	Bank Size	Variable Tested				
		ATDNE	SDNE	TDNE	CDNE	MCDNE
1973-74	S	5.134*	-1.144	2.325@	5.827*	NA
	M	5.739*	-4.422*	1.201	12.715*	NA
	L	2.492@	-7.743*	-5.986*	14.661*	NA
1974-75	S	-7.513*	2.708*	-1.308	-10.705*	NA
	M	-2.786*	5.701*	0.031	-10.233*	NA
	L	-4.017*	5.309*	4.653*	-11.562*	NA
1975-76	S	-4.906*	-2.832*	-4.302*	0.648	NA
	M	-9.257*	-1.580	-1.459#	-7.499*	NA
	L	0.470	3.768*	5.218*	-7.033*	NA
1976-77	S	-2.114@	-0.621	-2.896*	-0.477	NA
	M	-2.596*	-1.042	-2.574@	-0.350	NA
	L	-4.511	-0.955	-2.698*	-2.419@	NA
1977-78	S	-10.671*	-4.323*	-4.434*	-2.172@	NA
	M	-6.903*	-3.915*	1.792#	3.454*	NA
	L	-11.485*	-4.564*	-4.236*	1.146	NA
1978-79	S	-1.874	-4.231*	-2.601*	0.466	-22.871*
	M	-12.781*	-7.561*	-9.322*	-4.093*	-23.379*
	L	-12.411*	-4.829*	-10.985*	-3.099	-13.137*
1979-80	S	13.571*	-6.232*	-1.559	16.432*	-7.513*
	M	16.977*	-6.345*	-9.466*	20.156*	-5.880*
	L	11.857*	-3.431*	6.376*	9.481*	-0.686
1980-81	S	8.538*	-15.318*	-14.858*	16.036*	-5.798*
	M	1.583	-17.775*	-5.731*	8.357*	-7.401*
	L	-1.199	-8.020*	-5.260*	4.588*	-4.314*

* Significant at the .01 level.
@ Significant at the .05 level.
# Significant at the .10 level.
t-test value > (<) 0 means prior year's net earnings greater (less).
Key to Variables: ATDNE - average time deposit,
 SDNE- savings deposit, TDNE - time deposit,
 CDNE - certificate < $100K, and MCDNE - money market funds.
Bank Size: S, M, and L represent banks with deposits less than $50
million, between $50 million and $200 million, and over $200 million,
respectively.

Table 4.3: (cont.)

Years Compared	Bank Size	Variable Tested				
		ATDNE	SDNE	TDNE	CDNE	MCDNE
1981-82	S	5.469*	2.624*	16.546*	-4.203*	3.499*
	M	27.482*	9.340*	12.313*	5.393*	5.558*
	L	13.623*	5.226*	10.355*	2.812*	2.881*
1982-83	S	-5.655*	15.393*	-2.028@	-12.855*	5.532*
	M	-12.479*	18.316*	0.926	-17.627*	8.328*
	L	-3.135*	10.796*	-2.443@	-11.443*	4.628*
1983-84	S	6.739*	2.645*	4.320*	0.865	11.003*
	M	-2.909*	-1.895#	2.136@	-4.909*	15.034*
	L	-0.261	-0.851	-1.763#	0.342	8.478*
1984-85	S	-8.168*	5.410*	-6.719*	-6.507*	0.975
	M	-9.429*	7.109*	-9.464*	-6.423*	-0.180
	L	-6.376*	3.433*	-6.499*	-4.733*	-0.827
1985-86	S	-0.467	5.698*	-4.160*	-0.412	1.137
	M	-2.028@	8.072*	-3.531*	-4.239*	-0.478
	L	-0.797	6.224*	-1.533	-1.816#	1.365
1986-87	S	-7.989*	-1.042	3.715*	-8.637*	0.384
	M	-5.561*	2.103@	1.323	-6.393*	0.449
	L	-3.937*	0.059	-1.859#	-3.919*	-1.022
1987-88	S	2.521@	-2.065@	34.598*	2.239@	-1.084
	M	-1.413	-7.572*	11.354*	-1.293	0.107
	L	2.281@	-2.710*	NA	1.100	0.266

* Significant at the .01 level.
@ Significant at the .05 level.
# Significant at the .10 level.
t-test value > (<) 0 means prior year's net earnings greater   (less).
Key to Variables: ATDNE - average time deposit,
 SDNE- savings deposit, TDNE - time deposit,
 CDNE - certificate < $100K, and MCDNE - money market funds.
Bank Size: S, M, and L represent banks with deposits less than $50 million, between $50 million and $200 million, and over $200 million, respectively.

group size members decreases steadily from 147.3 in 1973 to 111.7 by 1976. After this period, the FCA reports no longer provide these numbers separately, but combine them with other account types given their decreasing importance.

Certificates of deposit less than $100,000 generally had significantly greater earnings in 1979, but significantly less in 1980, 1981, and 1982. However, earnings were generally significantly higher in 1983, 1984, and 1985. Some of these changes may be explained by the introduction of greater early withdrawal penalties in 1982 that were used to discourage customers from changing savings instruments with each change in market rates, thus making potentially higher earnings possible after 1982. It is expected that the changing earnings will be explained by the regression as these deposits are believed to be fairly competitive before any regulatory changes. However, they are thought to be less competitive than the money market funds that are included in the MCDNE category (includes CDs of $100,000 or more). MCDNE is found to be significantly greater in 1979, 1980, and 1981 before becoming significantly less in 1982, 1983 and 1984.[8] These results agree with CMT predictions since the earnings decrease in 1982-1984 and do not recover. This situation is somewhat surprising since money market funds are thought to have been highly competitive before the period studied and contestability was not expected to be increased as noted in Table 3.7.[9]

Table 4.4 provides the year by year comparison for the four types of checkable deposit accounts. Personal and interest-bearing accounts are found to have generally significantly greater net earnings in 1978, 1979, 1980, and 1981, but generally significantly lower net earnings in 1983 and for each year after 1985, as would be expected if contestable processes do not take hold immediately with deregulation. Commercial accounts are found to have significantly greater earnings in 1978-1981 and 1984, but generally lower in 1982, 1983, and 1985-1987. The average checkable deposit account results reflect the same findings as for personal and individual accounts with significantly greater net earnings in 1978, 1979, 1980, and 1981, but generally significantly lower net earnings in 1983 and 1985, 1986, and 1987. These results are also in agreement with the phase out of Regulation Q for the personal, interest-bearing, and average checkable deposits.

Table 4.5 presents the year by year comparison of net earnings for the four loan types examined. Credit card loans are expected to show results most like those predicted by CMT followed by installment,

Table 4.4: t-Tests Comparing Year by Year Commercial Bank
Checkable Deposit Net Earnings

Years Compared	Bank Deposit Size (millions)	ADDNE	Variable Tested CDDNE	PDDNE	IDDNE
1973-74	< $50	-2.297@	0.137	3.095*	NA
	$50 - $200	-4.540*	0.152	-0.091	NA
	> $200	-5.658*	-7.608*	2.021@	NA
1974-75	< $50	4.196*	5.689*	-10.276*	NA
	$50 - $200	5.269*	6.353*	0.780	NA
	> $200	4.292*	9.333*	-3.481*	NA
1975-76	< $50	-0.555	-8.382*	11.066*	NA
	$50 - $200	1.055	-2.738*	9.706*	NA
	> $200	2.062@	-0.514	6.790*	NA
1976-77	< $50	0.098	4.873*	-3.380*	-7.644 *
	$50 - $200	-1.506	-1.924#	7.417*	0.371
	> $200	0.684	1.085	-1.378	NA
1977-78	< $50	-2.674*	-11.722*	1.101	-4.197*
	$50 - $200	-0.150	-3.855*	-20.717*	-3.061*
	> $200	-4.561*	-3.771*	-3.548*	NA
1978-79	< $50	-9.850*	3.130*	-11.820*	-3.777*
	$50 - $200	-10.070*	-5.409*	-3.634*	-3.532*
	> $200	-4.090*	-3.960*	-4.818*	NA
1979-80	< $50	-11.619*	-11.374*	-4.473*	-15.421*
	$50 - $200	-9.928*	-11.149*	-2.961*	-15.827*
	> $200	-3.798 *	NA	NA	-12.799 *

* Significant at the .01 level.
@ Significant at the .05 level.
# Significant at the .10 level.
t-test value > (<) 0 means prior year's net earnings greater (less).
Key to Variables (all are net earnings)
ADDNE - average checkable deposits, CDDNE - commercial checkable deposits, PDDNE - personal checkable deposits IDDNE - interest-bearing checkable deposits.

Table 4.4: (cont.)

Years Compared	Bank Deposit Size (millions)	Variable Tested			
		ADDNE	CDDNE	PDDNE	IDDNE
1980-81	< $50	-11.340*	-13.810*	-6.091*	-23.347*
	$50 - $200	-3.850*	-9.931*	4.049*	-7.183*
	> $200	-1.165	NA	NA	2.946*
1981-82	< $50	4.071*	2.986*	1.700#	1.054
	$50 - $200	0.098	0.264	5.287*	-4.410*
	> $200	1.686#	NA	NA	-2.924 *
1982-83	< $50	17.687*	14.949*	15.847*	18.695*
	$50 - $200	20.108*	9.401*	5.232*	18.283*
	> $200	9.641*	-5.047*	10.122*	12.732*
1983-84	< $50	-1.532	-18.193*	-1.193	-1.648#
	$50 - $200	-6.890*	-8.042*	-9.726*	-5.994*
	> $200	-5.940*	-4.177*	4.095*	-6.231*
1984-85	< $50	3.464*	8.695*	2.653*	3.021*
	$50 - $200	6.759*	5.399*	3.997*	0.699
	> $200	3.801*	1.337	3.174*	1.912#
1985-86	< $50	8.590*	7.994*	28.657*	2.821*
	$50 - $200	7.175*	7.558*	3.750*	2.864*
	> $200	1.731#	2.183@	-7.986*	0.606
1986-87	< $50	6.918*	NA	NA	2.259@
	$50 - $200	10.298*	11.872*	2.968*	6.308*
	> $200	5.072*	5.344*	2.143@	0.147
1987-88	< $50	-2.221@	NA	NA	-1.998@
	$50 - $200	-1.354	-3.747*	1.865	-2.510@
	> $200	-0.467	-0.557	0.211	-0.282

* Significant at the .01 level.
@ Significant at the .05 level.
\# Significant at the .10 level.
t-test value > (<) 0 means prior year's net earnings greater (less).
Key to Variables (all are net earnings)
ADDNE - average checkable deposits, CDDNE - commercial checkable deposits, PDDNE - personal checkable deposits IDDNE - interest-bearing checkable deposits.

Table 4.5: t-Tests Comparing Year by Year Commercial Bank
Loan Net Earnings

Years Compared	Bank Deposit Size (millions)	Variable Tested			
		RENE	ILNE	CCNE	CLNE
1973-74	< $50	6.147*	4.853*	2.450@	-0.184
	$50 - $200	6.542*	8.899*	2.562@	-0.461
	> $200	6.399*	12.369*	1.326	-0.406
1974-75	< $50	-6.381*	-13.639*	22.713*	0.349
	$50 - $200	-6.512*	-9.026*	12.614*	0.612
	> $200	-5.572*	-9.422*	-8.673*	0.411
1975-76	< $50	-5.460*	3.897*	-22.603*	0.192
	$50 - $200	-4.351*	-4.393*	-16.066*	0.250
	> $200	-1.648#	-4.056*	5.247*	0.348
1976-77	< $50	-1.480	-2.233@	-2.020@	-0.010
	$50 - $200	-3.493*	-3.993*	-0.284	-0.002
	> $200	-4.220*	-5.187*	-0.640	-0.014
1977-78	< $50	-2.321@	-6.721*	0.862	-0.254
	$50 - $200	3.134*	3.990*	2.255@	-0.412
	> $200	6.092*	-1.351	0.759	-0.457
1978-79	< $50	7.064*	5.305*	1.176	-0.605
	$50 - $200	8.679*	5.077*	0.472	-0.879
	> $200	7.025*	7.301*	1.765#	-0.468
1979-80	< $50	10.769*	12.114*	0.322	-0.870
	$50 - $200	13.043*	6.188*	1.136	-0.551
	> $200	3.145*	10.042*	5.540*	-0.188

* Significant at the .01 level.
@ Significant at the .05 level.
# Significant at the .10 level.
t-test value > (<) 0 means prior year's net earnings greater   (less).
Key to Variables (all net earnings)
RENE - real estate loans, ILNE - installment loans,
CCNE - credit card loans, and CLNE - commercial loans.

Table 4.5: (cont.)

Years Compared	Bank Deposit Size (millions)	Variable Tested			
		RENE	ILNE	CCNE	CLNE
1980-81	< $50	14.130*	0.929	1.365	-0.676
	$50-$200	22.257*	17.898*	1.403	-0.721
	> $200	7.633*	-3.207*	-4.465*	-0.265
1981-82	< $50	-7.287*	-15.126*	-1.269	0.911
	$50-$200	-11.132*	-20.333*	-0.586	1.560
	> $200	-0.759	-14.492*	-2.539@	0.814
1982-83	< $50	-11.027*	-0.791	NA	1.072
	$50 - $200	-23.549*	-10.352*	-4.252*	1.339
	> $200	-13.250*	-4.949*	0.849	0.732
1983-84	< $50	0.895	13.010*	NA	-0.007
	$50 - $200	-0.839	7.475*	-0.253	-0.198
	> $200	0.930	4.616*	-2.078@	-0.220
1984-85	< $50	-4.990*	2.326@	NA	0.249
	$50 - $200	-9.212*	1.86#	-2.787*	0.687
	> $200	-8.678*	1.453	-0.399	0.176
1985-86	< $50	-2.161*	11.199*	NA	0.861
	$50 - $200	-6.072*	2.494@	0.880	0.617
	> $200	6.601*	1.456	1.148	0.132
1986-87	< $50	2.220@	-0.333	9.659*	-0.181
	$50 - $200	3.339*	13.204*	1.656	-0.438
	> $200	-7.999*	2.490@	-2.54 @	-0.116

* Significant at the .01 level.
@ Significant at the .05 level.
# Significant at the .10 level.
t-test value > (<) 0 means prior year's net earnings greater   (less).
Key to Variables (all net earnings)
RENE - real estate loans, ILNE - installment loans,
CCNE - credit card loans, and CLNE - commercial loans.

commercial, and finally real estate loans. Only the results for the larger two groups are discussed here since the smallest group has generally negative net earnings as shown in Table 3.5. The large size group has significantly lower earnings in 1980, but higher in 1981, 1982, and 1984. Otherwise, the earnings do not change significantly from year to year. The medium size group earned significantly less in 1981 and significantly more in 1983 and 1985; all other tests are not significant. In general, these results are not as CMT would predict.[10]

Net earnings from installment loans decrease in 1979 and 1980 as CMT would predict, but generally increase in 1982 and 1983 before falling again in 1984 and onward. The
results appear to be in agreement with Bailey and Baumol's argument that contestable processes do no take hold immediately with deregulation.

Net earnings from real estate loans are found to earn significantly less in 1979, 1980, and 1981 before increasing in 1982, 1983, 1985, and 1986. The results are similar to those for installment loans and again appear to be in agreement with the argument that contestable processes do not hold immediately with regulatory changes.

Net earnings from commercial loans do not change significantly during any of the yearly t-tests except for the medium deposit group which has marginally significant lower earnings in 1982 and 1983.

Overall, the results seem mixed as to whether banks reacted as CMT would predict. If banks' net earnings had been too high, CMT would predict that these earnings would decrease since new providers could underprice the incumbent firms. No consistent evidence is found to support this idea of increased bank competition in all areas. However, the preliminary results do give evidence to the importance of examining the different product areas separately to determine the effects of greater competition and regulatory change.

To improve interpretation of the t-test results, an investigation of the determinants of net earnings is undertaken with the general regression equation discussed in Chapter 3 and presented again below:

$$Earnings_i = \alpha_i + \beta_1(I_i) + \beta_2(GNP_i) + \beta_3(PC_i) + \beta_4(SC_i) + e_i$$

where: α is the intercept term,

β_i's are regression coefficients,

I is a variable for the general level of interest rates,

GNP is a variable for the general level of economic activity, and

PC is a variable for the processing costs of issuing and
maintaining deposit and loan accounts, and
SC is a variable for service charge income (used only for
checkable deposits).
$_l$ is a general designation for group size and/or year.

Figure 4.1 reports the results from the general regression equation
given above. The exhibit is broken down by product type. Each product
type is further divided by size group and each deposit group has
regressions run for the entire 1973-88 period and for pre-1980 and
post-1980 periods. Deposits are run without a general economic
variable since GNP or unemployment is not expected to have a direct
affect on net earnings for deposits as it is for loan net earnings. Results
for deposits are presented for one interest proxy (portfolio income for
all deposit types except money market funds which is reported using the
fed funds variable). Results for loans are presented for one interest
proxy (the average 6 month T-bill rate for all types except for
commercial loans which uses the average 3 month T-bill rate) and one
general economic condition proxy (real GNP for all except credit cards
which uses unemployment). Results are generally the same for the
various proxies unless in the manner discussed as expected.[11]

The regressions using average time deposit net earnings as the
dependent variable are found to be significant, as shown by F tests and
adjusted R^2's, only for the small deposit group for the 1973-88 period.
However, dividing the periods for before and after passage of
DIDMCA reveals that the two periods are different. Specifically, the
processing costs are found to be unexpectedly positively related to net
earnings before 1980 (significantly so for the medium deposit group)
while they are negatively signed (significantly so for the medium
deposit group) as expected after 1980. The pre-1980 regressions are
also significant at the .0731 level or better for all deposit groups, while
the post-1980 regressions are significant only for the medium and small
deposit groups.[12] The Farley-Hinich test, which is presented in Figure
4.2, shows no significant shift during the time period for any of the
deposit groups.[13] However, the Gujarati test, with results presented in
Figure 4.3, finds a significant difference in the intercept for all three
deposit groups and in the slope of the medium and large deposit
groups.[14] [15] The log likelihood calculations (with results presented in
Figure 4.4) show the shift as being between 1980 and 1981 for the
large deposit group, between 1976 and 1977 for the medium deposit
group, and between 1984 and 1985 for the small deposit group. These

Regression coefficients are reported with asterisks showing the level of significance for each coefficient. The interest proxy reported is portfolio income.

		Dependent Variable	= alpha	+ Interest Proxy	+ Process Cost	F VALUE	F Prob	ADJ R SQ
Small	1973-88	Average	1.44***	-10.41*	68.00	3.09	0.0797	0.2182
	Pre-1980	Time	-1.03	14.29	259.49	5.40	0.0731	0.5944
	Post-1980	Deposit Net	1.91*	-11.34	-8.54	6.14	0.0450	0.5950
Medium	1973-88	Earnings	1.35***	-14.42	198.77	0.97	0.4056	-0.0043
	Pre-1980		-0.60	-5.25	575.43*	13.84	0.0159	0.8106
	Post-1980		4.10***	3.45	-715.77***	29.83	0.0017	0.8917
Large	1973-88		0.68	-10.04	251.62*	2.67	0.1069	0.1820
	Pre-1980		-2.76**	41.26**	184.72	58.16	0.0011	0.9501
	Post-1980		1.99*	-5.15	-79.39	0.65	0.5598	-0.1101

*** t-test significant at the .01 level

** t-test significant at the .05 level

* t-test significant at the .10 level

Figure 4.1: Commercial Banking Deposit and Loan Net Earnings Regression Results

Regression coefficients are reported with asterisks showing the level of significance for each coefficient. The interest proxy reported is portfolio income.

	Dependent Variable	= alpha	+ Interest Proxy	+ Process Cost	F VALUE	F Prob	ADJ R SQ
Small	1973-88	-4.15***	95.42***	-259.86***	200.59	0.0001	0.9638
	Pre-1980	-2.19**	42.47**	62.55	13.34	0.0170	0.8045
	Post-1980	-4.69***	100.41***	-247.22***	300.87	0.0001	0.9885
Medium	1973-88	-4.43***	98.69***	-272.26***	184.95	0.0001	0.9608
	Pre-1980	-2.71**	42.43*	182.75	15.94	0.0124	0.8328
	Post-1980	-5.56***	105.55***	-238.43***	2049.70	0.0001	0.9983
Large	1973-88	-4.15***	100.92***	-331.21***	125.52	0.0001	0.9432
	Pre-1980	-3.70**	73.83**	-46.38	21.70	0.0071	0.8734
	Post-1980	-5.95***	105.09***	-217.08***	176.34	0.0001	0.9804

***   t-test significant at the .01 level
**   t-test significant at the .05 level
*   t-test significant at the .10 level

Figure 4.1: (cont.)

Regression coefficients are reported with asterisks showing the level of significance for each coefficient. The interest proxy reported is Fed Funds for money market funds and portfolio income for all other deposit types.

		Dependent Variable =	alpha	+ Interest Proxy	+ Process Cost	F VALUE	F Prob	ADJ R SQ
Small	1973-88	Time	-0.76	38.04***	-755.62**	5.81	0.0158	0.3905
	Pre-1980	Deposit	-1.02	14.56	862.28*	15.13	0.0136	0.8249
	Post-1980	Net Earnings	-2.16	51.78	-835.69	3.09	0.1336	0.3741
Medium	1973-88		-0.58	29.13***	-304.99	7.98	0.0055	0.4819
	Pre-1980		-1.43	39.07**	-322.90	5.66	0.0682	0.6082
	Post-1980		2.02	-0.28	-0.82	0.00	0.9997	-0.3998
Large	1973-88		-0.38	26.02*	-292.15	1.79	0.2066	0.0947
	Pre-1980		-4.84***	84.00***	-248.65	55.68	0.0012	0.9480
	Post-1980		6.80**	-59.23**	699.63	3.87	0.0966	0.4502

***   t-test significant at the .01 level

**   t-test significant at the .05 level

*   t-test significant at the .10 level

Figure 4.1: (cont.)

Regression coefficients are reported with asterisks showing the level of significance for each coefficient. The interest proxy reported is Fed Funds for money market funds and portfolio income for all other deposit types.

	Dependent Variable	=	alpha	+ Interest Proxy	+ Process Cost	F VALUE	F Prob	ADJ R SQ
Small	Certificate of Deposit Net Earnings	1973-88	1.56***	-35.01***	3559.84***	50.36	0.0001	0.8681
		Pre-1980	-0.07	-4.13	2106.47	2.26	0.2208	0.2951
		Post-1980	3.29**	-41.80***	1807.03	40.10	0.0008	0.9178
Medium	Earnings	1973-88	2.16***	-38.32***	3103.16***	11.86	0.0012	0.5915
		Pre-1980	0.48	-11.04	1958.94	0.99	0.4464	-0.0220
		Post-1980	5.60***	-52.11***	-401.08	34.76	0.0012	0.9061
Large		1973-88	1.69**	-32.11***	2913.44***	9.39	0.0030	0.5280
		Pre-1980	1.25	-25.59	2455.56	1.42	0.3423	0.1224
		Post-1980	5.15***	-48.38***	-364.32	31.71	0.0014	0.8977
Small	Money Market Funds Net Earnings	1973-88	-7.09**	1.37***		31.81	0.0005	0.7739
Medium		1973-88	-6.56**	1.36***		31.27	0.0005	0.7708
Large		1973-88	-6.92**	1.37***		29.49	0.0006	0.7599

***   t-test significant at the .01 level
**   t-test significant at the .05 level
*   t-test significant at the .10 level

Figure 4.1: (cont.)

Regression coefficients are reported with asterisks showing the level of significance for each coefficient. The interest proxy reported is portfolio income.

Dependent Variable	alpha	+ Interest Proxy	+ Process Cost	+ Service Charge	F VALUE	F Prob	ADJ R SQ
Small							
1973-88 Average	-0.01	1.05***	$-3.2*10^{-3}$	-2.40***	17.46	0.0001	0.7670
Pre-1980 Checkable	0.00	0.65	$4.0*10^{-4}$	-0.43	2.72	0.2168	0.4619
Post-1980 Deposit	-0.05	1.13***	0.82	-1.23	15.13	0.0120	0.8582
Medium Net							
1973-88 Earnings	0.00	1.00***	0.01	-3.05***	18.05	0.0001	0.7732
Pre-1980	0.00	0.96***	-1.31**	0.10	34.21	0.0081	0.9432
Post-1980	-0.01	1.06***	0.05	-3.08*	27.50	0.0039	0.9191
Large							
1973-88	0.00	0.80***	-0.08	-2.18**	23.18	0.0001	0.8160
Pre-1980	-0.01	0.99***	-0.03***	-1.60***	1236.40	0.0001	0.9984
Post-1980	0.02	0.75***	-1.06*	-2.03*	23.93	0.0051	0.9076

***   t-test significant at the .01 level

**   t-test significant at the .05 level

*   t-test significant at the .10 level

Figure 4.1: (cont.)

Regression coefficients are reported with asterisks showing the level of significance for each coefficient. The interest proxy reported is portfolio income.

		Dependent = Variable	alpha	+ Interest Proxy	+ Process Cost	+ Service Charge	F VALUE	F Prob	ADJ R SQ
Small	1973-88	Interest-Bearing Checkable	-0.05***	0.71***	-0.16	4.04	25.05	0.0001	0.8574
	Pre-1980		-0.04	0.59	-0.16		58.05	0.0924	0.9744
	Post-1980		-0.02***	0.00	7.91***	-6.12	42.25	0.0017	0.9465
Medium	1973-88	Deposit Net Earnings	-0.04***	0.69***	-0.05	-0.02	16.55	0.0005	0.7954
	Pre-1980		-0.03**	0.49**	0.01		146.90	0.0564	0.9905
	Post-1980		-0.02***	0.15	3.76**	-1.52	17.67	0.0090	0.8772
Large	1973-88		-0.05	0.63*	0.03	1.38	3.28	0.0887	0.4059

***   t-test significant at the .01 level
**   t-test significant at the .05 level
*   t-test significant at the .10 level

Figure 4.1: (cont.)

Regression coefficients are reported with asterisks showing the level of significance for each coefficient. The interest proxy reported is portfolio income.

	Dependent Variable	alpha	+ Interest Proxy	+ Process Cost	+ Service Charge	F VALUE	F Prob	ADJ R SQ
Small 1973-88	Commercial	0.01	0.80***	-2.33**	0.96**	58.26	0.0001	0.9296
Pre-1980	Demand	0.00	1.65*	-9.71*	-1.40	3.21	0.1819	0.5250
Post-1980	Deposit	-0.01	1.04*	-2.36	1.39	7.49	0.1200	0.7958
Medium 1973-88	Net Earnings	0.00	0.89***	-2.98**	0.41	128.18	0.0001	0.9622
Pre-1980		-0.02	1.26*	-2.96	3.74	3.35	0.1739	0.5398
Post-1980		-0.01	1.00***	-2.14	0.82	75.84	0.0006	0.9698
Large 1973-88		0.01	0.71***	-3.18**	1.32**	27.33	0.0001	0.8587
Pre-1980		0.04	0.26	-3.23	-5.76	6.92	0.0732	0.7474
Post-1980		-0.05	1.31**	-2.78	2.29**	10.60	0.0419	0.8275

***   t-test significant at the .01 level

**   t-test significant at the .05 level

*   t-test significant at the .10 level

Figure 4.1: (cont.)

Regression coefficients are reported with asterisks showing the level of significance for each coefficient. The interest proxy reported is portfolio income for deposits and the average 6 month T-bill rate for loans. The economic proxy reported for loans is real gross national product except for credit cards which uses unemployment.

		Dependent Variable	=	alpha	+ Interest Proxy	+ Process Cost	+ Service Charge	F VALUE	F Prob	ADJ R SQ
Small	1973-88	Personal		-0.05	1.21***	1.44	-2.63***	4.77	0.0259	0.4651
	Pre-1980	Checkable		-0.03**	1.90***	-1.13***	-1.81***	53.90	0.0042	0.9636
	Post-1980	Deposit		-0.17*	2.05**	2.12	-1.91	10.45	0.0886	0.8501
Medium	1973-88	Net Earnings		0.01	0.32	-0.33	-0.61	0.81	0.5133	-0.0399
	Pre-1980			0.02**	0.73*	-1.66***	0.06	65.17	0.0031	0.9698
	Post-1980			-0.01	-0.23	1.14	0.94	2.69	0.1816	0.4200
Large	1973-88			0.01	0.09	-0.33	-0.22	0.21	0.8891	-0.2239
	Pre-1980			0.01	0.73**	-1.61**	0.82	16.94	0.0220	0.8885
	Post-1980			-0.08	1.05	-0.73	1.33	0.10	0.9566	-0.8232

***   t-test significant at the .01 level
**   t-test significant at the .05 level
*   t-test significant at the .10 level

Figure 4.1: (cont.)

Regression coefficients are reported with asterisks showing the level of significance for each coefficient. The interest proxy reported is portfolio income for deposits and the average 6 month T-bill rate for loans. The economic proxy reported for loans is real gross national product except for credit cards which uses unemployment.

Dependent Variable		alpha	+ Interest Proxy	+ Economy Proxy	+ Process Cost	F VALUE	F Prob	ADJ R SQ
Small	1973-88 Real	1.98*	-0.17***	7.3×10^{-4}	-67.53	17.78	0.0001	0.7704
	Pre-1980 Estate	-0.25	-0.10**	1.4×10^{-3}***	-82.61	15.62	0.0246	0.8796
	Post-1980 Loan	3.41	-0.17	-9.0×10^{-5}	52.54	19.81	0.0073	0.8896
Medium	1973-88 Net	3.03**	-0.28***	5.2×10^{-4}***	-3.23	29.15	0.0001	0.8492
	Pre-1980 Earnings	0.51	-0.17**	1.3×10^{-3}***	-63.22	15.28	0.0254	0.8772
	Post-1980	4.48	-0.35***	2.5×10^{-4}	-3.35	23.34	0.0054	0.9054
Large	1973-88	3.25*	-0.27***	6.2×10^{-4}	-88.38	18.77	0.0001	0.7805
	Pre-1980	1.53	-0.23**	1.3×10^{-3}	-195.45	9.44	0.0489	0.8084
	Post-1980	2.34	-0.11	-1.5×10^{-3}	582.53	12.40	0.0171	0.8301

***   t-test significant at the .01 level

**   t-test significant at the .05 level

*   t-test significant at the .10 level

Figure 4.1: (cont.)

Regression coefficients are reported with asterisks showing the level of significance for each coefficient. The interest proxy reported is portfolio income for deposits and the average 6 month T-bill rate for loans. The economic proxy reported for loans is real gross national product except for credit cards which uses unemployment.

		Dependent Variable =	alpha +	Interest Proxy +	Economy Proxy +	Process Cost	F VALUE	F Prob	ADJ R SQ
Small	1973-88	Credit Card	0.35	-0.33	-1.86*	93.65	1.48	0.2929	0.1147
Medium	1973-88	Loan	1.08	-0.16	-0.15	15.63	0.29	0.8323	-0.1657
	Pre-1980	Net	11.00	-1.93*	-2.91**	203.17*	6.75	0.0756	0.7418
	Post-1980	Earnings	24.86**	-0.56**	-0.69	-99.58**	7.85	0.0376	0.7459
Large	1973-88		3.88	-0.46**	0.53	-10.92	3.38	0.0542	0.3228
	Pre-1980		3.02	0.52	1.84**	-186.85	7.98	0.0610	0.7772
	Post-1980		5.13	-0.26	-0.12	11.71	1.83	0.2814	0.2630

***   t-test significant at the .01 level

**   t-test significant at the .05 level

*   t-test significant at the .10 level

Figure 4.1: (cont.)

Regression coefficients are reported with asterisks showing the level of significance for each coefficient. The interest proxy reported is the average 6 month T-bill rate except for commercial loans which uses the average 3 month T-bill rate. The economic proxy reported is real gross national product.

Dependent Variable		=	alpha	+ Interest Proxy	+ Economy Proxy	+ Process Cost	F VALUE	F Prob	ADJ R SQ
Small	1973-88	Installment	5.75^{***}	0.04	$-1.1 \times 10^{-3}{}^{*}$	9.58	6.47	0.0075	0.5225
	Pre-1980	Loan	0.73	-0.06	9.3×10^{-4}	-3.18	1.54	0.3655	0.2128
	Post-1980	Net	8.79	-0.03	$-2.6 \times 10^{-3}{}^{**}$	78.96	9.97	0.0250	0.7935
Medium	1973-88	Earnings	4.95^{***}	-0.08	$-7.3 \times 10^{-4}{}^{*}$	21.32	3.02	0.0717	0.2876
	Pre-1980		0.59	-0.15^{**}	$1.0 \times 10^{-3}{}^{**}$	8.46	7.97	0.0611	0.7770
	Post-1980		18.98	-0.25^{**}	$-3.0 \times 10^{-3}{}^{**}$	-118.43	4.29	0.0966	0.5852
Large	1973-88		0.70	-0.15^{*}	2.2×10^{-4}	78.81	2.12	0.1509	0.1832
	Pre-1980		-2.09	-0.20^{**}	$2.4 \times 10^{-3}{}^{**}$	-50.64	5.16	0.0972	0.6931
	Post-1980		13.25	-0.24^{**}	-2.2×10^{-3}	-23.69	2.97	0.1604	0.4574

***   t-test significant at the .01 level

**   t-test significant at the .05 level

*   t-test significant at the .10 level

Figure 4.1: (cont.)

Regression coefficients are reported with asterisks showing the level of significance for each coefficient. The interest proxy reported is the average 6 month T-bill rate except for commercial loans which uses the average 3 month T-bill rate. The economic proxy reported is real gross national product.

	Dependent Variable	= alpha	+ Interest Proxy	+ Economy Proxy	+ Process Cost	F VALUE	F Prob	ADJ R SQ
Small	1973-88 Commercial	2.47	0.48***	-8.2×10^{-4}	-84.05	38.80	0.0001	0.8832
	Pre-1980 Loan	1.54***	0.19***	-3.8×10^{-4}***	44.87***	755.43	0.0001	0.9974
	Post-1980 Net	-1.37	0.59**	1.9×10^{-6}	-85.75	23.90	0.0051	0.9075
Medium	1973-88 Earnings	4.80***	0.44***	-1.8×10^{-3}***	2.34	24.05	0.0001	0.8217
	Pre-1980	2.31	0.37***	-9.4×10^{-4}	60.89	46.64	0.0051	0.9580
	Post-1980	-8.76*	0.73***	1.2×10^{-3}	5.26	32.50	0.0029	0.9310
Large	1973-88	1.61*	0.56***	-3.7×10^{-4}	-194.88***	51.15	0.0001	0.9093
	Pre-1980	2.20	0.50***	-1.2×10^{-3}	74.45	22.83	0.0144	0.9161
	Post-1980	-4.05	0.63***	8.5×10^{-4}	-149.95**	46.94	0.0014	0.9517

*** t-test significant at the .01 level

** t-test significant at the .05 level

* t-test significant at the .10 level

Figure 4.1: (cont.)

The test results are only for the regressions reported in Figure 4.1.

Dependent Variable	Independent Variables	Size	Test Statistic
Average Time Deposit Net Earnings	Portfolio Income, Processing Cost	Small Medium Large	0.2624 1.3964 0.5959
Savings Deposit Net Earnings	Portfolio Income, Processing Cost	Small Medium Large	1.7568 4.6385 @ 6.0123 @
Time Deposit Net Earnings	Portfolio Income, Processing Cost	Small Medium Large	12.5048 * 1.1790 2.2864
Certificates of Deposit Net Earnings	Portfolio Income, Processing Cost	Small Medium Large	3.2496 # 6.6724 * 2.7113
Money Market Deposit Net Earnings	Federal Funds	Small Medium Large	0.4275 0.5879 3.7223
Average Checkable Deposit Net Earnings	Portfolio Income, Processing Cost, Service Charge	Small Medium Large	4.8000 @ 3.5000 # 0.3636
Interest-Bearing Checkable Deposit Net Earnings	Portfolio Income, Processing Cost, Service Charge	Small Medium Large	1.5278 0.7812 0.9000

*   Significant at the .01 level
@   Significant at the .05 level
#   Significant at the .10 level

Figure 4.2: Results from the Farley-Hinich Test for Commercial Banking Deposit and Loan Net Earnings Regressions

The test results are only for the regressions reported in Figure 4.1.

Dependent Variable	Independent Variables	Size	Test Statistic
Commercial Demand Deposit Net Earnings	Portfolio Income, Processing Cost, Service Charge	Small Medium Large	0.6429 1.0000 0.8182
Personal Checkable Deposit Net Earnings	Portfolio Income, Processing Cost, Service Charge	Small Medium Large	4.6714 @ 13.7778 * 2.4429
Real Estate Loan Net Earnings	6-month T-bill, real GNP, Processing Cost	Small Medium Large	4.8984 @ 4.3246 @ 1.8273
Credit Card Loan Net Earnings	6-month T-bill, unemployment rate, Processing Cost	Small Medium Large	0.2845 11.0324 * 2.3979
Installment Loan Net Earnings	6-month T-bill, real GNP, Processing Cost	Small Medium Large	1.5175 3.2148 # 5.2989 @
Commercial Loan Net Earnings	3-month T-bill, real GNP, Processing Cost	Small Medium Large	1.4085 1.3182 2.1898

* Significant at the .01 level
@ Significant at the .05 level
\# Significant at the .10 level

Figure 4.2: (cont.)

The test results are only reported in a general fashion for the regressions reported in Figure 4.1. The model form is presented with the significant variables listed (with its significance level in parenthesis).

Independent Variable	Size Group	Results
Time Deposit Net Earnings $= \alpha_i + \beta_1(D) + \beta_2(I_i) + \beta_3(DI_i) + \beta_4(PC_i) + \beta_5(DPC_i) + e_i$		
Average Time	Small	Intercept (.05)
	Medium	Intercept (.01), DPC (.01)
	Large	Intercept (.01), DPI (.10)
Savings	Small	Intercept (.01), DPI (.01), DPC (.05)
	Medium	Intercept (.01), DPI (.01), DPC (.05)
	Large	None Significant
Time	Small	None Significant
	Medium	None Significant
	Large	Intercept (.01), DPI (.01)
Small Certificates of Deposit	Small	Intercept (.05)
	Medium	Intercept (.05)
	Large	None Significant

D equals 1 for years 1973 through 1979, else it equals 0. I_i is the interest proxy, GNP_i is the economic activity proxy, PC_i is the processing cost proxy, and SC_i is the service charge proxy. The variable DX_i (where X can be I, GNP, PC, or SC) is the value of D times the value of the variable for the given year. (See Chapter 3 for a more complete discussion of the Gujarati Test.)

Figure 4.3: Results from the Gujarati Test for Commercial Banking Deposit and Loan Net Earnings Regression Results

The test results are only reported in a general fashion for the regressions reported in Figure 4.1. The model form is presented with the significant variables listed (with its significance level in parenthesis).

Independent Variable	Size Group	Results
Money Market Fund Net Earnings $= \alpha_i + \beta_1(D) + \beta_2(I_i) + \beta_3(DI_i) + e_i$		
Money Market	All	None Significant
Checkable Deposit NE $= \alpha_i + \beta_1(D) + \beta_2(I_i) + \beta_3(DI_i) + \beta_4(PC_i) + \beta_5(DPC_i) + \beta_6(SC_i) + \beta_7(DSC_i) + e_i$		
Average	Small	DSC (.01)
	Medium	DPC (.10), DSC (.01)
	Large	Intercept (.05), DPC (.05), DSC (.01)
Interest-Bearing	All	None Significant
Commercial	Small	DPC (.05), DSC (.05)
	Medium	None Significant
	Large	DSC (.05)
Personal	Small	DSC (.05)
	Medium	None Significant
	Large	None Significant

D equals 1 for years 1973 through 1979, else it equals 0. I_i is the interest proxy, GNP_i is the economic activity proxy, PC_i is the processing cost proxy, and SC_i is the service charge proxy. The variable DX_i (where X can be I, GNP, PC, or SC) is the value of D times the value of the variable for the given year. (See Chapter 3 for a more complete discussion of the Gujarati Test.)

Figure 4.3: (cont.)

The test results are only reported in a general fashion for the regressions reported in Figure 4.1. The model form is presented with the significant variables listed (with its significance level in parenthesis).

Independent Variable	Size Group	Results
Loan Net Earnings $= \alpha_i + \beta_1(D) + \beta_2(I_i) + \beta_3(DI_i) + \beta_4(GNP_i) + \beta_5(DGNP_i) + \beta_6(PC_i) + \beta_7(DPC_i) + e_i$		
Real Estate	Small	Intercept (.05)
	Medium	None Significant
	Large	None Significant
Credit Card	Small	Intercept (.01), DTB6 (.05), DUNEMP (.01), DPC (.05)
	Medium	DTB6(.05), DUNEMP (.01), DPC (.01)
	Large	DTB6 (.10)
Installment	Small	Intercept (.10), DGNP (.01)
	Medium	Intercept (.05), DGNP (.01)
	Large	None Significant
Commercial	Small	DI (.05)
	Medium	Intercept (.10), DI (.05)
	Large	DPC (.10)

D equals 1 for years 1973 through 1979, else it equals 0. I_i is the interest proxy, GNP_i is the economic activity proxy, PC_i is the processing cost proxy, and SC_i is the service charge proxy. The variable DX_i (where X can be I, GNP, PC, or SC) is the value of D times the value of the variable for the given year. (See Chapter 3 for a more complete discussion of the Gujarati Test.)

Figure 4.3: (cont.)

Dep Var	Size Group	Ind Var	73-75 and 76-88	73-76 and 77-88	73-77 and 78-88	73-78 and 79-88	73-79 and 80-88	73-80 and 81-88	73-81 and 82-88	73-82 and 83-88	73-83 and 84-88	73-84 and 85-88	73-85 and 86-88
ATDNE	Small	PI PC	47.86	-12.24	-16.14	-13.61	-14.18	-10.75	-12.25	-9.94	-8.53	-6.43	-48.04
	Medium	PI PC	-55.41	-14.84	-22.26	-25.41	-23.41	-20.01	-28.72	-18.26	-15.02	-16.78	-51.20
	Large	PI PC	-47.17	-11.41	-12.36	-13.63	-17.91	-10.67	-18.44	-13.15	-11.40	-16.01	-52.80
SDNE	Small	PI PC	NA	-14.50	-15.15	-12.95	-12.97	-13.12	-11.80	-13.34	-9.98	-10.44	NA
	Medium	PI PC	-56.03	-14.33	-14.72	-16.32	-19.16	-20.00	-18.30	-16.01	-12.81	-11.76	-47.86
	Large	PI PC	-51.44	-9.77	-11.36	-10.34	-10.07	-12.14	-12.64	-20.26	-26.31	-34.80	-55.47
TDNE	Small	PI PC	-53.69	-10.68	-13.01	-16.00	-16.90	-17.10	-19.89	-20.09	-19.45	-30.03	-62.33
	Medium	PI PC	NA	-14.06	-12.17	-15.19	-14.27	-14.69	-16.37	-17.20	-14.97	-15.07	-58.38
	Large	PI PC	-51.28	-10.48	-14.62	-20.02	-21.41	-15.48	-19.50	-14.97	-17.39	-19.70	-57.16
CDNE	Small	PI PC	-52.21	-7.62	-9.14	-9.66	-9.90	-8.41	-9.03	-9.81	-9.59	-9.41	-56.06
	Medium	PI PC	-52.44	-22.93	-28.36	-12.50	-10.32	-12.63	-12.39	-13.98	-18.95	-16.10	-59.38
	Large	PI PC	-51.81	-13.24	-14.97	-19.69	-10.20	-11.29	-11.32	-12.89	-12.31	-10.62	-50.07

The test results are reported for the regressions presented in Figure 4.1

Key to Dependent Variables (all net earnings)

ATDNE - average time deposits, SDNE - savings deposits, TDNE - time deposits, and CDNE - certificates < $100K.

Key to Independent Variables

PC - processing cost and PI - portfolio income.

Figure 4.4: Results from the Log Likelihood Ratio Test for Commercial Banking Deposit and Loan Net Earnings Regressions

Dep Var	Size Group	Ind Var	73-75 and 76-88	73-76 and 77-88	73-77 and 78-88	73-78 and 79-88	73-79 and 80-88	73-80 and 81-88	73-81 and 82-88	73-82 and 83-88	73-83 and 84-88	73-84 and 85-88	73-85 and 86-88
MCDNE	Small	FF	NA	NA	NA	NA	NA	-33.92	-7.71	-5.33	-20.22	-15.64	-13.08
	Medium	FF	NA	NA	NA	NA	NA	-34.50	-13.25	-6.64	-24.71	-15.01	-11.24
	Large	FF	NA	NA	NA	NA	NA	-35.37	-6.05	-6.92	-6.92	-9.38	-7.12
ADDNE	Small	PI PC SC	NA	-23.67	-6.64	-3.49	-3.62	-1.87	-4.87	-13.68	-27.55	-62.65	NA
	Medium	PI PC SC	NA	NA	-16.44	-18.99	-20.65	-11.15	-11.86	-32.06	-24.59	NA	NA
	Large	PI PC SC	NA	NA	-28.34	-26.28	-30.00	-33.83	-14.44	-11.37	-14.19	-68.84	NA
IDDNE	Small	PI PC SC	NA	NA	NA	NA	-23.55	-9.83	-11.57	-13.52	-10.48	NA	NA
	Medium	PI PC SC	NA	NA	NA	NA	NA	-12.91	-12.79	-11.52	-12.84	NA	NA
	Large	PI PC SC	NA	NA	NA	NA	NA	NA	-144.21	-22.86	-22.42	NA	NA
CDDNE	Small	PI PC SC	NA	NA	-9.14	-3.76	-4.32	-2.46	-6.12	-96.25	NA	NA	NA
	Medium	PI PC SC	NA	NA	-8.55	-8.88	-7.18	-6.94	-8.73	-7.79	-8.56	NA	NA
	Large	PI PC SC	NA	NA	NA	-9.55	-14.33	-14.23	-14.14	-20.05	-12.92	-66.07	NA

The test results are reported for the regressions presented in Figure 4.1

Key to Dependent Variables (all net earnings)

MCDNE - money market funds, ADDNE - average checkable deposits, IDDNE - interest-bearing checkable deposits, and CDDNE - commercial checkable deposits.

Key to Independent Variables

PC - processing cost, FF - federal funds rate, PI - portfolio income, and SC - service charge.

Figure 4.4: (cont.)

Dep Var	Size Group	Ind Var	73-75 and 76-88	73-76 and 77-88	73-77 and 78-88	73-78 and 79-88	73-79 and 80-88	73-80 and 81-88	73-81 and 82-88	73-82 and 83-88	73-83 and 84-88	73-84 and 85-88	73-85 and 86-88
PDDNE	Small	PI PC SC	NA	-19.11	-16.62	-19.11	-20.90	-9.07	-10.65	NA	NA	NA	NA
	Medium	PI PC SC	NA	NA	-27.06	-30.73	-22.34	-12.62	-17.80	-17.59	-15.48	-61.28	NA
	Large	PI PC SC	NA	NA	-11.79	-14.16	-16.09	-18.00	-19.92	-30.39	-18.25	NA	NA
RENE	Small	TB6 G PC	NA	-58.15	-14.87	-15.54	-17.33	-13.18	-8.64	-12.64	-11.17	NA	NA
	Medium	TB6 G PC	NA	-53.98	-11.55	-13.24	-16.13	-12.87	-6.90	-11.42	-22.06	-67.83	NA
	Large	TB6 G PC	NA	NA	-10.81	-10.92	-15.81	-13.97	-18.90	-11.70	-15.61	NA	NA
CCNE	Small	TB6 G PC	NA	NA	-45.53	-12.41	-13.76	-18.36	-17.35	-19.46	-20.14	NA	NA
	Medium	TB6 G PC	NA	NA	-17.30	-20.43	-20.42	-17.75	-16.85	-15.69	-13.94	-65.43	NA
	Large	TB6 G PC	NA	-72.47	-34.94	-28.37	-33.38	NA	NA	NA	NA	NA	NA

The test results are reported for the regressions presented in Figure 4.1

Key to Dependent Variables (all net earnings)

PDDNE - personal checkable deposits, RENE - real estate loans, and CCNE - credit card loans.

Key to Independent Variables

PC - processing cost, PI - portfolio income, SC - service charge, TB6 - six-month T-bill rate, and G - real GNP.

Figure 4.4: (cont.)

Dep Var	Size Group	Ind Var	73-75 and 76-88	73-76 and 77-88	73-77 and 78-88	73-78 and 79-88	73-79 and 80-88	73-80 and 81-88	73-81 and 82-88	73-82 and 83-88	73-83 and 84-88	73-84 and 85-88	73-85 and 86-88
ILNE	Small	TB6 G PC	NA	-65.85	-17.08	-14.69	-16.95	-15.93	-18.88	-16.32	-24.81	-66.12	NA
	Medium	TB6 G PC	NA	-64.61	-30.46	-17.34	-18.04	-20.35	-18.22	-19.99	-20.18	-65.06	NA
	Large	TB6 G PC	NA	-66.17	-22.43	-15.25	-14.45	-15.98	-19.22	-23.29	-21.60	-64.89	NA
CLNE	Small	TB3 G PC	NA	NA	-46.25	-35.29	-30.64	-13.71	-12.61	-19.02	-19.51	-60.68	NA
	Medium	TB3 G PC	NA	-66.18	-21.79	-17.67	-20.50	-24.60	-25.97	-19.36	-23.40	-69.87	NA
	Large	TB3 G PC	NA	-65.26	-13.73	-13.40	-12.17	-13.71	-12.48	-15.57	-17.05	-65.25	NA

The test results are reported for the regressions presented in Figure 4.1
Key to Dependent Variables (all net earnings)
    ILNE - installment loans, and CLNE - commercial loans.
Key to Independent Variables
    PC - processing cost, TB6 - six-month T-bill rate, TB3 - three-month T-bill rate, and G - real GNP.

Figure 4.4: (cont.)

results hold no matter which set of variables is used in the regression estimations. The Chow test (results presented in Table 4.6) comparing pre- and post-1980 periods is significant (at the .10 level for the large and small deposit groups, and at the .05 level for the medium deposit group) as well. These results hold at the given significance level or better for all combinations of independent variables tested in the regressions. Further interpretation is sought by looking at the components of average time deposits.

The regressions for savings deposits are significant as expected, with all of the regressions for the 1973-88 time period significant at the alpha = .0001 level. Signs are as expected for the independent variables with the portfolio income interest rate proxy significant at the .01 level. When the regressions are run for the pre- and post-1980 periods, it is found that the interest proxy is less significant for the pre-1980 period than the post-1980 period. This result is surprising. The existence of Regulation Q before 1980 should result in little change in the payout to customers from higher general interest rates. Therefore, higher earnings for banks would be expected. After Regulation Q, higher rates could be passed on to customers more readily and lower earnings would be expected. The existence of implicit interest payments via convenience or other services before 1980 could help to explain lower net earnings during a time of higher market rates.[16] The Farley-Hinich test shows significant structural breaks for the medium and large deposit groups and the Gujarati test shows significant structural breaks for the small and medium deposit groups. The log likelihood function shows the shift between 1983 and 1984 for the small deposit group, between 1984 and 1985 for the medium deposit group, and between 1976 and 1977 for the large deposit group. The Chow test comparing pre- and post-1980 periods is not significant for any deposit group.[17]

Time deposit regressions for the entire period are significant for the small and medium deposit groups with variable signs as expected for all deposit groups. The large and medium groups exhibit the expected result for interest proxies for before and after 1980. The proxies are positively signed in the pre-1980 period, but negatively signed in the post-1980 period in agreement with CMT expectations as well as with the phase out of Regulation Q.[18] The Farley-Hinich test is significant for only the small deposit group, while the Gujarati test is significant for only the large deposit group. The Gujarati test shows a shift in the intercept and the interest proxy of the model. The log likelihood test generally shows the shift as being between 1976 and

Table 4.6: Results from the Chow Test Comparing Pre- and Post-1980 Periods for Commercial Banking Deposit and Loan Net Earnings Regressions

Ind Var	Size Group	Dep Variables	SSE 1973-88	SSE 1973-79	SSE 1981-88	F Stat
ATDNE	Small	PI PC	0.4605	0.0692	0.0799	6.2656#
	Medium	PI PC	1.0151	0.0640	0.0478	24.2388@
	Large	PI PC	1.6663	0.0548	0.3981	8.0375#
SDNE	Small	PI PC	0.4010	0.0630	0.0932	4.7017
	Medium	PI PC	0.4422	0.0921	0.0127	-3.0000
	Large	PI PC	0.8341	0.1706	0.1792	4.1535
TDNE	Small	PI PC	6.7442	0.0683	5.2064	0.8358
	Medium	PI PC	2.3660	0.0959	1.1783	-3.0000
	Large	PI PC	7.2264	0.0964	1.2259	13.3951@
CDNE	Small	PI PC	0.4874	0.0739	0.2047	2.2484
	Medium	PI PC	1.7398	0.3999	0.2584	-3.0000
	Large	PI PC	2.5168	1.4694	0.2562	1.3755
MCDNE	Small	FF	42.1643	NA	41.9148	0.0149
	Medium	FF	42.3806	NA	41.6215	-2.3955
	Large	FF	45.8363	NA	41.8365	0.2390
ADDNE	Small	PI PC SC	0.0003	0.0000	0.0001	2.6411
	Medium	PI PC SC	0.0002	0.0000	0.0000	23.7708*
	Large	PI PC SC	0.0001	0.0000	0.0000	5.8081

The test results are for the regressions reported in Figure 4.1.

* Significant at the .01 level.
@ Significant at the .05 level.
# Significant at the .10 level.

Key to Dependent Variables
   ATDNE - average time deposits, SDNE - savings deposits, TDNE - time deposits, CDNE - certificates of deposit (< $100,000), MCDNE - money market funds, and ADDNE - average checkable deposits.
Key to Independent Variables
   PI - portfolio income, PC - processing cost, FF - federal funds rate, and SC - service charge.

Table 4.6: (cont.)

Ind Var	Size Group	Dep Variables	SSE 1973-88	SSE 1973-79	SSE 1981-88	F Stat
IDDNE	Small	PI PC SC	0.0002	0.0000	0.0000	7.3333@
	Medium	PI PC SC	0.0001	0.0000	0.0000	4.2632#
	Large	PI PC SC	0.0002	NA	0.0001	0.3462
CDDNE	Small	PI PC SC	0.0001	0.0000	0.0000	0.8333
	Medium	PI PC SC	0.0001	0.0000	0.0000	1.6528
	Large	PI PC SC	0.0002	0.0000	0.0000	2.7500
PDDNE	Small	PI PC SC	0.0014	0.0000	0.0002	8.0764@
	Medium	PI PC SC	0.0007	0.0000	0.0001	15.2816*
	Large	PI PC SC	0.0009	0.0000	0.0007	0.5909
RENE	Small	TB6 G PC	0.5667	0.0169	0.1470	4.3008#
	Medium	TB6 G PC	0.9762	0.0258	0.3643	2.6293
	Large	TB6 G PC	1.4297	0.1040	0.5205	2.2564
CCNE	Small	TB6 U PC	88.6521	9.9581	NA	NA
	Medium	TB6 U PC	70.4547	5.1812	3.9106	11.8112@
	Large	TB6 U PC	24.4409	1.6655	3.2550	6.9425@

The test results are for the regressions reported in Figure 4.1.

*   Significant at the .01 level.
@   Significant at the .05 level.
#   Significant at the .10 level.

Key to Dependent Variables
    IDDNE - interest-bearing checkable deposits, CDDNE - commercial demand deposits, PDDNE - personal checkable deposits, RENE - real estate loans, and CCNE - credit card loans.
Key to Independent Variables
    PI - portfolio income, PC - processing cost, SC - service charge, TB6 - six-month Treasury bill rate, G - real GNP, and U - unemployment rate.

Table 4.6: (cont.)

Ind Var	Size Group	Dep Variables	SSE 1973-88	SSE 1973-79	SSE 1981-88	F Stat
ILNE	Small	TB6 G PC	1.6402	0.0929	0.3347	4.9627#
	Medium	TB6 G PC	1.4140	0.0349	0.3434	4.7911#
	Large	TB6 G PC	2.8776	0.2025	0.4853	5.5716#
CLNE	Small	TB3 G PC	2.4013	0.0010	1.0875	2.1106
	Medium	TB3 G PC	4.3095	0.0471	0.8323	6.8259@
	Large	TB3 G PC	1.6667	0.1792	0.3782	3.4827

The test results are for the regressions reported in Figure 4.1.

* Significant at the .01 level.
@ Significant at the .05 level.
# Significant at the .10 level.

Key to Dependent Variables
  ILNE - installment loans, and CLNE - commercial loans.
Key to Independent Variables
  TB6 - six-month Treasury bill rate, TB3 - three-month Treasury bill rate, G - real GNP, and PC - processing cost.

1977 for the small and large deposit groups and between 1977 and 1978 for the medium deposit group. The Chow test comparing pre- and post-1980 regressions is only significant for the large deposit group.[19]

The small certificates of deposit regressions are found to be significant for the entire period as expected, but only the interest proxy has the expected sign. It is found that the pre-1980 period's interest proxy is negatively signed, but is not significant while the post-1980 interest rate proxy is negatively significant. Such a result is compatible with CMT expectations as well as with the phase out of Regulation Q.[20] The Farley-Hinich and Gujarati tests show significant differences for the small and medium deposit groups with the Gujarati test showing the shift to be in the intercept. The log likelihood ratio test shows a switch occurring between 1979 and 1980 for the medium and large deposit groups and between 1976 and 1977 for the small deposit group. The Chow tests are not significant.[21]

Money market deposits (such as CDs of $100,000 or more) are found to have significant regressions as expected and all interest proxies are also significant at the .01 level. However, the interest proxies are unexpectedly positively signed. It is expected that higher interest rates would lead to higher costs for money market funds and lower net earnings as in Flannery (1980). A positive sign for these deposits suggests that margins increase as interest levels rise.[22][23] Pre- and post-1980 comparisons are unavailable due to insufficient data during the pre-1980 period.[24] The log likelihood test does show that any change in the process underlying the regression occurs between 1982 and 1983 for the small and medium deposit groups and between 1981 and 1982 for the large deposit group.

The regressions for average checkable deposits are highly significant for all time periods, size groups, and proxies used, except for the pre-1980 period for the small deposit group and then only for the regression using portfolio income as the interest proxy. Interest proxies are uniformly of the expected signs and generally highly significant. Processing costs are generally of the expected sign and are only significant when it is negatively signed. The service charge variable is unexpectedly negatively signed and is often significant. Little difference is found between the time periods, except that processing costs are more likely to be significant during the pre-1980 period. The Farley-Hinich test is significant for the small and medium deposit groups with the Gujarati test showing the shift to be in the service charge variable at the .01 level for all three deposit groups. Processing costs were significantly different for the medium and large deposit groups as well. The log likelihood test shows any shift as generally between 1980 and 1981 for the small and medium deposit groups, but between 1982 and 1983 for the large deposit group. The Chow test for pre- and post-1980 periods is generally not significant except for the medium deposit group. Decomposing the average checking deposits into its components should provide added information.[25]

The regressions for interest-bearing checkable accounts are generally significant. The interest proxies are positively significant, as expected, for the 1973-1988 period for all deposit groups and for the pre-1980 period for the medium deposit group, but are not significant for the post-1980 period. This result is consistent with CMT expectations in that, after 1980, increases in interest rates are now more likely passed on to consumers in the more contestable environment as well as the phase out of Regulation Q.[26] Data limit the usefulness of the parameter shift tests. They are reported for completeness, but no interpretation is given here.[27]

Commercial checking accounts (true demand deposit accounts) are found to have significant regressions for the 1973-88 period, generally with the expected signs on the independent variables. Surprisingly, the interest proxy is generally greater in the post-1980 period for those regressions reported in Figure 4.1.[28] The Farley-Hinich results show no significant changes in the regressions for all deposit groups, while the Gujarati test shows significant differences for the small and large deposit groups in the service charge variable as well as the processing cost variable for the medium deposit group. The log likelihood test shows any change to be between 1980 and 1981 for the small and medium deposit groups and between 1978 and 1979 for the large deposit group. The Chow test comparing pre- and post-1980 is found to be significant for the small and medium deposit groups.[29]

The personal checkable deposit regressions are generally not significant, as expected. Interest rate proxies are positively significant for the pre-1980 period for all the deposit groups. The post-1980 regressions perform worse for all three deposit groups and exhibit the same pattern for interest proxies as seen for interest checking, which is again consistent with CMT expectations as well as the phase out of Regulation Q.[30] The Farley-Hinich test is significant for the small and medium deposit groups and the Gujarati test suggests that the any switch is from changes in the service charge variable. The log likelihood test shows a switch between 1980 and 1981 for the small and medium deposit groups and between 1977 and 1978 for the large deposit group. The Chow test comparing pre- and post-1980 is significant for the small and medium deposit groups as would be expected from the Farley-Hinich and log likelihood tests.[31]

Real estate loans are found to have significant regressions for the entire period with signs on variables as expected, in general. Interest rate proxies are uniformly significant. The pre- and post-1980 periods generally show the same results, but the sign of the processing cost variable changes to positive (although still not significant).[32] The Farley-Hinich tests are significant for the two smaller deposit groups, but the Gujarati test is only significant for the small size group and shows a shift in the intercept. The log likelihood test shows any shift to have occurred between 1981 and 1982 for the smaller deposit groups and between 1977 and 1978 for the large deposit group. The Chow test is generally not significant except for the small deposit group.[33]

In general, the regression results for the 1973-88 period credit card net earnings are poor, as expected. The economic proxy, unemployment, is negatively significant, as expected, only for the small deposit group, while interest proxies are significantly negative and processing costs negatively signed, as expected, only for the large deposit group. The regressions for the divided periods perform statistically better; however, the signs in the pre-1980 period are generally the opposite of those of the post-1980 period. The results are consistent with CMT expectations in that the given general economic variables can not explain well the changes in net earnings for credit cards.[34] The Farley-Hinich test is significant only for the medium deposit group. The Gujarati test reveals significant changes in the interest proxy for all deposit groups as well as the unemployment and processing cost variables for the two smaller deposit groups. The intercept is also significantly different for the small deposit group. The log likelihood test shows any switch to occur most likely between 1978 and 1979 for the small and large deposit groups and between 1983 and 1984 for the medium deposit group. The Chow test comparing the pre- and post-1980 periods is significant for the medium and large deposit groups.[35]

The 1973-88 period regressions for installment loans are more significant the smaller the deposit group. General economic conditions are typically significant for the small deposit group, but are of the wrong sign. Dividing the period produces no improvement in the regression results in either sub-period. These poor regressions are consistent with CMT in that an added independent variable for competition could prove useful.[36] The Farley-Hinich test is significant for the two larger deposit groups with the Gujarati test showing shifts in the intercept and the GNP proxy variables. The log likelihood test shows shifts between 1978 and 1979 for the two smaller deposit groups and between 1979 and 1980 for the large deposit group. The Chow test finds the pre- and post-1980 periods marginally significantly different for all three deposit groups.[37]

Regressions for commercial loan net earnings for the 1973-1988 period are generally highly significant and with positively significant interest proxies, as expected. GNP variables, though, are unexpectedly negatively signed. Dividing the time periods results in the interest proxies generally being more significant during the pre-1980 period, but GNP proxies are more likely to be positively signed, as expected, in the post-1980 period. The regressions for both time periods are generally significant.[38] Farley-Hinich test results are uniformly insignificant. The Gujarati test shows a switch in the interest proxy for the two smaller deposit groups and in the processing cost for the large deposit group. The log likelihood test shows the switch occurring between 1981 and 1982 for the small deposit group, between 1978 and 1979 for the medium deposit group, and between 1979 and 1980 for the large deposit group. Chow tests are uniformly significant when using Fed Funds as the interest rate proxy, otherwise generally only the medium size group showed significant difference between the pre- and post-1980 periods.[39]

Summary and Conclusions for the Profitability Tests

Thus far, the results of applying Contestable Markets Theory to the U.S. commercial banking industry are consistent with the expectations that because threat of entry and actual entry were both occurring during the test period, evidence would be found to support imperfectly contestable and competitive market forces. Net earnings generally decreased after the passage of DIDMCA in 1980 in products specifically addressed by that legislation (savings, time, checkable and certificates of deposit less than $100,000 and real estate, installment, credit card, and commercial loans). A result consistent with both contestable and competitive markets as well as the confounding factors addressed earlier such as the phaseout of Regulation Q. Year-to-year changes in net earnings provide further evidence consistent with imperfectly contestable markets for all these products except commercial loans.

Regression analysis is used to determine if the results of the year-to-year net earnings changes could be explained by general economic variables such as the level of GNP and interest rates. If the regression proves to be well specified, then contestability is not expected to be an important explanatory variable for that product. As such, poor regression results are expected for those products thought to be the most likely to be contestable: installment and credit card loans and personal and interest-bearing checkable deposits. Of course, poor results would also be generated from poorly specified regressions. Generally poor regression results are obtained for both installment and credit card loans. The regression results for personal and interest-bearing checkable deposits are generally significant over the entire test period, but are strikingly different for pre- and post-1980 periods and different in a manner consistent with CMT expectations.

Overall, these results provide evidence for imperfectly contestable markets in commercial banking. Therefore, further deregulation that allows the possibility of new entry—either geographical or product—should provide additional benefit to consumers as evidenced by lower net earnings margins for the individual banking products.

ONE FACTOR MODEL

As reported in Chapter 3, the one factor model is used to examine the effects of pre- and post-product entry on commercial bank's stock returns. The emphasis on the use of the model in this study focuses on possible changes in the intercept and slope coefficients. CMT would infer a greater β as potential competition is increased as discussed in Chapter 3. This prediction includes not only the allowance of new competitors via the deregulatory acts of 1980 and 1982, but also the form of the banking company (bank holding company or not, multistate operation or not) and the branching allowed in its main state of operation (unit banking, limited, or statewide branching). The basic data on the number of observations in each category are presented in Table 3.8, Table 3.9, and Table 3.10 and the mean betas for each category are presented in Table 3.11 and Table 3.12, and Table 3.13. The mean betas in Table 3.11, Table 3.12, and Table 3.13 are also disaggregated for companies whose stock is traded on the New York or American Stock Exchanges (NYSE/AMEX) as opposed to the OTC market.

Inspection of Table 3.12 suggests that multibank holding companies have greater betas on average than the one bank holding companies which are greater than those for individual banks and inspection of Table 3.11 suggests that multistate operations have greater betas than one-state operations. These results support the argument presented in Chapter 3 that MBHCs face greater as opposed to less potential competition. If that argument is correct, these results agree with CMT predictions. The pattern for the type of branching is not as easily discerned just by reviewing the data in the tables. It is interesting to note that companies traded on NYSE/AMEX seem to have higher betas than those traded in the OTC market (although that observation is not tested).

The t-tests comparing each year's mean with the previous year's for beta, alpha, and total assets for the combined data and the OTC and NYSE/AMEX subsets are presented in Figure 4.5 through Figure 4.13. The figures consist of nine parts which examine the data in sets ranging from the entire data set to those observations in the unit banking subset. In examining Figure 4.5 containing all data, no clear pattern emerges; this result is not unexpected given the number of possible confounding factors to be examined later. The closest example of any pattern is the general increase in beta for the years 1985-1987, followed by a significant decrease in 1988 for all three categories. It should be noted that the OTC market subset is more variable from year to year than the NYSE/AMEX subset. This pattern is noted since OTC data makes up the majority of observations.

The alphas are generally negative for 1973 and 1974, positive from 1975-1985, negative for 1986 and 1987, and then positive again in 1988 with slight variations given the subset being examined. This pattern can be interpreted as showing the market being fooled by unexpectedly high inflation in 1973-1974 and then earning positive real risk-free returns for the subsequent period as inflation was generally below estimations. The alphas are generally very close to zero in the 1979 and 1980 period, which again had high inflation. This

YEAR	BETA MEAN	t^1	ALPHA MEAN	t	TOTAL ASSETS MEAN	t
Combined Data						
1973	0.37		-0.0003		2,631,651	
1974	0.52	-4.10*	-0.0008	5.19*	3,018,711	-0.65
1975	0.47	1.36	0.0003	-12.88*	3,088,217	-0.11
1976	0.40	1.89	0.0008	-6.78*	3,155,544	-0.10
1977	0.34	1.58	0.0003	6.91*	3,888,591	-0.91
1978	0.42	-2.48@	0.0003	0.00	4,202,407	-0.33
1979	0.48	-1.66#	0.0000	3.28*	4,547,148	-0.33
1980	0.40	2.85*	0.0002	-2.22@	4,996,703	-0.39
1981	0.37	1.18	0.0010	-8.94*	5,421,536	-0.35
1982	0.43	-2.24@	0.0004	6.74*	5,954,829	-0.42
1983	0.32	4.19*	0.0012	-8.93*	6,542,585	-0.44
1984	0.33	-0.34	0.0006	6.65*	6,867,727	-0.23
1985	0.44	-3.75*	0.0011	-5.52*	7,610,998	-0.49
1986	0.54	-2.81*	0.0002	9.87*	6,087,042	1.17
1987	0.57	-1.17	-0.0002	4.35*	8,895,073	-1.96@
1988	0.47	3.13*	0.0007	-6.03*	9,308,285	-0.21

[1]   t-test compares 1973 with 1974, 1974 with 1975, et cetera.

*   Significant at the .01 level.
@   Significant at the .05 level.
#   Significant at the .10 level.

Figure 4.5: Comparison of Mean α's, β's, and Total Assets (in millions of dollars) for One Factor Model Data: All Data

YEAR	BETA MEAN	t^1	ALPHA MEAN	t	TOTAL ASSETS MEAN	t
OTC Data						
1973	0.35		-0.0003		1,349,519	
1974	0.49	-3.38*	-0.0008	4.46*	1,430,876	-0.45
1975	0.42	1.54	0.0004	-11.89*	1,506,413	-0.39
1976	0.36	1.57	0.0008	-4.90*	1,461,914	0.23
1977	0.30	1.43	0.0003	6.22*	1,582,147	-0.63
1978	0.39	-2.47@	0.0003	0.00	1,724,279	-0.68
1979	0.44	-1.41	0.0000	4.53*	1,725,199	0.00
1980	0.38	2.01@	0.0001	-1.40	1,890,579	-0.90
1981	0.33	1.82#	0.0010	-11.22*	2,080,783	-0.93
1982	0.38	-1.85#	0.0005	5.51*	2,307,741	-0.99
1983	0.24	5.67*	0.0013	-8.29*	2,579,112	-1.01
1984	0.24	0.00	0.0007	6.55*	2,701,353	-0.42
1985	0.37	-4.51*	0.0012	-5.19*	3,101,159	-1.24
1986	0.50	-3.53*	0.0004	6.83*	3,438,254	-0.83
1987	0.51	-0.53	0.0001	2.35@	3,772,961	-0.67
1988	0.42	2.41@	0.0008	-3.85*	3,318,896	0.89

[1] t-test compares 1973 with 1974, 1974 with 1975, et cetera.

*   Significant at the .01 level.
@   Significant at the .05 level.
#   Significant at the .10 level.

Figure 4.5: (cont.)

YEAR	BETA MEAN	t^1	ALPHA MEAN	t	TOTAL ASSETS MEAN	t
NYSE/AMEX Data						
1973	0.48		-0.0004		9,002,242	
1974	0.67	-2.55@	-0.0010	2.49@	10,056,682	-0.38
1975	0.68	-0.12	0.0000	-4.33*	10,081,454	-0.01
1976	0.59	1.25	0.0010	-4.36*	10,821,446	-0.25
1977	0.51	1.05	0.0000	4.52*	13,166,786	-0.64
1978	0.56	-0.79	0.0000	0.00	14,492,028	-0.32
1979	0.63	-1.06	0.0000	0.00	16,571,106	-0.44
1980	0.48	2.72*	0.0000	0.00	17,359,074	-0.15
1981	0.52	-0.77	0.0010	-5.02*	18,457,023	-0.21
1982	0.60	-1.26	0.0000	5.14*	19,216,968	-0.14
1983	0.59	0.12	0.0010	-5.22*	20,488,138	-0.24
1984	0.65	-0.89	0.0000	5.15*	22,571,749	-0.37
1985	0.74	-1.25	0.0010	-4.94*	26,532,717	-0.62
1986	0.75	-0.08	-0.0010	9.25*	19,463,418	1.19
1987	0.82	-1.03	-0.0010	0.00	29,494,873	-1.58
1988	0.62	2.68*	0.0000	-2.95*	31,176,518	-0.21

[1]   t-test compares 1973 with 1974, 1974 with 1975, et cetera.

*   Significant at the .01 level.
@   Significant at the .05 level.
#   Significant at the .10 level.

Figure 4.5: (cont.)

interpretation is at best an ex post explanation to fit a story to the data. Another problem with the t-tests comparing the alphas is that a very small difference in absolute percentage (two basis points) is often significant. It is doubtful that a great deal can be made of changes if those changes are of such a small amount. Therefore, the tests comparing the alpha means will not be discussed below.

Figure 4.6 presents the same yearly t-tests for multibank holding companies (MBHCs) as well as comparing MBHCs with one bank holding companies (OBHCs) and also with banks for each year.[40] The same pattern of rising betas and greater variability for the OTC subset are present. The t-tests comparing MBHCs and OBHCs show that for the combined and OTC data sets the MBHCs mean betas are uniformly greater and more often significantly so from 1980 onward. This result is in accordance with CMT expectations if the argument that MBHCs face greater potential competition is considered to be correct. The NYSE/AMEX data set shows MBHCs with significantly lower average betas in 1975, 1976, and 1977, but showing a pattern of generally increasing betas relative to the OBHCs from 1979 onward (with 1986 significantly greater). This pattern also agrees with CMT predictions. MBHCs total assets are found to be uniformly significantly greater for the OTC during the test period while the NYSE/AMEX MBHCs are found to be uniformly smaller (except for 1985) than their OBHC counterparts, although not significantly. Not surprisingly, given the difference of the two subsets, the combined data set shows MBHCs to be generally greater than OBHCs, but not significantly.

The tests comparing MBHCs to banks for each year reveal that the MBHC's betas are greater for each year as CMT would predict. A surprising result is that the MBHC average asset level is not significantly greater than that for banks for the combined data and is not significantly greater except for 1979 after 1976 for the OTC data set. This result is noted more out of the unexpectedness of the result than its implications to CMT.

Figure 4.7 examines OBHCs and compares them to banks. The same general pattern for the average beta over time as in the first two parts holds again and will not be discussed further. The comparison of OBHC average betas to bank's shows OBHC's to be uniformly greater (except for 1977 for the OTC data set) as CMT would predict. However, this difference is rarely statistically significant. The comparison of average total assets again shows that banks are smaller than OBHCs, but generally not significantly so.

Year	Beta	t¹	t²	t³	Alpha	t¹	t²	t³	Total Assets	t¹	t²	t³
Combined Data												
1973	0.42		2.35@	3.55*	-0.0003		0.66	1.55	2,878,753		0.63	1.43
1974	0.57	-3.66*	2.04@	2.44@	-0.0008	4.16*	1.14	-1.43	3,113,606	-0.37	0.00	1.27
1975	0.49	1.73#	0.92	1.64	0.0002	-9.36*	-2.60@	-2.19@	3,207,374	-0.14	0.09	1.29
1976	0.43	1.41	1.01	4.56*	0.0008	-7.46*	0.00	1.35	3,232,630	-0.04	-0.06	1.21
1977	0.36	1.81#	1.23	0.92	0.0002	8.18*	-1.75#	-2.18@	4,096,365	-0.98	0.26	1.03
1978	0.43	-1.89#	0.34	1.14	0.0003	-1.10	0.00	0.00	4,429,487	-0.31	0.28	0.99
1979	0.48	-1.31	0.00	0.97	0.0000	2.81*	-0.66	0.86	4,685,746	-0.22	0.05	0.94
1980	0.42	1.92#	1.88#	1.72#	0.0003	-2.84*	2.06@	1.14	5,222,701	-0.43	0.31	0.73
1981	0.39	0.98	1.97#	0.89	0.0010	-6.66*	0.00	-1.70#	5,716,854	-0.37	0.41	0.76
1982	0.45	-1.91#	1.64	1.45	0.0004	5.75*	0.00	-1.63	6,313,250	-0.43	0.58	0.58
1983	0.34	3.56*	2.36@	1.16	0.0011	-6.72*	-0.67	-0.60	6,877,038	-0.39	0.55	0.47
1984	0.35	-0.27	2.04@	1.15	0.0006	4.80*	0.68	0.24	7,335,055	-0.31	0.76	0.48
1985	0.47	-3.47*	2.12@	1.72#	0.0010	-3.84*	-2.58@	-0.01	8,162,391	-0.54	0.79	0.72
1986	0.58	-2.59*	2.40@	1.77#	0.0001	8.51*	-2.95*	-1.45	7,336,681	0.58	2.90*	1.26
1987	0.61	-0.82	.	2.56@	-0.0003	3.70*	-2.64*	-1.93#	9,927,775	-1.71#	1.13	1.15
1988	0.50	2.50@	1.41		0.0007	-5.72*	0.00	0.23	10,051,738	-0.06	0.68	0.94

* Significant at the .01 level.
@ Significant at the .05 level.
# Significant at the .10 level.
1 t-test compares 1973 with 1974, 1974 with 1975, et cetera.
2 t-test compares Multibank Holding Company (MBHC) vs One Bank Holding Company (OBHC) for the given year.
3 t-test compares MBHC vs Bank for the given year.

Figure 4.6: Comparison of Mean α's, β's, and Total Assets (in millions of dollars) for One Factor Model Data: MBHC

Year	Beta	t¹	t²	t³	Alpha	t¹	t²	t³	Total Assets	t¹	t²	t³
OTC Data												
1973	0.41		2.79*	3.42*	-0.0002		2.14@	2.02@	1,611,908		2.77#	2.02@
1974	0.55	-3.05*	2.53@	2.24@	-0.0008	4.68*	0.89	-1.43	1,673,629	-0.26	2.53@	1.79#
1975	0.45	1.86#	1.54	1.38	0.0003	-9.21*	-1.90#	-1.81#	1,773,915	-0.39	2.55@	1.69#
1976	0.41	1.05	1.73#	4.27*	0.0007	-4.14*	-1.18	0.86	1,685,428	0.34	2.35@	1.75#
1977	0.34	1.68#	2.05@	0.71	0.0003	4.48*	-0.84	-1.74#	1,818,916	-0.53	2.31@	1.63
1978	0.41	-1.87#	1.17	0.96	0.0002	1.35	-0.99	-0.38	1,998,022	-0.64	2.48@	1.56
1979	0.45	-0.90	0.43	0.72	-0.0001	4.17*	-1.98@	0.97	1,930,325	0.26	2.26@	1.88#
1980	0.40	1.25	2.06@	1.58	0.0002	-3.30*	1.47	1.04	2,152,057	-0.94	2.81*	1.35
1981	0.36	1.68#	1.81#	0.63	0.0010	-7.87*	0.00	-2.05@	2,387,081	-0.90	2.92*	1.46
1982	0.41	-1.73#	2.00@	1.31	0.0005	4.92*	0.00	-1.65	2,648,011	-0.90	3.00*	1.08
1983	0.26	5.04*	2.22@	1.20	0.0013	-8.28*	0.00	-0.57	2,964,463	-0.94	3.00*	0.87
1984	0.26	0.05	1.73#	1.19	0.0007	6.67*	1.39	0.42	3,171,849	-0.56	3.75*	0.90
1985	0.40	-4.09*	1.81#	1.54	0.0011	-3.50*	-1.72#	0.11	3,649,509	-1.17	3.62*	1.24
1986	0.52	-2.78*	1.19	1.48	0.0003	6.11*	-2.08@	-0.95	4,257,878	-1.16	3.78*	1.57
1987	0.53	-0.35	0.98	2.32*	0.0000	2.14@	-1.08	-1.12	4,673,799	-0.62	3.43*	1.45
1988	0.46	1.57	1.87#	1.22	0.0008	-3.35*	0.27	0.27	3,928,284	1.11	2.96*	1.45

* Significant at the .01 level.
@ Significant at the .05 level.
# Significant at the .10 level.
1 t-test compares 1973 with 1974, 1974 with 1975, et cetera.
2 t-test compares Multibank Holding Company (MBHC) vs One Bank Holding Company (OBHC) for the given year.
3 t-test compares MBHC vs Bank for the given year.

Figure 4.6: (cont.)

Year	Beta	t¹	t²	t³	Alpha	t¹	t²	t³	Total Assets	t¹	t²	t³
NYSE/AMEX Data												
1973	0.46		-0.89	.	-0.0005		-1.02	.	8,238,479	-0.86	.	.
1974	0.63	-2.20@	-1.13	.	-0.0008	-3.46	0.50	.	8,923,167	-0.01	-1.06	.
1975	0.63	0.07	-1.76#	.	0.0001	-2.71	0.25	.	8,941,210	-0.23	-1.10	.
1976	0.54	1.13	-1.98#	.	0.0008	3.22	-0.50	.	9,576,160	-0.76	-1.09	.
1977	0.47	0.88	-1.49	.	0.0000	0.00	0.00	.	12,360,251	-0.29	-0.57	.
1978	0.51	-0.59	-2.17@	.	0.0000	0.00	-2.80	.	13,615,019	-0.39	-0.53	.
1979	0.60	-1.23	-1.25	.	0.0000	0.00	0.00	.	15,554,348	-0.09	-0.53	.
1980	0.48	2.03@	-0.44	.	0.0000	-4.50	0.00	.	16,046,721	-0.20	-0.72	.
1981	0.53	-0.90	0.20	.	0.0010	4.63	0.00	.	17,086,811	-0.14	-0.74	.
1982	0.57	-0.76	-1.13	.	0.0000	-4.74	0.00	.	17,797,668	-0.21	-0.82	.
1983	0.59	-0.30	0.26	.	0.0010	4.72	0.00	.	18,875,601	-0.36	-0.96	.
1984	0.65	-0.70	-0.26	.	0.0000	0.00	0.00	.	20,770,854	-0.54	-1.03	.
1985	0.73	-1.08	-0.79	.	0.0000	4.35	-2.11	.	23,792,373	0.79	-1.63	.
1986	0.80	-0.98	2.91*	.	-0.0010	0.00	-2.09	.	19,651,893	-1.55	0.17	.
1987	0.86	-0.82	1.64	.	-0.0010	-2.67	0.00	.	27,901,905	-0.28	-0.64	.
1988	0.64	2.84*	0.65	.	0.0000	.	-2.55	.	29,646,793	.	-0.54	.

* Significant at the .01 level.
@ Significant at the .05 level.
# Significant at the .10 level.
1 t-test compares 1973 with 1974, 1974 with 1975, et cetera.
2 t-test compares Multibank Holding Company (MBHC) vs One Bank Holding Company (OBHC) for the given year.
3 t-test compares Multibank Holding Company vs Bank for the given year.

Figure 4.6: (cont.)

Year	Beta	t¹	t²	Alpha	t¹	t²	Total Assets	t¹	t²
Combined Data									
1973	0.30		2.25@	-0.0004		1.15	2,301,994		0.83
1974	0.43	-1.64	1.46	-0.0010	3.25*	-2.30@	3,112,842	-0.51	0.82
1975	0.43	-0.03	1.07	0.0005	-9.17*	-1.03	3,104,623	0.00	0.81
1976	0.38	0.70	3.60*	0.0008	-1.98#	1.12	3,300,383	-0.11	0.79
1977	0.30	1.06	0.34	0.0004	2.23@	-0.79	3,694,881	-0.19	0.74
1978	0.41	-1.63	0.85	0.0003	0.52	0.00	3,965,747	-0.12	0.72
1979	0.48	-0.93	0.87	0.0001	1.07	1.09	4,598,395	-0.25	0.71
1980	0.35	2.21@	1.07	0.0000	0.55	0.54	4,624,080	-0.01	0.50
1981	0.32	0.76	0.35	0.0010	-5.68*	-1.60	4,887,834	-0.10	0.52
1982	0.38	-1.20	1.00	0.0004	3.45*	-1.62	5,117,176	-0.08	0.37
1983	0.25	2.43@	0.78	0.0012	-4.50*	-0.50	5,626,433	-0.16	0.29
1984	0.26	-0.23	0.81	0.0005	3.85*	0.14	5,549,540	0.02	0.26
1985	0.36	-1.53	1.33	0.0014	-4.82*	0.54	6,010,647	-0.11	0.33
1986	0.45	-1.52	1.26	0.0006	3.33*	-0.30	2,982,960	0.96	0.75
1987	0.51	-1.04	2.06@	0.0001	2.15@	-1.12	6,535,070	-1.01	0.46
1988	0.37	2.14@	0.82	0.0007	-3.12*	0.46	7,656,158	-0.21	0.42

* Significant at the .01 level.
@ Significant at the .05 level.
# Significant at the .10 level.
1 t-test compares 1973 with 1974, 1974 with 1975, et cetera.
2 t-test compares One Bank Holding Company (OBHC) vs Bank for the given year.

Figure 4.7: Comparison of Mean α's, β's, and Total Assets (in millions of dollars) for One Factor Model Data: OBHC

Year	Beta	t¹	t²	Alpha	t¹	t²	Total Assets	t¹	t²
OTC Data									
1973	0.27		2.04@	-0.0005		0.83	837,132		1.83#
1974	0.36	-1.19	1.07	-0.0010	2.40@	-2.38@	902,276	-0.40	1.76#
1975	0.35	0.09	0.60	0.0005	-8.91*	-0.89	908,964	-0.04	1.60
1976	0.30	0.59	3.29*	0.0009	-1.97#	1.28	978,310	-0.39	1.73#
1977	0.22	1.14	-0.18	0.0004	2.56@	-0.90	1,055,907	-0.41	1.53
1978	0.34	-1.75#	0.40	0.0003	0.65	0.00	1,115,014	-0.29	1.33
1979	0.42	-1.07	0.48	0.0001	1.62	1.66	1,272,217	-0.67	1.39
1980	0.32	1.62	0.87	0.0000	0.76	0.74	1,293,634	-0.08	0.84
1981	0.29	0.86	0.09	0.0010	-6.94*	-1.87#	1,399,278	-0.36	0.77
1982	0.32	-0.80	0.90	0.0005	2.74*	-1.34	1,523,028	-0.36	0.62
1983	0.19	2.88*	0.90	0.0013	-3.61*	-0.33	1,580,951	-0.15	0.63
1984	0.20	-0.09	0.76	0.0005	3.55*	0.13	1,485,067	0.27	0.68
1985	0.30	-2.03@	1.41	0.0014	-4.50*	0.60	1,623,617	-0.39	0.90
1986	0.45	-2.57@	1.27	0.0007	2.86*	-0.17	1,675,966	-0.13	1.29
1987	0.49	-0.55	2.02#	0.0002	2.07@	-1.01	1,746,614	-0.18	1.43
1988	0.33	2.29@	0.73	0.0007	-2.94*	0.66	1,901,318	-0.35	1.09

* Significant at the .01 level.
@ Significant at the .05 level.
# Significant at the .10 level.
1 t-test compares 1973 with 1974, 1974 with 1975, et cetera.
2 t-test compares One Bank Holding Company (OBHC) vs Bank for the given year.

Figure 4.7: (cont.)

Year	Beta	t¹	t²	Alpha	t¹	t²	Total Assets	t¹	t²
NYSE/AMEX Data									
1973	0.57	·	·	0.0000	·	·	12,311,884	·	·
1974	0.78	-1.16	·	-0.0010	1.85#	·	14,165,673	-0.20	·
1975	0.85	-0.45	·	0.0000	-2.00#	·	14,357,371	-0.02	·
1976	0.77	0.65	·	0.0010	-2.00#	·	15,491,267	-0.12	·
1977	0.67	0.58	·	0.0000	2.06#	·	16,303,311	-0.07	·
1978	0.75	-0.52	·	0.0010	-2.18@	·	17,649,262	-0.12	·
1979	0.74	0.09	·	0.0000	2.24@	·	20,231,433	-0.20	·
1980	0.51	1.99#	·	0.0000	0.00	·	22,608,489	-0.16	·
1981	0.51	0.05	·	0.0010	-2.24@	·	24,074,892	-0.09	·
1982	0.70	-1.18	·	0.0000	2.24@	·	25,603,820	-0.09	·
1983	0.56	0.68	·	0.0010	-2.18@	·	28,550,828	-0.16	·
1984	0.68	-0.56	·	0.0000	2.06#	·	32,476,672	-0.18	·
1985	0.86	-0.69	·	0.0010	-1.75#	·	49,003,539	-0.50	·
1986	0.39	1.61	·	0.0000	1.58	·	18,144,097	0.94	·
1987	0.65	-1.22	·	-0.0010	1.03	·	37,061,472	-0.59	·
1988	0.54	0.49	·	0.0010	-2.53@	·	37,869,068	-0.02	·

* Significant at the .01 level.
@ Significant at the .05 level.
# Significant at the .10 level.
1 t-test compares 1973 with 1974, 1974 with 1975, et cetera.
2 t-test compares One Bank Holding Company (OBHC) vs Bank for the given year.

Figure 4.7: (cont.)

Figure 4.8 reports the yearly averages for banks. Given the small number of observations in this subset, little can be said regarding the results of these tests except that the general pattern found for the average beta in the Figure 4.5 through Figure 4.7 does not hold as well for this group.

Figure 4.9 reports the results of the yearly comparisons for multistate operations and compares multistate and one-state operations. The general pattern for the average betas is the same as Figure 4.5 through Figure 4.7. More interestingly, the comparison of the multistate operation average beta with that of the one-state operation shows that the multistate beta is uniformly greater, and it is significantly greater at the .01 level for all tests of the combined and OTC data sets. This result is in agreement with CMT predictions. As expected, the average total assets of the multistate operation category are uniformly greater and generally significant at the .01 level.

Figure 4.10 presents the results of the yearly tests for the one-state operation category. The same general pattern for the average betas is again found.

Figure 4.11 reports the yearly tests for those banks in statewide branching states for the given year and compares the averages for statewide branching to those for limited branching and unit banking states. The discussion of tests comparing the various levels of permissible branching needs to be taken remembering the warning concerning the difficulty of comparing these various levels as was discussed earlier. The same pattern for the average betas is found in the yearly tests. The comparison of statewide versus limited branching average betas for the combined data set shows a change from significantly lower average betas for the statewide branching set in 1973 and 1975 to significantly greater average betas by 1984, 1985, and 1986. This pattern of greater betas for the statewide branching group is supportive of CMT. The pattern, however, does not hold as well when the OTC and NYSE/AMEX subsets are examined. As expected the average assets for the statewide group is found to be generally significantly greater than those in limited branching states for the combined data set. When the data are separated into OTC and NYSE/AMEX subsets, it appears that this difference comes from the NYSE/AMEX subset. Indeed the OTC subset has uniformly lower total assets for the statewide group, although this difference is usually not statistically significant.

Year	Beta Mean	t[1]	Alpha Mean	t	Total Assets Mean	t
Combined Data[2]						
1973	0.07		-0.0008		367,657	
1974	0.19	-2.12#	-0.0002	-1.21	394,017	-0.16
1975	0.25	-0.57	0.0008	-2.69@	420,016	-0.16
1976	-0.17	2.26@	0.0004	0.77	436,098	-0.11
1977	0.25	-1.77	0.0007	-0.62	519,082	-0.56
1978	0.29	-0.22	0.0003	0.61	583,643	-0.40
1979	0.36	-0.51	-0.0003	0.90	605,522	-0.14
1980	0.21	0.96	-0.0003	-0.08	732,240	-0.62
1981	0.28	-0.47	0.0019	-1.83	731,065	0.00
1982	0.15	0.85	0.0016	0.20	683,028	0.13
1983	0.03	0.68	0.0017	-0.11	306,772	0.49
1984	0.00	.	0.0004	.	354,124	.
1985	0.03	-0.09	0.0010	-0.43	368,024	-0.19
1986	0.24	-0.78	0.0008	0.21	304,617	0.35
1987	0.18	0.31	0.0007	0.21	331,641	-0.16
1988	0.18	0.02	0.0004	0.37	414,539	-0.38

* Significant at the .01 level.
@ Significant at the .05 level.
# Significant at the .10 level.
1 t-test compares 1973 with 1974, 1974 with 1975, et cetera.
2 Combined and OTC data are the same. NYSE/AMEX has no observations.

Figure 4.8: Comparison of Mean α's, β's, and Total Assets (in millions of dollars) for One Factor Model Data: Banks

Year	Beta	t¹	t²	Alpha	t¹	t²	Total Assets	t¹	t²
Combined Data									
1973	0.50		3.73*	-0.0001		2.31@	5,339,130		4.47*
1974	0.77	-3.85*	5.56*	-0.0004	1.69#	3.77*	5,974,682	-0.33	4.10*
1975	0.70	0.82	5.53*	0.0001	-2.59@	-2.39@	6,428,404	-0.22	4.57*
1976	0.58	1.58	4.45*	0.0008	-3.60*	0.00	6,698,355	-0.12	4.46*
1977	0.49	1.38	3.64*	0.0001	3.64*	-2.46@	7,492,780	-0.32	3.30*
1978	0.56	-1.11	3.44*	0.0001	0.00	-1.68#	8,468,127	-0.34	3.51*
1979	0.60	-0.74	3.28*	-0.0002	1.59	-1.84#	9,204,917	-0.23	3.34*
1980	0.51	1.76#	4.10*	0.0000	-1.06	-1.44	10,189,883	-0.27	3.50*
1981	0.50	0.23	4.19*	0.0009	-4.72*	-0.65	11,456,694	-0.45	5.36*
1982	0.57	-1.31	4.31*	0.0005	2.10@	0.67	12,338,356	-0.28	3.92*
1983	0.45	2.18@	4.06*	0.0010	-2.66*	-1.31	13,840,837	-0.35	4.21*
1984	0.50	-0.74	4.98*	0.0010	0.00	3.33*	14,637,012	-0.17	4.40*
1985	0.64	-2.17@	5.12*	0.0010	0.00	-0.67	16,565,663	-0.39	4.74*
1986	0.69	-0.68	3.64*	0.0001	4.87*	-1.01	12,331,496	1.03	5.62*
1987	0.71	-0.50	4.04*	0.0000	0.55	0.68	19,543,968	-1.61	5.33*
1988	0.62	1.65	3.45*	0.0000	0.00	-2.81*	21,414,651	-0.31	5.19*

* Significant at the .01 level.
@ Significant at the .05 level.
# Significant at the .10 level.
1 t-test compares 1973 with 1974, 1974 with 1975, et cetera.
2 t-test compares Multistate Operation vs One-state Operation for the given year.

Figure 4.9: Comparison of Mean α's, β's, and Total Assets (in millions of dollars) for One Factor Model Data: Multistate Operation

Year	Beta	t¹	t²	Alpha	t¹	t²	Total Assets	t¹	t²
OTC Data									
1973	0.47		2.90*	-0.0001	0.96	1.86#	2,412,512	-0.21	5.28*
1974	0.76	-3.51*	5.05*	-0.0003		3.78*	2,537,312	-0.58	5.27*
1975	0.65	1.05	4.71*	0.0002	-2.53@	-1.57	2,915,944	0.30	5.98*
1976	0.54	1.20	3.85*	0.0008	-4.47*	0.70	2,716,537	-0.38	5.89*
1977	0.44	1.27	3.16*	0.0001	5.25*	-2.57@	2,973,964	-0.56	5.93*
1978	0.54	-1.36	3.31*	0.0001	0.00	-1.64	3,397,699	0.33	6.35*
1979	0.55	-0.14	2.42*	-0.0002	2.26@	-1.98@	3,169,382	-0.54	6.77*
1980	0.48	1.14	3.20*	0.0000	-1.51	-1.34	3,507,411	-0.72	6.76*
1981	0.43	0.95	2.88*	0.0009	-5.74*	-0.71	3,986,708	-0.86	6.70*
1982	0.52	-1.46	3.74*	0.0005	2.20@	0.00	4,610,288	-0.89	7.89*
1983	0.33	3.69*	2.98*	0.0013	-4.89*	0.00	5,382,846	-0.30	7.87*
1984	0.34	-0.35	3.16*	0.0009	3.21*	2.00@	5,587,952	-1.41	12.81*
1985	0.54	-3.19*	3.70*	0.0010	-0.54	-1.03	6,721,343	-0.93	8.54*
1986	0.65	-1.61	3.13*	0.0003	4.03*	-0.45	8,002,372	-0.49	8.64*
1987	0.64	0.11	3.16*	-0.0001	3.01*	-1.03	8,825,096	1.24	8.23*
1988	0.55	1.50	2.04@	0.0003	-2.59@	-1.46	6,719,411		6.23*

* Significant at the .01 level.
@ Significant at the .05 level.
# Significant at the .10 level.
1 t-test compares 1973 with 1974, 1974 with 1975, et cetera.
2 t-test compares Multistate Operation vs One-state Operation for the given year.

Figure 4.9: (cont.)

Year	Beta	t¹	t²	Alpha	t¹	t²	Total Assets	t¹	t²
NYSE/AMEX Data									
1973	0.59		1.90#	0.0000		1.67	13,893,860		2.34@
1974	0.81	-1.60	2.01#	-0.0010	2.55@	0.00	16,815,619	-0.47	2.62@
1975	0.85	-0.31	2.57@	0.0000	-2.55@	-1.01	17,235,973	-0.06	2.79*
1976	0.70	1.23	1.74#	0.0010	-2.55@	0.36	18,950,105	-0.23	2.88*
1977	0.62	0.63	1.39	0.0000	2.60@	-0.93	20,726,455	-0.22	1.91#
1978	0.62	0.01	0.71	0.0000	0.00	0.00	23,679,409	-0.32	2.03#
1979	0.77	-1.16	2.02#	0.0000	0.00	0.00	27,311,524	-0.34	2.04#
1980	0.60	1.70	2.37@	0.0000	0.00	0.00	28,900,806	-0.13	2.17@
1981	0.68	-0.87	2.58@	0.0010	-2.74@	0.00	30,380,658	-0.12	2.12@
1982	0.71	-0.36	1.74#	0.0010	0.00	3.37*	32,624,532	-0.18	2.45@
1983	0.76	-0.36	2.34@	0.0000	2.83*	-3.36*	34,457,191	-0.14	2.53@
1984	0.84	-0.72	2.99*	0.0000	0.00	0.00	34,746,034	-0.02	2.24@
1985	0.85	-0.04	1.77#	0.0010	-3.08*	3.36*	35,762,087	-0.08	1.68
1986	0.79	0.51	0.63	0.0000	2.98*	3.10*	23,695,445	1.05	1.21
1987	0.86	-0.75	0.76	-0.0010	3.01*	0.00	40,981,712	-1.37	2.03#
1988	0.72	1.32	1.92#	0.0000	-3.28*	0.00	42,789,547	-0.13	2.11@

* Significant at the .01 level.
@ Significant at the .05 level.
# Significant at the .10 level.
1 t-test compares 1973 with 1974, 1974 with 1975, et cetera.
2 t-test compares Multistate Operation vs One-state Operation for the given year.

Figure 4.9: (cont.)

Year	Beta Mean	t¹	Alpha Mean	t	Total Assets Mean	t
Combined Data						
1973	0.33		-0.0004		1,645,355	
1974	0.43	-2.62*	-0.0010	5.07*	1,932,844	-0.82
1975	0.39	1.08	0.0004	-14.09*	1,931,159	0.00
1976	0.34	1.29	0.0008	-4.68*	1,959,563	-0.08
1977	0.30	1.05	0.0004	4.79*	2,694,432	-1.16
1978	0.38	-2.37@	0.0003	1.33	2,882,627	-0.23
1979	0.44	-1.56	0.0000	4.41*	3,144,809	-0.29
1980	0.37	2.35@	0.0002	-2.53@	3,454,977	-0.32
1981	0.34	1.13	0.0010	-8.29*	3,797,864	-0.34
1982	0.39	-1.78#	0.0004	5.95*	4,075,415	-0.26
1983	0.28	3.73*	0.0012	-7.86*	4,418,755	-0.32
1984	0.28	0.18	0.0005	6.81*	4,496,050	-0.07
1985	0.38	-3.15*	0.0011	-5.77*	4,675,858	-0.16
1986	0.49	-3.00*	0.0003	6.26*	4,118,681	0.57
1987	0.52	-0.87	-0.0001	3.06*	4,901,738	-0.80
1988	0.41	2.75*	0.0008	-5.14*	4,830,588	0.06

* Significant at the .01 level.
@ Significant at the .05 level.
# Significant at the .10 level.
1 t-test compares 1973 with 1974, 1974 with 1975, et cetera.

Figure 4.10: Comparison of Mean α's, β's, and Total Assets (in millions of dollars) for One Factor Model Data: One-state Operation

Year	Beta Mean	t¹	Alpha Mean	t	Total Assets Mean	t
OTC Data						
1973	0.32		-0.0004		1,015,687	
1974	0.40	-1.91#	-0.0010	4.90*	1,062,064	-0.43
1975	0.35	1.15	0.0004	-12.70*	1,065,935	-0.04
1976	0.30	1.12	0.0007	-3.07*	1,081,726	-0.15
1977	0.26	0.96	0.0004	3.24*	1,162,555	-0.79
1978	0.35	-2.22@	0.0003	1.23	1,252,576	-0.81
1979	0.41	-1.56	0.0000	4.01*	1,331,331	-0.65
1980	0.35	1.72#	0.0002	-2.30@	1,458,051	-0.98
1981	0.31	1.48	0.0010	-8.38*	1,630,938	-1.07
1982	0.35	-1.25	0.0005	4.94*	1,695,671	-0.36
1983	0.22	4.63*	0.0013	-7.38*	1,854,968	-0.84
1984	0.22	0.20	0.0006	6.81*	1,961,200	-0.53
1985	0.33	-3.60*	0.0012	-5.26*	2,184,359	-1.00
1986	0.46	-3.22*	0.0004	5.62*	2,240,173	-0.22
1987	0.48	-0.54	0.0001	1.99@	2,289,117	-0.18
1988	0.39	1.94#	0.0009	-3.63*	2,448,365	-0.50

* Significant at the .01 level.
@ Significant at the .05 level.
# Significant at the .10 level.
1 t-test compares 1973 with 1974, 1974 with 1975, et cetera.

Figure 4.10: (cont.)

NYSE/AMEX Data

Year	Beta Mean	t[1]	Alpha Mean	t	Total Assets Mean	t
1973	0.40		-0.0006		5,655,346	
1974	0.59	-2.39@	-0.0010	1.38	6,395,591	-0.41
1975	0.58	0.07	0.0003	-5.35*	6,361,105	0.02
1976	0.52	0.71	0.0009	-2.82*	6,594,543	-0.13
1977	0.45	0.79	0.0003	2.53@	9,638,941	-0.93
1978	0.54	-1.05	0.0000	1.18	10,472,549	-0.20
1979	0.57	-0.45	0.0000	0.00	11,872,172	-0.30
1980	0.43	2.24@	0.0000	0.00	12,412,618	-0.11
1981	0.46	-0.41	0.0010	-4.21*	13,488,842	-0.22
1982	0.55	-1.32	0.0000	4.33*	13,716,429	-0.05
1983	0.52	0.40	0.0010	-4.39*	14,606,432	-0.19
1984	0.55	-0.40	0.0000	4.24*	16,126,540	-0.30
1985	0.66	-1.33	0.0000	0.00	19,433,202	-0.56
1986	0.72	-0.66	-0.0010	3.53*	16,642,068	0.49
1987	0.79	-0.65	-0.0010	0.00	19,845,928	-0.59
1988	0.51	2.63@	0.0000	-1.69#	19,010,488	0.12

* Significant at the .01 level.
@ Significant at the .05 level.
# Significant at the .10 level.
1 t-test compares 1973 with 1974, 1974 with 1975, et cetera.

Figure 4.10: (cont.)

Year	Beta	t¹	t²	t³	Alpha	t¹	t²	t³	Total Assets	t¹	t²	t³
Combined Data												
1973	0.30		-2.35@	-0.53	-0.0004		-3.35*	-3.26*	1,974,217		-0.98	0.09
1974	0.46	-2.36@	-1.55	0.21	-0.0009	3.16*	7.57*	6.38*	2,156,735	-0.27	-0.13	-0.68
1975	0.40	0.76	-1.76#	-0.22	0.0004	-8.89*	3.81*	2.13@	2,151,027	0.01	1.22	1.22
1976	0.46	-0.80	1.26	2.24@	0.0008	-2.63*	-2.98*	-3.17*	5,247,022	-2.02@	3.43*	1.46
1977	0.36	1.57	-0.02	1.43	0.0003	3.04*	-0.86	-1.07	6,958,401	-0.78	3.47*	1.42
1978	0.47	-1.77	0.99	1.56	0.0002	0.62	-2.48@	-1.72#	7,749,786	-0.30	3.50*	1.44
1979	0.54	-1.36	1.64	2.30@	0.0000	1.23	1.82#	-0.58	8,628,260	-0.29	3.49*	1.26
1980	0.39	3.15*	-1.03	1.57	0.0001	-0.63	6.61*	2.27@	8,840,492	-0.06	3.25*	1.08
1981	0.41	-0.40	1.53	1.13	0.0010	-5.94*	-4.00*	-3.20*	8,713,026	0.04	2.94*	0.56
1982	0.46	-1.11	1.28	0.49	0.0005	3.56*	4.88*	8.32*	8,203,381	0.17	2.28@	1.24
1983	0.33	2.98*	0.75	0.11	0.0012	-5.19*	-4.47*	-0.95	8,980,875	-0.27	2.42@	0.94
1984	0.38	-1.12	2.47@	1.09	0.0006	4.46*	3.85*	5.77*	9,715,852	-0.25	2.87*	0.97
1985	0.52	-2.77*	2.81*	1.03	0.0012	-4.43*	-3.54*	3.02*	11,097,594	-0.43	1.85#	-0.02
1986	0.55	-0.75	0.65	-0.03	0.0006	4.36*	-1.26	2.14@	7,083,332	1.47	2.93*	0.92
1987	0.62	-1.33	2.05@	-0.62	-0.0002	5.92*	6.57*	2.57@	12,550,340	-1.91#	2.72*	0.57
1988	0.47	2.99*	0.42	-0.82	0.0010	-8.83*	.	.	12,846,433	-0.08	.	.

* Significant at the .01 level.
@ Significant at the .05 level.
# Significant at the .10 level.
1 t-test compares 1973 with 1974, 1974 with 1975, et cetera.
2 t-test compares Statewide Branching (SB) vs Limited Branching (LB) for the given year.
3 t-test compares SB vs Unit Banking (UB) for the given year.

Figure 4.11: Comparison of Mean α's, β's, and Total Assets (in millions of dollars) for One Factor Model Data: SB

OTC Data

Year	Beta	t¹	t²	t³	Alpha	t¹	t²	t³	Total Assets	t¹	t²	t³
1973	0.28		-2.23@	-0.97	-0.0003		0.63	-0.47	1,181,977		-0.65	-0.87
1974	0.43	-1.93#	-1.42	0.14	-0.0009	3.31*	-0.53	-0.83	1,297,429	-0.25	-0.51	-0.51
1975	0.37	0.63	-1.39	0.10	0.0004	-7.97*	0.00	0.00	1,318,052	-0.04	-0.72	-0.52
1976	0.39	-0.24	0.31	1.56	0.0008	-2.73*	0.72	-0.57	1,413,502	-0.20	-0.37	0.21
1977	0.27	1.75#	-1.67#	1.50	0.0004	2.56@	1.74#	-0.54	1,561,453	-0.31	-0.26	0.37
1978	0.39	-2.04@	-0.32	1.38	0.0001	2.08@	-1.73#	-1.33	1,699,092	-0.26	-0.28	0.40
1979	0.47	-1.28	0.40	2.08@	0.0000	0.80	1.01	-1.49	1,368,041	0.78	-1.82#	-1.09
1980	0.35	2.32@	-1.81#	1.14	0.0001	-0.80	0.74	-3.10*	1,406,324	-0.19	-2.34@	-1.50
1981	0.35	-0.10	0.23	1.57	0.0010	-7.19*	0.00	-0.60	1,730,031	-1.18	-1.39	-1.81#
1982	0.39	-1.00	0.44	0.27	0.0006	2.59@	0.00	3.31*	1,781,808	-0.16	-2.70*	-0.96
1983	0.24	3.98*	-0.16	0.54	0.0013	-4.62*	0.00	0.99	2,183,275	-1.07	-1.63	-0.65
1984	0.27	-0.75	1.25	1.03	0.0006	5.62*	-1.56	1.92#	2,577,655	-0.87	-0.42	-0.49
1985	0.42	-3.47*	1.50	1.20	0.0013	-5.29*	0.70	3.75*	3,084,984	-0.92	-0.06	-0.01
1986	0.51	-1.87#	0.72	-0.58	0.0007	3.64*	2.78*	2.92*	3,526,375	-0.59	-0.20	0.26
1987	0.54	-0.57	1.39	-1.05	0.0000	4.16*	-0.58	0.85	4,241,336	-0.79	-1.10	0.18
1988	0.40	2.72*	-0.43	-1.37	0.0007	-4.87*	-0.58	3.23*	3,486,498	0.87	-0.43	0.60

* Significant at the .01 level.
@ Significant at the .05 level.
# Significant at the .10 level.
1 t-test compares 1973 with 1974, 1974 with 1975, et cetera.
2 t-test compares Statewide Branching (SB) vs Limited Branching (LB) for the given year.
3 t-test compares SB vs Unit Banking (UB) for the given year.

Figure 4.11: (cont.)

Year	Beta	t¹	t²	t³	Alpha	t¹	t²	t³	Total Assets	t¹	t²	t³
NYSE/AMEX Data												
1973	0.43		-0.71	0.91	-0.0008		-2.12@	-1.86#	5,847,391		-1.09	-0.44
1974	0.62	-1.82#	-0.62	0.10	-0.0009	0.25	0.27	0.24	5,937,678	-0.03	-1.27	-0.80
1975	0.54	0.66	-1.59	-1.07	0.0006	-5.02*	1.90#	1.28	5,482,928	0.18	-1.57	-0.87
1976	0.64	-0.79	0.65	1.36	0.0010	-1.27	0.30	0.23	14,739,549	-1.76#	2.05@	0.77
1977	0.59	0.44	1.67	0.58	0.0000	3.28*	-1.26	0.00	19,960,138	-0.83	2.24@	1.45
1978	0.65	-0.51	1.89#	0.79	0.0000	0.00	-1.36	-0.63	22,876,520	-0.38	2.46@	1.47
1979	0.71	-0.60	1.50	1.10	0.0000	0.00	-0.68	0.00	26,118,788	-0.36	2.43@	1.41
1980	0.50	2.44@	0.00	1.18	0.0000	0.00	-0.26	-2.75*	26,806,400	-0.07	2.44@	1.34
1981	0.57	-0.77	1.40	0.13	0.0010	-3.50*	0.92	0.00	27,706,774	-0.09	2.47@	1.14
1982	0.62	-0.63	0.54	0.49	0.0000	3.69*	-3.23*	2.87*	25,755,681	0.21	1.55	1.31
1983	0.59	0.35	-0.36	0.58	0.0010	-3.81*	0.00	2.65@	28,402,590	-0.29	1.71#	1.55
1984	0.73	-1.29	0.97	1.65	0.0010	0.00	5.35*	9.10*	31,385,378	-0.31	1.94#	1.49
1985	0.83	-1.02	1.54	1.52	0.0010	0.00	0.00	4.28*	36,737,946	-0.50	1.89#	1.49
1986	0.75	0.78	-0.13	1.48	0.0000	3.23*	1.92#	2.19@	24,472,897	1.13	1.46	0.99
1987	0.84	-0.97	0.62	.	-0.0010	3.31*	2.25@	.	37,774,104	-1.19	1.99#	.
1988	0.66	1.88#	0.99	.	0.0010	-7.48*	2.20@	.	38,251,970	-0.04	1.69#	.

* Significant at the .01 level.
@ Significant at the .05 level.
# Significant at the .10 level.
1 t-test compares 1973 with 1974, 1974 with 1975, et cetera.
2 t-test compares Statewide Branching (SB) vs Limited Branching (LB) for the given year.
3 t-test compares SB vs Unit Banking (UB) for the given year.

Figure 4.11: (cont.)

The comparison of the statewide branching group with the unit banking group shows the average betas of the statewide group to be greater during the 1976-1985 period for all data sets, as CMT would predict. Surprisingly, the relationship for 1986-1988 is reversed, although the differences are not statistically significant. Interestingly, no significant difference is generally found between the average total asset size of the groups in the statewide branching and unit banking states.

Figure 4.12 presents the results for the yearly limited branching state group and also compares this group with the unit banking group. The same general pattern for average betas is found again. The comparison of the average betas of the limited branching group with those of the unit banking group brings an interesting result. While the limited branching group's average betas are greater for the 1973-1981 period, the unit banking group's average betas are greater from 1982 onward for the combined data set. This result is not as CMT would expect. The average assets of the limited branching group are generally greater than the unit banking groups, but not significantly.

Finally, Figure 4.13 presents the yearly results for the unit banking group. The same general pattern for the average betas is found once again.

EXCESS MARKET VALUE

Excess Market Value (EMV) is calculated according to the general formula given in Chapter 3. Gross income less investment income, gross income, and total loans are each used as the normalizing variable. Table 3.14 listed the mean and number of observations under each of these computational methods for the combined data and Table 3.15, Table 3.16, and Table 3.17 provide the same information for the data separated by state(s) of operation, organizational form (MBHC, BHC, or bank), and the degree of branching allowed, respectively. A quick inspection of the table shows a pattern of negative to positive EMVs for virtually every classification with the change from negative to positive occurring around 1982 or 1983. Given the upward trend in stock prices during this time as well as the downward trend in interest rates, the expansion of the economy, and the write down of loan values discussed in Chapter 3, the results are not surprising, but generally are not as

Year	Beta	t^1	t^2	Alpha	t^1	t^2	Total Assets	t^1	t^2
Combined Data									
1973	0.42		1.26	-0.0004		-1.02	3,070,905		0.09
1974	0.57	-3.23*	1.52	-0.0008	3.00*	-0.46	3,486,568	-0.06	-0.68
1975	0.51	1.18	1.22	0.0003	-8.76*	-0.67	3,593,285	-0.01	1.22
1976	0.39	2.55@	1.37	0.0007	-3.74*	-1.32	1,806,711	2.31@	1.46
1977	0.36	0.56	1.72#	0.0003	4.18*	-0.83	1,950,192	-0.55	1.42
1978	0.42	-1.23	0.84	0.0003	0.00	0.00	2,137,073	-0.65	1.44
1979	0.46	-1.00	1.06	-0.0001	4.89*	-2.78*	2,263,669	-0.41	1.26
1980	0.43	0.82	2.49@	0.0001	-1.95#	-2.91*	2,552,284	-0.84	1.08
1981	0.35	2.41@	0.07	0.0010	-7.42*	-0.58	2,583,714	-0.08	0.56
1982	0.40	-1.43	-0.37	0.0006	3.53*	6.17*	4,128,074	-2.43@	1.24
1983	0.30	2.62*	-0.38	0.0012	-4.89*	1.90#	4,346,955	-0.25	0.94
1984	0.28	0.70	-0.39	0.0007	3.88*	3.70*	4,053,959	0.34	0.97
1985	0.38	-2.49@	-0.37	0.0011	-2.98*	4.55*	4,545,923	-0.58	-0.02
1986	0.52	-3.00*	-0.23	0.0000	6.81*	1.90#	5,438,281	-1.00	0.92
1987	0.53	-0.12	-1.25	-0.0002	1.04	0.32	5,442,279	0.00	0.57
1988	0.45	1.53	-0.72	0.0008	-3.31*	1.07	5,647,219	-0.17	.

* Significant at the .01 level.
@ Significant at the .05 level.
# Significant at the .10 level.
1 t-test compares 1973 with 1974, 1974 with 1975, et cetera.
2 t-test compares Limited Branching (LB) vs Unit Banking (UB) for the given year.

Figure 4.12: Comparison of Mean α's, β's, and Total Assets (in millions of dollars) for One Factor Model Data: LB

Year	Beta	t¹	t²	Alpha	t¹	t²	Total Assets	t¹	t²
OTC Data									
1973	0.39		0.81	-0.0004		-0.97	1,370,079		-0.70
1974	0.54	-2.74*	1.38	-0.0008	2.70*	-0.41	1,459,319	-0.45	-0.31
1975	0.46	1.39	1.38	0.0004	-8.64*	0.00	1,573,606	-0.49	0.00
1976	0.37	1.84#	1.37	0.0007	-2.60@	-1.19	1,527,936	0.19	0.71
1977	0.36	0.11	2.86*	0.0002	4.94*	-2.16@	1,648,260	-0.56	0.86
1978	0.41	-1.03	1.55	0.0003	-1.10	0.00	1,801,308	-0.65	0.92
1979	0.45	-0.77	1.68#	-0.0001	4.61*	-2.41@	1,903,000	-0.40	0.59
1980	0.42	0.74	2.65@	0.0000	-0.99	-3.29*	2,152,676	-0.88	0.70
1981	0.34	2.30@	1.45	0.0010	-8.18*	-0.53	2,185,377	-0.11	-0.76
1982	0.38	-0.91	-0.01	0.0006	3.45*	4.76*	2,796,849	-1.69#	0.99
1983	0.25	3.60*	0.63	0.0013	-5.53*	0.80	2,909,131	-0.26	0.35
1984	0.23	0.71	0.44	0.0008	3.59*	2.61@	2,764,073	0.34	-0.29
1985	0.35	-2.94*	0.49	0.0012	-2.94*	3.10*	3,114,090	-0.83	0.02
1986	0.48	-2.66*	-0.77	0.0002	6.25*	1.86#	3,392,790	-0.59	0.31
1987	0.48	-0.11	-1.67#	0.0001	0.55	0.79	3,368,792	0.04	-0.08
1988	0.43	0.89	-0.84	0.0009	-2.43@	1.07	3,215,286	0.26	0.53

* Significant at the .01 level.
@ Significant at the .05 level.
# Significant at the .10 level.
1 t-test compares 1973 with 1974, 1974 with 1975, et cetera.
2 t-test compares Limited Branching (LB) vs Unit Banking (UB) for the given year.

Figure 4.12: (cont.)

Year	Beta	t^1	t^2	Alpha	t^1	t^2	Total Assets	t^1	t^2
NYSE/AMEX Data									
1973	0.51		0.95	0.0000		-0.54	10,441,151		0.27
1974	0.70	-1.84#	0.46	-0.0010	3.28*	0.00	12,148,452	-0.41	0.44
1975	0.73	-0.32	0.07	0.0000	-3.28*	-0.44	12,922,276	-0.17	0.67
1976	0.57	1.53	0.84	0.0009	-2.73@	0.00	4,214,309	1.88#	-1.67
1977	0.36	2.36@	-0.84	0.0004	2.00#	1.80#	4,441,132	-0.17	-1.56
1978	0.45	-0.98	-0.62	0.0004	0.00	1.26	4,751,244	-0.21	-1.68
1979	0.55	-1.15	-0.17	0.0001	1.30	0.29	5,252,063	-0.32	-1.78#
1980	0.50	0.49	0.76	0.0001	0.00	-1.82#	5,562,662	-0.18	-2.07@
1981	0.43	0.82	-0.98	0.0007	-1.35	-0.99	5,345,515	0.12	-2.54@
1982	0.57	-1.34	0.04	0.0010	-0.83	5.58*	11,865,823	-1.88#	0.30
1983	0.63	-0.52	0.67	0.0010	0.00	2.39@	12,704,303	-0.19	0.43
1984	0.61	0.19	0.74	0.0000	2.78*	0.00	12,137,247	0.13	-0.08
1985	0.65	-0.35	0.28	0.0010	-2.69@	3.78*	15,110,213	-0.63	0.39
1986	0.77	-0.99	1.23	-0.0010	3.45*	0.61	16,055,354	-0.22	1.25
1987	0.78	-0.16	.	-0.0020	1.56	.	16,616,070	-0.14	.
1988	0.54	2.05@	.	0.0000	-2.86*	.	17,969,009	-0.27	.

* Significant at the .01 level.

@ Significant at the .05 level.

\# Significant at the .10 level.

1 t-test compares 1973 with 1974, 1974 with 1975, et cetera.

2 t-test compares Limited Branching (LB) vs Unit Banking (UB) for the given year.

Figure 4.12: (cont.)

Year	Beta Mean	t^1	Alpha Mean	t	Total Assets Mean	t
Combined Data						
1973	0.34		-0.0002		2,079,633	
1974	0.44	-1.18	-0.0007	1.97#	2,769,528	-0.65
1975	0.42	0.20	0.0004	-5.37*	2,844,201	-0.06
1976	0.29	1.51	0.0009	-3.61*	2,842,588	0.00
1977	0.25	0.50	0.0004	3.30*	3,457,919	-0.46
1978	0.36	-1.53	0.0003	0.70	3,685,865	-0.16
1979	0.39	-0.49	0.0002	0.86	4,297,661	-0.38
1980	0.32	1.37	0.0006	-2.85*	4,937,598	-0.35
1981	0.35	-0.59	0.0011	-2.55@	6,252,913	-0.65
1982	0.43	-1.15	-0.0004	6.66*	4,404,196	0.99
1983	0.33	1.31	0.0008	-5.17*	5,653,262	-0.81
1984	0.30	0.32	0.0000	3.60*	6,285,516	-0.33
1985	0.42	-1.09	-0.0002	0.73	7,146,293	-0.36
1986	0.56	-0.83	-0.0011	1.72#	2,542,397	1.37
1987	0.75	-1.73	-0.0005	-0.81	3,570,480	-0.75
1988	0.61	0.59	-0.0005	0.00	1,297,804	2.26#

* Significant at the .01 level.
@ Significant at the .05 level.
# Significant at the .10 level.
1 t-test compares 1973 with 1974, 1974 with 1975, et cetera.

Figure 4.13: Comparison of Mean α's, β's, and Total Assets (in millions of dollars) for One Factor Model Data:
Unit Banking

Year	Beta Mean	t^1	Alpha Mean	t	Total Assets Mean	t
OTC Data						
1973	0.34		-0.0002		1,578,725	
1974	0.41	-0.75	-0.0007	1.75#	1,553,879	0.07
1975	0.36	0.51	0.0004	-4.72*	1,571,976	-0.05
1976	0.26	1.06	0.0009	-3.64*	1,311,729	0.76
1977	0.16	1.46	0.0005	2.34@	1,364,208	-0.18
1978	0.30	-2.06@	0.0003	1.19	1,464,613	-0.32
1979	0.33	-0.47	0.0002	0.73	1,662,401	-0.57
1980	0.29	0.72	0.0006	-2.43@	1,835,934	-0.46
1981	0.27	0.35	0.0011	-2.47@	2,561,281	-1.33
1982	0.38	-1.51	-0.0002	5.51*	2,213,320	0.59
1983	0.22	1.88#	0.0011	-5.40*	2,636,469	-0.70
1984	0.20	0.17	0.0002	4.31*	2,973,044	-0.42
1985	0.29	-0.67	0.0002	0.00	3,097,363	-0.12
1986	0.61	-1.63	-0.0009	2.69@	2,878,445	0.15
1987	0.75	-1.51	-0.0005	-0.57	3,570,480	-0.49
1988	0.61	0.59	-0.0005	0.00	2,346,225	0.79

* Significant at the .01 level.
@ Significant at the .05 level.
# Significant at the .10 level.
1 t-test compares 1973 with 1974, 1974 with 1975, et cetera.

Figure 4.13: (cont.)

Year	Beta Mean	t[1]	Alpha Mean	t	Total Assets Mean	t
NYSE/AMEX Data						
1973	0.29		0.0004		8,090,526	
1974	0.61	-0.95	-0.0010	3.21@	9,090,901	-0.12
1975	0.72	-0.48	0.0002	-2.83@	8,569,211	0.09
1976	0.43	1.47	0.0009	-1.50	9,221,168	-0.12
1977	0.50	-0.42	0.0000	3.31*	8,692,198	0.11
1978	0.54	-0.29	0.0002	-1.58	9,683,246	-0.24
1979	0.58	-0.24	0.0000	0.63	11,412,864	-0.35
1980	0.41	1.60	0.0010	-2.29@	12,832,743	-0.27
1981	0.55	-1.65	0.0010	0.00	15,314,192	-0.44
1982	0.56	-0.09	-0.0010	13.35*	10,489,963	0.92
1983	0.52	0.37	0.0000	-2.50@	10,781,812	-0.08
1984	0.49	0.22	0.0000	0.00	12,542,408	-0.43
1985	0.60	-0.76	-0.0010	1.94#	12,930,478	-0.08
1986	0.32	0.78	-0.0023	0.84	862,156	1.17
1987	.		.		.	
1988	.		.		.	

* Significant at the .01 level.
@ Significant at the .05 level.
# Significant at the .10 level.
1 t-test compares 1973 with 1974, 1974 with 1975, et cetera.

Figure 4.13: (cont.)

CMT would predict. According to CMT, EMV should be decreasing, not increasing, with the threat of entry.[41] Given that the confounding factors biased the results to finding increasing EMV measurements, comparing the various possible structures with one another should provide information to examine CMT's predictions.

Figure 4.14 through Figure 4.17 provide a year-by-year comparison for each EMV measurement type and compare the EMVs of different structural types for each year when applicable. Figure 4.14 lists the EMVs for the three normalizing proxies and presents the yearly t-tests for the combined data. The general form of a worsening (lower) number in 1974 followed be a gradual (insignificant) improvement through 1981 before generally significantly greater EMVs for 1982 through 1986 is found for all three measures. Again, the general pattern is not as CMT would predict, given that added competition was threatened through the deregulatory actions of the 1980s, but not surprising given the confounding factors discussed above.

Figure 4.15 presents the comparison of MBHCs, BHCs, and banks.[42] The general pattern of yearly t-tests for each category is the same as reported above for the combined data except for the banks. The banks begin with positive EMVs before generally turning to negatives for 1976 through 1985. The general pattern agrees with CMT predictions, but must be discounted given the small sample size and the lack of significance in the changes. Comparison of the MBHCs and BHCs with the banks reveals generally higher EMVs for the banks in 1973 through 1978 and generally lower EMVs for banks after that point. This pattern is in agreement with the theory that the market believed the bank holding company form of ownership allowed greater potential for growth. If banks would be threatened more by new competition given their more limited scope of activities, then the results would also be supportive of CMT, although weakly. Comparison of the MBHC and BHC groups reveals that the MBHC group generally has greater EMVs for 1973 through 1977, but generally lower after 1978. It would seem reasonable to assume that if there were a difference in the reaction between MBHCs and BHCs to threatened entry, the MBHCs would be affected less given the greater options open to them. However, these results do not support that expectation. It is possible that a more precisely defined BHC group could help the interpretation of this comparison.

Year	N	EMV_III	t¹	N	EMV_GI	t	N	EMV_L	t
1973	203	-0.093		207	-0.036		209	-0.009	
1974	208	-0.377	2.53@	211	-0.257	3.27*	212	-0.036	3.17*
1975	216	-0.303	-1.47	218	-0.206	-1.59	219	-0.028	-1.13
1976	223	-0.274	-0.58	225	-0.183	-0.70	228	-0.024	-0.61
1977	235	-0.282	0.19	235	-0.195	0.42	240	-0.026	0.46
1978	248	-0.308	0.62	249	-0.206	0.43	256	-0.030	1.04
1979	251	-0.255	-1.43	252	-0.183	-1.11	258	-0.042	0.80
1980	258	-0.195	-1.47	259	-0.138	-1.78#	266	-0.029	-0.83
1981	264	-0.158	-0.92	267	-0.103	-1.39	273	-0.022	-1.28
1982	258	-0.067	-2.96*	260	-0.047	-2.85*	267	-0.007	-2.98*
1983	265	0.024	-2.27@	268	0.055	-2.04@	271	0.012	-2.36@
1984	258	0.201	-2.03@	259	0.129	-1.05	262	0.029	-1.38
1985	254	0.387	-1.56	256	0.272	-1.72#	264	0.053	-1.59
1986	245	0.215	1.69#	247	0.143	1.74#	252	0.028	1.88#
1987	232	0.624	-1.03	232	0.434	-1.06	235	0.059	-0.85
1988	203	0.227	0.90	205	0.145	0.95	208	0.017	1.08

* Significant at the .01 level.
@ Significant at the .05 level.
# Significant at the .10 level.
1 t-test compares 1973 with 1974, 1974 with 1975, et cetera.

Figure 4.14: Comparison of Excess Market Value (EMV) using the following normalizing variables: Gross Income less Investment Income (EMV_GIII), Gross Income (EMV_GI), and Loans (EMV_L): All Combined Data

Multibank Holding Companies

Year	EMV_III	t^1	t^2	t^3	EMV_GI	t^1	t^2	t^3	EMV_L	t^1	t^2	t^3
1973	-0.071		-0.40	0.54	-0.008		-0.42	0.93	-0.006		-0.60	0.96
1974	-0.387	2.16@	-3.95*	0.89	-0.265	2.91*	-3.86*	0.72	-0.037	2.79*	-3.83*	1.10
1975	-0.322	-1.21	-2.75*	0.13	-0.219	-1.29	-2.59@	-0.05	-0.025	-1.51	1.15	0.58
1976	-0.264	-0.95	-0.29	0.67	-0.178	-1.04	-0.27	0.58	-0.024	-0.11	-1.90#	0.57
1977	-0.283	0.32	-0.66	0.22	-0.194	0.44	-0.62	0.30	-0.027	0.58	-3.01*	0.12
1978	-0.323	0.74	-0.37	-0.74	-0.215	0.66	-0.45	-0.97	-0.032	1.07	-3.04*	-0.69
1979	-0.256	-1.39	0.17	-0.12	-0.183	-1.23	0.35	-0.07	-0.050	0.89	-0.64	-0.78
1980	-0.179	-1.45	0.34	0.72	-0.128	-1.69#	0.45	0.73	-0.029	-1.01	-1.40	0.41
1981	-0.168	-0.22	0.02	-0.90	-0.109	-0.60	0.03	-0.76	-0.025	-0.56	-3.17*	-1.09
1982	-0.088	-2.28@	.	-2.06@	-0.059	-2.20@	.	-1.83#	-0.013	-2.38@	-12.76*	-2.93*
1983	0.018	-2.26@	.	-0.33	0.064	-1.90#	.	0.32	0.003	-2.81*	-7.62*	-3.13*
1984	0.089	-1.44	2.01@	-10.00*	0.058	0.09	1.99@	-9.31*	0.012	-1.36	-10.15*	-11.25*
1985	0.298	-2.81*	0.50	-3.20*	0.215	-2.57@	0.51	-2.46@	0.035	-2.59*	-6.41*	-3.08*
1986	0.152	1.57	-1.46	-2.04@	0.103	1.52	-1.66#	-1.75#	0.019	1.43	-5.67*	-1.52
1987	0.731	-1.07	0.10	0.42	0.504	-1.07	0.09	0.40	0.062	-0.88	-0.71	0.32
1988	0.201	0.88	0.19	-0.55	0.121	0.92	0.13	-0.72	0.011	0.96	0.21	-2.44@

* Significant at the .01 level.   @ Significant at the .05 level.   # Significant at the .10 level.

1 t-test compares 1973 with 1974, 1974 with 1975, et cetera.
2 t-test compares Multibank Holding Company or Bank Holding Company vs Bank for the given year.
3 t-test compares Multibank Holding Company vs One Bank Holding Company for the given year.

Figure 4.15: Comparison of Excess Market Value (EMV) using the following normalizing variables: Gross Income less Investment Income (EMV_GIII), Gross Income (EMV_GI), and Loans (EMV_L): MBHC vs BHC vs Bank

Year	EMV_III	t¹	t²	t³	EMV_GI	t¹	t²	t³	EMV_L	t¹	t²	t³
Bank Holding Companies												
1973	-0.211		-2.03@		-0.148		-2.22@		-0.024		-2.80*	
1974	-0.444	2.41@	-5.76*		-0.296	2.32@	-6.30*		-0.044	2.26@	-5.62*	
1975	-0.332	-1.55	-4.63*		-0.216	-1.78#	-4.32*		-0.032	-1.63	.	
1976	-0.317	-0.23	-1.06		-0.207	-0.21	-0.93		-0.028	-0.69	-5.00*	
1977	-0.296	-0.39	-1.49		-0.208	0.01	-1.44		-0.028	-0.05	-7.05*	
1978	-0.270	-0.60	-0.37		-0.182	-0.80	-0.26		-0.028	0.12	-4.67*	
1979	-0.251	-0.45	0.27		-0.181	-0.05	0.49		-0.023	-0.58	-1.69#	
1980	-0.237	-0.30	0.36		-0.163	-0.56	0.52		-0.033	1.10	-4.02*	
1981	-0.129	-2.25@	0.22		-0.088	-2.24@	0.18		-0.018	-2.46@	-4.67*	
1982	-0.007	-1.90#	.		-0.011	-1.79#	.		0.002	-2.29@	-9.58*	
1983	0.041	-0.64	.		0.029	-0.80	.		0.029	-1.20	-2.60@	
1984	0.550	-1.62	0.57		0.355	-1.61	0.59		0.071	-0.94	-0.87	
1985	0.693	-0.33	0.45		0.471	-0.41	0.56		0.081	-0.20	-2.45@	
1986	0.369	1.08	-1.65		0.235	1.16	-1.51		0.038	1.29	-15.59*	
1987	0.333	0.35	0.08		0.241	-0.07	0.04		0.035	0.27	-20.68*	
1988	0.316	0.13	0.57		0.219	0.24	0.52		0.034	0.11	0.58	

* Significant at the .01 level.
@ Significant at the .05 level.
# Significant at the .10 level.
1 t-test compares 1973 with 1974, 1974 with 1975, et cetera.
2 t-test compares Multibank Holding Company or Bank Holding Company vs Bank for the given year.
3 t-test compares Multibank Holding Company vs One Bank Holding Company for the given year.

Figure 4.15: (cont.)

Year	EMV_III	t¹	t²	t³	EMV_GI	t¹	t²	t³	EMV_L	t¹	t²	t³
Banks												
1973	0.179				0.149				0.019			
1974	0.209	-0.05			0.134	0.04			0.020	-0.01		
1975	0.124	0.14			0.054	0.22			-0.056	0.73		
1976	-0.209	0.80			-0.144	0.79			0.006	-0.67		
1977	-0.154	-0.43			-0.112	-0.37			0.020	-0.25		
1978	-0.233	0.55			-0.163	0.51			0.011	0.18		
1979	-0.291	0.42			-0.231	0.72			0.022	-0.19		
1980	-0.277	-0.10			-0.205	-0.27			0.019	0.05		
1981	-0.174	-0.67			-0.113	-0.85			0.064	-0.50		
1982	.				.				0.292	-1.05		
1983	.				.				0.502	-0.43		
1984	-0.464	.			-0.326	.			0.224	0.49		
1985	-0.038	-0.61			-0.020	-0.80			0.337	-0.36		
1986	1.026	-1.11			0.810	-1.45			0.292	0.16		
1987	0.306	1.05			0.233	1.00			0.293	0.00		
1988	0.040	0.63			0.047	0.52			0.003	0.98		

* Significant at the .01 level.
@ Significant at the .05 level.
# Significant at the .10 level.
1 t-test compares 1973 with 1974, 1974 with 1975, et cetera.
2 t-test compares Multibank Holding Company or Bank Holding Company vs Bank for the given year.
3 t-test compares Multibank Holding Company vs One Bank Holding Company for the given year.

Figure 4.15: (cont.)

Figure 4.16 presents the results for multistate versus one-state operations. The yearly mean EMVs show the same general pattern as for the combined data for both multistate and one-state operations. The comparison of multistate and one-state operations with each other for given years is more interesting. For 1973 through 1979, the multistate subset has generally significantly greater EMVs than the one-state subset. However, from 1980 through 1988 the one-state subset has the greater EMVs and significantly so for 1981 and after. CMT would predict that the EMVs of the multistate operations would be open to greater potential competition and, therefore, should be lower. This pattern is found after 1979.

Figure 4.17 compares the various degrees of branching. The yearly means show the same pattern as the combined data for statewide and limited branching, but the unit banking EMVs are generally negative for the entire test period. The discussion of these results is made more difficult given the following argument. First, in a unit banking state the threat of entry from another bank can only come with the creation of a new bank; thus yielding lower expected competition and greater EMVs for banks in unit banking states. However, since the banking organization in a unit banking state is limited to one office it could possibly be more affected by the threat of entry of a S&L or credit union into its traditional product areas; thus yielding an expectation of lower EMV.[43] Given the possibility of multibank holding companies and other combined ownership form, the a priori expectation is that banking companies in unit banking states will have less threatened competition and, therefore, greater EMVs. This expectation is confirmed for the 1973 through 1983 period when comparing banking companies in statewide and limited branching states with those in unit banking states. From 1984 through 1988, the organizations in statewide branching state have significantly greater EMVs than those in unit banking states. Organizations in limited branching states have greater, but not significantly greater, EMVs for this same period. These results are not generally consistent with CMT expectations, but would agree with the idea that organizations in states allowing some form of branching have greater opportunities than those in unit banking states.[44]

Overall, the results from the EMV calculations are mixed. Support is received in meeting CMT expectations when the various operation levels are compared, but the results that do not control for the various categories are not supportive. This result is not surprising given the

Year	N	EMV_III	t¹	t²	N	EMV_GI	t¹	t²	N	EMV_L	t¹	t²
Multistate												
1973	54	0.320		3.03*	54	0.244		2.90*	54	0.023		2.79*
1974	54	-0.254	1.79#	3.61*	54	-0.169	1.81#	3.70*	54	-0.023	1.66#	3.96*
1975	54	-0.117	-1.11	4.63*	54	-0.076	-1.10	4.75*	54	-0.009	-1.11	4.86*
1976	55	-0.066	-0.35	4.35*	55	-0.041	-0.35	4.57*	55	-0.005	-0.32	4.31*
1977	56	-0.113	0.33	4.52*	56	-0.078	0.39	4.49*	56	-0.011	0.48	4.03*
1978	58	-0.294	1.23	0.30	58	-0.160	1.06	2.33@	58	-0.021	0.87	2.69*
1979	58	-0.181	-0.84	2.71*	58	-0.132	-0.44	2.88*	58	-0.085	0.97	-1.59
1980	57	-0.196	0.18	-0.06	57	-0.138	0.09	0.00	58	-0.027	-0.89	0.80
1981	58	-0.219	0.29	-2.67*	58	-0.126	-0.26	-1.87#	58	-0.036	0.79	-3.79*
1982	59	-0.115	-1.50	-2.83*	59	-0.076	-1.22	-2.58@	59	-0.018	-1.76#	-6.85*
1983	61	-0.054	-1.18	-6.39*	61	-0.040	-1.07	-6.89*	61	-0.007	-2.06@	-13.65*
1984	61	0.098	-3.04*	-7.34*	61	0.058	-3.15*	-8.97*	61	0.011	-3.05*	-16.80*
1985	63	0.239	-2.24@	-7.68*	63	0.157	-2.55@	-10.08*	63	0.024	-2.08@	-19.38*
1986	66	0.062	1.23	-2.61@	66	0.026	1.30	-2.82*	66	0.005	1.48	-4.73*
1987	64	0.181	-0.81	-31.39*	65	0.111	-0.85	.	65	0.013	-0.70	.
1988	57	0.056	1.11	-3.99*	57	-0.001	2.00	-7.51*	57	0.004	1.63	-9.11*

* Significant at the .01 level.
@ Significant at the .05 level.
# Significant at the .10 level.
1 t-test compares 1973 with 1974, 1974 with 1975, et cetera.
2 t-test compares Multistate Operation vs One-state Operation for the given year.

Figure 4.16: Comparison of Excess Market Value (EMV) using the following normalizing variables: Gross Income less Investment Income (EMV_GIII), Gross Income (EMV_GI), and Loans (EMV_L): Multistate vs One-state Operations

Year	N	EMV_III	t¹	t²	N	EMV_GI	t¹	t²	N	EMV_L	t¹	t²
One-state												
1973	149	-0.243			153	-0.135			155	-0.020		
1974	154	-0.420	1.80#		157	-0.288	3.56*		158	-0.041	3.27*	
1975	162	-0.365	-1.07		164	-0.248	-1.24		165	-0.034	-0.77	
1976	168	-0.342	-0.53		170	-0.229	-0.71		173	-0.030	-0.55	
1977	179	-0.335	-0.21		179	-0.232	0.12		184	-0.030	0.13	
1978	190	-0.313	-0.77		191	-0.220	-0.60		198	-0.032	0.58	
1979	193	-0.278	-1.33		194	-0.198	-1.15		200	-0.029	-0.66	
1980	201	-0.195	-1.79#		202	-0.138	-2.11@		208	-0.030	0.06	
1981	206	-0.140	-1.17		209	-0.097	-1.40		215	-0.018	-1.81#	
1982	199	-0.052	-2.58@		201	-0.038	-2.59@		208	-0.004	-2.50@	
1983	204	0.047	-2.02@		206	0.029	-2.01@		210	0.017	-2.07@	
1984	197	0.233	-1.65		198	0.151	-1.65		201	0.034	-1.09	
1985	191	0.436	-1.30		193	0.309	-1.46		201	0.062	-1.41	
1986	179	0.271	1.29		181	0.185	1.32		186	0.037	1.52	
1987	168	0.793	-0.96		167	0.559	-0.99		170	0.077	-0.81	
1988	146	0.294	0.81		148	0.201	0.85		151	0.021	1.02	

* Significant at the .01 level.
@ Significant at the .05 level.
# Significant at the .10 level.
1 t-test compares 1973 with 1974, 1974 with 1975, et cetera.
2 t-test compares Multistate Operation vs One-state Operation for the given year.

Figure 4.16: (cont.)

Year	EMV_III	t¹	t²	t³	EMV_GI	t¹	t²	t³	EMV_L	t¹	t²	t³
Statewide Branching												
1973	-0.235		-1.32	-6.82*	-0.163		-1.28	-8.62*	-0.023		-1.13	-7.26*
1974	-0.411	2.44@	-0.92	-1.96#	-0.281	2.48@	-0.89	-2.10@	-0.039	2.44@	-0.55	-1.66#
1975	-0.321	-1.66#	-1.76#	-0.27	-0.213	-1.93#	-1.27	-0.14	-0.030	-1.71#	-10.35*	2.06@
1976	-0.270	-1.01	-0.18	0.44	-0.185	-0.84	-0.59	0.10	-0.019	-1.57	0.49	1.82#
1977	-0.296	0.64	-0.96	-0.85	-0.210	0.86	-0.96	-1.49	-0.024	0.71	0.01	0.84
1978	-0.380	1.06	-1.20	-1.73#	-0.230	0.83	-1.96#	-2.52@	-0.030	0.85	-0.24	0.24
1979	-0.284	-1.24	-3.63*	-0.72	-0.204	-1.04	-3.87*	-0.84	-0.024	-0.67	-0.49	7.42*
1980	-0.171	-1.26	-0.88	1.20	-0.127	-1.45	-1.14	1.16	-0.022	-0.18	-0.58	2.27@
1981	-0.152	-0.23	-3.34*	2.49@	-0.107	-0.40	-3.40*	1.43	-0.020	-0.20	-2.19@	2.27@
1982	0.013	-3.76*	1.37	4.65*	0.006	-3.80*	1.42	4.55*	0.006	-2.98*	1.12	3.85*
1983	0.078	-1.35	-1.69#	4.40*	0.047	-1.24	-1.99@	0.15	0.016	-1.10	-0.22	1.80#
1984	0.251	-2.74*	2.69*	0.88	0.165	-2.82*	2.68*	1.07	0.038	-1.98@	2.19@	1.19
1985	0.486	-1.87#	2.33@	1.00	0.352	-1.83#	2.12@	1.01	0.075	-1.94#	2.43@	1.90#
1986	0.343	1.11	2.15@	4.33*	0.240	1.08	2.71*	4.72*	0.048	1.29	1.48	3.18*
1987	0.238	1.39	1.98@	-15.04*	0.163	1.52	2.17@	-31.17*	0.032	1.03	1.20	-7.54*
1988	0.147	1.06	1.81#	-2.87*	0.097	1.16	1.92#	-2.64*	0.017	1.23	1.62	-0.33

* Significant at the .01 level.   @ Significant at the .05 level.   # Significant at the .10 level.
1 t-test compares 1973 with 1974, 1974 with 1975, et cetera.
2 t-test compares Statewide Branching (SB) or Limited Branching (LB) vs Unit Banking (UB) for the given year.
3 t-test compares SB vs LB for the given year.

Figure 4.17: Comparison of Excess Market Value (EMV) using the following normalizing variables: Gross Income less Investment Income (EMV_GIII), Gross Income (EMV_GI), and Loans (EMV_L): SB vs LB vs UB

Year	EMV III	t¹	t²	t³	EMV GI	t¹	t²	t³	EMV L	t¹	t²	t³
Limited Branching												
1973	-0.020		0.31		0.037		0.62		-0.001		0.54	
1974	-0.365	1.86#	0.03		-0.248	2.55@	0.07		-0.035	2.41@	0.14	
1975	-0.314	-0.67	-0.70		-0.211	-0.73	-0.52		-0.035	-0.06	-2.22@	
1976	-0.281	-0.40	-0.18		-0.187	-0.44	-0.29		-0.027	-0.76	-0.40	
1977	-0.280	-0.01	-0.20		-0.190	0.05	-0.07		-0.027	0.02	-0.35	
1978	-0.283	0.04	-0.45		-0.198	0.21	-0.34		-0.030	0.53	-0.31	
1979	-0.270	-0.27	-1.95#		-0.193	-0.16	-2.14@		-0.060	1.04	-0.79	
1980	-0.250	-0.44	-3.64*		-0.172	-0.74	-3.78*		-0.039	-0.74	-2.39@	
1981	-0.207	-0.98	-3.24*		-0.129	-1.65	-3.54*		-0.030	-1.16	-3.22*	
1982	-0.148	-1.28	-1.39		-0.098	-1.12	-1.30		-0.021	-1.46	-1.95#	
1983	-0.067	-1.74	-3.98*		0.044	-1.44	-0.47		0.006	-1.92#	-0.51	
1984	0.207	-1.60	0.69		0.130	-0.60	0.68		0.027	-0.88	0.70	
1985	0.380	-0.79	1.51		0.262	-0.92	1.70#		0.045	-0.67	1.72#	
1986	0.123	1.60	0.83		0.076	1.67#	0.97		0.013	1.75#	1.11	
1987	1.043	-1.18	0.30		0.722	-1.21	0.31		0.089	-1.08	0.31	
1988	0.363	0.72	0.97		0.229	0.76	1.01		0.019	0.83	1.86#	

* Significant at the .01 level.
@ Significant at the .05 level.
# Significant at the .10 level.
1 t-test compares 1973 with 1974, 1974 with 1975, et cetera.
2 t-test compares Statewide Branching (SB) or Limited Branching (LB) vs Unit Banking (UB) for the given year.
3 t-test compares SB vs LB for the given year.

Figure 4.17: (cont.)

Year	EMV_III	t¹	t²	t³	EMV_GI	t¹	t²	t³	EMV_L	t¹	t²	t³
Unit Banking												
1973	-0.132				-0.094				-0.015			
1974	-0.368	2.21@			-0.253	2.25@			-0.036	2.02#		
1975	-0.238	-1.26			-0.175	-1.32			-0.001	-1.21		
1976	-0.261	0.23			-0.167	-0.13			-0.023	0.78		
1977	-0.262	0.01			-0.185	0.39			-0.024	0.18		
1978	-0.253	-0.18			-0.183	-0.07			-0.028	0.62		
1979	-0.148	-1.81#			-0.105	-1.79#			-0.018	-1.35		
1980	-0.067	-0.73			-0.048	-0.79			-0.014	-0.37		
1981	-0.023	-0.37			-0.017	-0.41			-0.002	-0.74		
1982	-0.070	0.52			-0.052	0.54			-0.008	0.38		
1983	0.185	-1.23			0.130	-1.23			0.019	-1.01		
1984	-0.044	0.98			-0.031	0.97			-0.004	0.78		
1985	-0.221	1.90#			-0.174	2.16@			-0.032	2.16@		
1986	-0.223	0.01			-0.206	0.28			-0.028	-0.19		
1987	-0.302	0.43			-0.226	0.16			-0.033	0.29		
1988	-0.442	0.97			-0.325	0.84			-0.040	0.36		

* Significant at the .01 level.
@ Significant at the .05 level.
# Significant at the .10 level.
1 t-test compares 1973 with 1974, 1974 with 1975, et cetera.
2 t-test compares Statewide Branching (SB) or Limited Branching (LB) vs Unit Banking (UB) for the given year.
3 t-test compares SB vs LB for the given year.

Figure 4.17: (cont.)

confounding factors that bias EMVs upward and that the earlier profitability portion of this study found evidence of imperfect contestability in only certain areas and not for all products of the banking firm. Hence, examining the firm as a whole would likely yield mixed results.

TOBIN'S q APPROXIMATION

The computational method for Tobin's q approximation was presented and discussed in Chapter 3. The mean and number of observations used in the calculations are presented in Table 3.19 and show a general pattern for q's less than 1.0 before 1983 and greater than one after 1982. This pattern is not uniformly followed, however, as will be discussed below.

Figure 4.18 through Figure 4.21 present the year-by-year t-tests for the combined data and each subset as well as the comparison of the relevant subsets. Figure 4.18 presents the results for the combined data and shows that after a significant drop in 1974 from 1973, the approximation measure is generally greater for each year from 1979 through 1987, but only significantly greater in 1982, 1983, and 1985. This general pattern is again likely owing to the general rise in the stock market during the early and mid-1980s as well as the lowering of interest rates, the expansion of the economy, and the write down of loan values as discussed above. CMT would predict lower q approximations with greater threat of entry. That result is not found for the combined data which is not surprising given the confounding factors as well as the expectation that the q approximations will follow the same general pattern as the EMV results. As with the EMV results, examining the q approximations in the context of operating levels is expected to provide more information concerning CMT expectations.

Figure 4.19 examines MBHC, BHC, and bank ownership forms. MBHCs and BHCs show the same general pattern of improving q measurements during the test period—moving from q values below 1.0 to over 1.0 after 1982. During this same period, the q values for banks never changed significantly on a year-to-year basis, but are greater than 1.0 for all years except 1975 and 1976. These patterns do not support CMT, but are not surprising given the confounding factors discussed above. The comparison of MBHC and BHC forms with banks generally

YEAR	N	q Approximation	STD DEV	t^1
1973	209	0.995	0.063	
1974	212	0.981	0.024	3.15*
1975	219	0.985	0.044	-1.30
1976	228	0.988	0.026	-0.81
1977	240	0.987	0.023	0.55
1978	256	0.984	0.021	1.33
1979	258	0.985	0.029	-0.41
1980	266	0.986	0.034	-0.21
1981	273	0.989	0.026	-1.20
1982	268	0.995	0.027	-2.91*
1983	272	1.010	0.092	-2.44@
1984	263	1.014	0.083	-0.60
1985	264	1.029	0.098	-1.87#
1986	252	1.018	0.061	1.56
1987	235	1.036	0.350	-0.81
1988	209	1.010	0.046	1.04

* Significant at the .01 level.
@ Significant at the .05 level.
# Significant at the .10 level.
1 t-test compares 1973 with 1974, 1974 with 1975, et cetera.

Figure 4.18: Comparison of Tobin's q Approximations: All Combined Data

YEAR	N	q Approximation	STD DEV	t^1	t^2	t^3
Multibank Holding Companies						
1973	149	0.997	0.072	-0.47	0.91	
1974	155	0.980	0.023	2.71*	-3.06*	1.01
1975	158	0.987	0.039	-1.75#	1.74#	0.57
1976	164	0.988	0.027	-0.31	-1.27	0.62
1977	174	0.986	0.024	0.62	-2.30@	0.32
1978	186	0.983	0.021	1.33	-2.38@	-0.61
1979	189	0.984	0.023	-0.16	-2.41@	-1.31
1980	193	0.986	0.038	-0.90	-1.14	1.05
1981	196	0.988	0.026	-0.36	-2.49@	-0.81
1982	196	0.993	0.021	-2.20@	-6.65*	-2.54@
1983	203	1.007	0.092	-2.13@	-1.46	-0.64
1984	194	1.006	0.027	0.13	-3.37*	-8.62*
1985	195	1.021	0.077	-2.48@	-3.22*	-2.47@
1986	183	1.013	0.063	1.02	-3.47*	-1.18
1987	172	1.039	0.407	-0.83	-0.36	0.33
1988	153	1.007	0.044	0.96	0.10	-2.05@

* Significant at the .01 level.
@ Significant at the .05 level.
\# Significant at the .10 level.
1 t-test compares 1973 with 1974, 1974 with 1975, et cetera.
2 t-test compares MBHC or BHC vs Bank for the given year.
3 t-test compares MBHC vs BHC for the given year.

Figure 4.19: Comparison of Tobin's q Approximations: MBHC vs
BHC vs Bank

YEAR	N	q Approximation	STD DEV	t^1	t^2	t^3
Bank Holding Companies						
1973	50	0.988	0.027		-2.37@	
1974	49	0.977	0.017	2.39@	-4.88*	
1975	51	0.984	0.015	-2.08@	3.85*	
1976	54	0.986	0.014	-0.70	-3.02*	
1977	58	0.985	0.012	0.18	-4.73*	
1978	62	0.985	0.014	0.21	-3.15*	
1979	63	0.987	0.040	-0.48	-1.17	
1980	67	0.982	0.018	1.08	-3.02*	
1981	73	0.990	0.022	-2.48@	-2.68@	
1982	70	0.999	0.031	-2.08@	-4.28*	
1983	68	1.014	0.091	-1.31	-1.26	
1984	66	1.035	0.156	-0.93	-0.26	
1985	63	1.045	0.138	-0.39	-1.37	
1986	65	1.023	0.035	1.26	-5.65*	
1987	59	1.022	0.036	0.18	-4.81*	
1988	53	1.020	0.051	0.23	0.50	

* Significant at the .01 level.
@ Significant at the .05 level.
\# Significant at the .10 level.
1 t-test compares 1973 with 1974, 1974 with 1975, et cetera.
2 t-test compares MBHC or BHC vs Bank for the given year.
3 t-test compares MBHC vs BHC for the given year.

Figure 4.19: (cont.)

YEAR	N	q Approximation	STD DEV	t^1	t^2	t^3
Banks						
1973	10	1.008	0.049			
1974	8	1.006	0.053	0.08		
1975	10	0.965	0.139	0.78		
1976	10	0.999	0.054	-0.71		
1977	8	1.006	0.046	-0.28		
1978	8	1.001	0.044	0.21		
1979	6	1.007	0.056	-0.22		
1980	6	1.004	0.050	0.08		
1981	4	1.020	0.064	-0.44		
1982	2	1.094	0.128	-1.01		
1983	1	1.149	1.149	-0.35		
1984	3	1.059	0.164	0.48		
1985	6	1.122	0.154	-0.57		
1986	4	1.124	0.175	-0.01		
1987	4	1.112	0.176	0.10		
1988	3	1.005	0.038	1.01		

* Significant at the .01 level.

@ Significant at the .05 level.

Significant at the .10 level.

1 t-test compares 1973 with 1974, 1974 with 1975, et cetera.

2 t-test compares MBHC or BHC vs Bank for the given year.

3 t-test compares MBHC vs BHC for the given year.

Figure 4.19: (cont.)

shows the banks to have significantly greater q approximations for most years. If MBHCs and BHCs are considered as having greater potential competition than the banks, then this result is in agreement with CMT predictions. The comparison of MBHCs and BHCs provides additional evidence to support this viewpoint. The q approximations of the BHCs are generally greater than those of the MBHCs for the 1978-1988 period. Also, the only times that the difference between the two groups is significant are when the BHC's q approximations are greater than the MBHC's.

Figure 4.20 compares multistate and one-state operations. The same general pattern for the mean q approximations of the combined data is found again, with the multistate's q measures not being greater than 1.0 until 1984. The comparison of the two subsets is interesting in that the multistate subset's q approximations are uniformly statistically greater from 1973 through 1978, but uniformly statistically less from 1981 through 1988. This result is more readily explained by the possibility that the stock market anticipated greater opportunities for the multistate operations in the period after the regulatory acts of the 1980s. Most likely, the result is much more related to the possibility of interstate acquisitions than competitive changes in products. The general result is not supportive of CMT, but not surprising given the possibility of acquisition.

Figure 4.21 compares statewide branching, limited branching, and unit banking states. The combined data's general pattern is found for the statewide and limited branching states, but the unit banking states subset shows q approximations that are uniformly less than 1.0 except for 1983. These q approximation are generally lower during this time, but the results for the later years must be discounted given the decrease in observations after 1981. The comparison of statewide branching and limited branching states to unit banking states shows the branching states to have generally greater q approximations from 1973 to 1983, but lower from 1984 to 1988. Assuming greater potential threats of competition for the states with branching, CMT expectations are not fulfilled. Comparing statewide and limited branching states does not show a well-defined pattern. This result is not surprising given the earlier discussion of the degrees of branching possible in a limited branching state.

Overall, the results for Tobin's q approximation as like those for EMV. The results are mixed in any support for CMT. Again, this result is not surprising given the confounding factors affecting market

YEAR	N	q Approximation	STD DEV	t^1	t^2
Multistate					
1973	54	1.015	0.111		2.92*
1974	54	0.988	0.033	1.69#	3.75*
1975	54	0.996	0.035	-1.16	5.04*
1976	55	0.998	0.040	-0.32	4.34*
1977	56	0.994	0.034	0.49	4.01*
1978	58	0.989	0.030	0.97	2.69*
1979	58	0.989	0.033	-0.03	2.07@
1980	58	0.986	0.028	0.45	0.39
1981	58	0.984	0.028	0.34	-2.90*
1982	59	0.990	0.017	-1.40	-5.53*
1983	61	0.996	0.016	-1.78#	-16.27*
1984	61	1.005	0.017	-3.17*	-9.68*
1985	63	1.013	0.021	-2.26@	-14.03*
1986	66	1.001	0.057	1.52	-5.29*
1987	65	1.007	0.018	-0.77	-24.15*
1988	58	1.003	0.017	1.32	-7.43*

* Significant at the .01 level.
@ Significant at the .05 level.
\# Significant at the .10 level.
1 t-test compares 1973 with 1974, 1974 with 1975, et cetera.
2 t-test compares Multistate Operation vs One-state Operation for the given year.

Figure 4.20: Comparison of Tobin's q Approximations: Multistate vs One-state Operations

YEAR	N	q Approximation	STD DEV	t^1	t^2
One-state					
1973	155	0.989	0.031		
1974	158	0.978	0.020	3.52*	
1975	165	0.982	0.047	-0.89	
1976	173	0.985	0.019	-0.79	
1977	184	0.984	0.017	0.23	
1978	198	0.983	0.017	0.89	
1979	200	0.984	0.028	-0.49	
1980	208	0.985	0.036	-0.47	
1981	215	0.990	0.025	-1.48	
1982	209	0.997	0.029	-2.59@	
1983	211	1.014	0.104	-2.26@	
1984	202	1.017	0.094	-0.33	
1985	201	1.034	0.111	-1.66#	
1986	186	1.023	0.062	1.14	
1987	170	1.047	0.411	-0.77	
1988	151	1.013	0.053	1.00	

* Significant at the .01 level.

@ Significant at the .05 level.

\# Significant at the .10 level.

1 t-test compares 1973 with 1974, 1974 with 1975, et cetera.

2 t-test compares Multistate Operation vs One-state Operation for the given year.

Figure 4.20: (cont.)

YEAR	N	q Approximation	STD DEV	t¹	t²	t³
Statewide						
1973	55	0.987	0.022		-1.29	-6.52*
1974	55	0.978	0.015	2.45@	-1.30	-2.22@
1975	56	0.984	0.014	-2.03@	-5.57*	1.21
1976	79	0.989	0.021	-1.56	0.06	1.02
1977	79	0.986	0.018	0.82	-0.37	-0.14
1978	82	0.983	0.018	1.02	-0.66	-0.43
1979	83	0.986	0.038	-0.64	-0.66	1.19
1980	87	0.988	0.047	-0.19	-0.74	1.43
1981	102	0.989	0.024	-0.19	-2.52@	1.41
1982	119	1.001	0.032	-3.31*	1.12	4.14*
1983	116	1.007	0.029	-1.45	-1.08	-1.61
1984	118	1.018	0.042	-2.34@	2.54@	1.10
1985	116	1.040	0.102	-2.13@	2.37@	1.61
1986	115	1.026	0.061	1.26	1.67#	2.62*
1987	115	1.017	0.046	1.25	1.57	-9.06*
1988	112	1.010	0.048	1.12	1.58	-0.52

* Significant at the .01 level.

@ Significant at the .05 level.

Significant at the .10 level.

1 t-test compares 1973 with 1974, 1974 with 1975, et cetera.

2 t-test compares Statewide Branching or Limited Branching vs Unit Banking for the given year.

3 t-test compares Statewide Branching vs Limited Branching for the given year.

Figure 4.21: Comparison of Tobin's q Approximations: Statewide Branching vs Limited Branching vs Unit Banking

YEAR	N	q Approximation	STD DEV	t^1	t^2	t^3
Limited						
1973	123	1.000	0.080		0.53	
1974	124	0.981	0.029	2.41@	-0.08	
1975	128	0.982	0.045	-0.23	-1.89#	
1976	113	0.987	0.031	-0.88	-0.35	
1977	124	0.987	0.027	0.08	-0.20	
1978	136	0.984	0.024	0.80	-0.33	
1979	136	0.983	0.025	0.53	-1.98@	
1980	137	0.982	0.022	0.21	-3.27*	
1981	129	0.986	0.023	-1.37	-3.40*	
1982	113	0.989	0.019	-1.17	-1.97#	
1983	125	1.011	0.125	-1.86#	-0.06	
1984	119	1.014	0.116	-0.17	0.74	
1985	131	1.025	0.099	-0.86	1.85#	
1986	131	1.012	0.062	1.33	1.09	
1987	116	1.056	0.496	-1.02	0.30	
1988	92	1.013	0.044	0.84	1.87#	

* Significant at the .01 level.
@ Significant at the .05 level.
\# Significant at the .10 level.
1 t-test compares 1973 with 1974, 1974 with 1975, et cetera.
2 t-test compares Statewide Branching or Limited Branching vs Unit Banking for the given year.
3 t-test compares Statewide Branching vs Limited Branching for the given year.

Figure 4.21: (cont.)

YEAR	N	q Approximation	STD DEV	t^1	t^2	t^3
Unit						
1973	31	0.992	0.024			
1974	33	0.982	0.016	2.04#		
1975	35	0.997	0.067	-1.28		
1976	36	0.989	0.015	0.72		
1977	37	0.988	0.014	0.36		
1978	38	0.985	0.014	0.66		
1979	39	0.991	0.019	-1.33		
1980	42	0.993	0.035	-0.41		
1981	42	0.998	0.036	-0.63		
1982	36	0.995	0.026	0.36		
1983	31	1.013	0.092	-1.08		
1984	26	0.997	0.017	0.85		
1985	17	0.981	0.030	2.24@		
1986	6	0.984	0.015	-0.23		
1987	4	0.981	0.018	0.30		
1988	5	0.976	0.018	0.43		

* Significant at the .01 level.
@ Significant at the .05 level.
# Significant at the .10 level.
1 t-test compares 1973 with 1974, 1974 with 1975, et cetera.
2 t-test compares Statewide Branching or Limited Branching vs Unit Banking for the given year.
3 t-test compares Statewide Branching vs Limited Branching for the given year.

Figure 4.21: (cont.)

and book values and the earlier finding of imperfect contestability for only certain products. Examination for CMT implications at the firm level is, therefore, much less likely to provide support for CMT.

NOTES

1. The pre- and post-DIDMCA periods are used as proxies for pre- and post-entry periods for the products.

2. Competition for time deposits, CDs, et cetera should have been only slightly affected by DIDMCA.

3. One possible area for additional competition for commercial loans is from finance companies. The Bankruptcy Reform Act which was passed in 1978 and was effective in October of 1980 allowed greater protection for individuals when they filed for bankruptcy. Many finance companies decreased their personal lending operations and put greater emphasis on commercial lending. For example, in 1980, 50.4% of finance company loans were to individuals and 48.1% to businesses. By 1983, only 38.3% of loans were to individuals and 52.2% to businesses. This trend continued to 34.3%, and 55.5% for personal and commercial loans, respectively by 1988. (Source: *Federal Reserve Bulletin* Federal Reserve System, 1975-1990.) This environment leads to an expectation of greater potential change in the commercial loan net earnings, but of uncertain affect on installment loan net earnings. Commercial loans would face greater competition. Installment loans would possibly face less competition, which would allow increased net earnings, but the bankruptcy changes could lower earnings by making collection processes more difficult.

4. Tests on interest-bearing checkable accounts are not possible due to lack of pre-1980 data.

5. Lack of data precludes a test for the largest asset groups for both personal and commercial checkable deposits.

6. See Flannery (1980) for a discussion of bank profits and changing interest rates under Regulation Q.

7. Two economic factors helped to bring about their elimination: 1) some actually paid no interest such that the public demanded these products less; and 2) the average balances in the accounts were so small that banks found them too costly to maintain.

8. Tests are not possible for 1973-1974 through 1977-1978 because of lack of data.

9. Possible explanations for the lower net earnings in the later period include the increase in the number of MMMFs during the period and the increase in use of brokered deposits with the change in the deposit insurance level to $100,000 enacted by DIDMCA in 1980. These two conditions allowed for greater competition for the funds and possibly better information as to the maximum rates being paid allowing depositors to better shop for the best yields.

10. One possible explanation for greater credit card loan net earnings after 1980, but one not thought too likely, is that DIDMCA included the elimination of usury ceiling laws in all the states unless a state passed a new law replacing the ceilings. The ability to charge higher rates than possible before DIDMCA could yield the greater net earnings in the later periods.

11. The unemployment variable did have the opposite sign, as expected, from real GNP and the one year lag of real GNP. Also as expected, real GNP was generally more significant than the one year lag of real GNP. The results from the other interest proxies will be included in the footnotes as the primary regression results are presented.

12. The results when using the other three interest proxies (three and six month maturity Treasury bills and the average federal funds rate) only differ slightly from those results reported above. No deposit group's regressions are significant for the 1973-1988 period. The interest rate proxies are still negatively related to net earnings for the two smaller deposit groups, but not for the large deposit group. All of the interest proxies are insignificantly related to net earnings no matter the deposit group. Processing costs are negatively related to net earnings, as expected, for the two smaller deposit groups, but still positively related for the large deposit group. This variable is not significant in any of the 1973-1988 period regressions. The pre-1980 regressions are virtually identical to the results reported above for the two smaller deposit groups. The other interest proxies for the large deposit group are still positively related to net earnings, but no longer significant. However, the F-tests still show significance at the .01 level or better. The post-1980 regressions are virtually identical to the above reported results for the two larger deposit groups. The interest proxies for the small deposit group are still negatively related to net earnings, but not significantly.

13. In fact, the results of the Farley-Hinich test are not significant for any size group of any variation of the regression variables run for average time deposits.

14. All Gujarati and Farley-Hinich tests are conducted for 1973-1988 when data are available for the full period. Table 3.3, Table 3.4, and Table 3.5 show the years for which data are available for the various categories. The tests can point out significant shifts in the regression or its variables, as discussed in Chapter 3, but can not pinpoint the specific period of any shift. The log likelihood ratio test is conducted to find any such shift.

15. The results of the Gujarati tests are more significant for the regressions using another interest proxy than portfolio income. In those regressions, the intercept was significantly different at the .01 level and processing cost was different at the .05 level or better for all three size groups.

16. The results of the regressions when using the other interest proxies for the 1973-1988 period are virtually identical to the above reported results for all deposit groups except for the processing cost variable. While still negatively

related to net earnings, it is no longer significant for any of the regressions using the other interest proxies. The R^2s of the regressions are slightly lower, but generally still above .7500. The pre- and post-1980 regressions for all deposit groups are virtually identical to the ones reported above, except the interest rate proxies are generally less significant.

17. The Farley-Hinich test is significant for the small deposit group and remain so for the larger two groups when the other interest proxies are used in the saving deposit regressions. The results for the Gujarati test change when using the other interest proxies in that only the slope of the interest rate variable is found to be significantly different (and not the intercept or other slope variables), and it is significant for the large deposit group as well. The log likelihood ratio test does change dramatically for the other interest rate proxies. Any change is found to be between 1976 and 1977 for the small and medium deposit groups and between 1983 and 1984 for the large deposit group. This relationship holds for all three of the other interest proxies. The Chow test results are similar to the ones discussed above, with only one of the other tests showing marginal significance.

18. The 1973-1988 regression results for the other interest proxies are virtually identical to the above reported results for the small deposit group. The medium and large deposit groups' results for the same period have the same signs for the variables as reported above, but the interest proxies are no longer significant. The pre-1980 results are virtually identical as those reported above for the small and large deposit groups. The medium deposit group's interest rate proxies are no longer significant, but are of the same sign as reported above. The regressions for the post-1980 period are still insignificant, but the interest proxies and processing cost variables are significant for the small deposit group (with the same signs as reported above) while the large deposit group's interest proxies are no longer significant.

19. When other interest proxies are used in the time deposit regressions, the Farley-Hinich test is uniformly significant for all deposit groups. The Gujarati test results are virtually identical with only a marginal significance for the small deposit group in the slope of the regression using federal funds as the interest proxy. The log likelihood test results differ markedly in that a shift is found between 1977 and 1978 for the small deposit group and between 1980 and 1981 for the medium and large deposit groups. These differences hold for all of the other interest proxies. The Chow test results are the same for the other interest proxies—they are uniformly insignificant for the small and medium deposit groups and significant for the large deposit group.

20. The only difference for the 1973-1988 period regression results when using the other interest proxies than those reported above is that processing costs, while still positively related to net earnings, are no longer significant for the small and medium deposit groups. The pre-1980 regressions are virtually identical to the above reported results for all deposit groups, with the

processing cost variable marginally significant for the small deposit group. The post-1980 period regression results are virtually identical as those reported above.

21. The Farley-Hinich test results for certificates of deposit when the other interest proxies are used are uniformly insignificant. The Gujarati test still shows changes in the intercept for small and medium deposit groups, but also shows a significant change in the interest and processing cost variables for the two groups as well. The large deposit group still shows no significant changes for any interest proxy. The log likelihood results for the other three interest proxies show any switch to have occurred between 1984 and 1985 for the small deposit group and between 1976 and 1977 for the medium deposit group. The test results for the large deposit group finds the switch between 1976 and 1977 for two interest proxy regressions (federal funds and 3-month T-bill) and between 1984 and 1985 for the third. The Chow tests are uniformly insignificant for the small and large deposit groups while the two regressions using treasury bill rates are significant (.05 level) for the medium deposit group.

22. It is possible that at higher interest rates, the banks are able to attract more funds and take advantage of scale economies, thus yielding a greater net earnings level, all else held constant. It is not believed that such scale economies could solely explain the significantly positive interest proxies.

23. The regression results using the other interest proxies are virtually identical to the above reported results for all deposit groups.

24. The results for the Farley-Hinich, Gujarati, and Chow tests are presented for completeness, but are uniformly insignificant as would be expected given the lack of pre-1980 data.

25. The Farley-Hinich test is uniformly not significant for the small and medium deposit groups and uniformly insignificant except for two cases for the large deposit group when other interest proxies are used in the average checkable deposit regressions. Only the large deposit group shows significant changes from the Gujarati test and the service charge variable and the intercept remain the sources of that change. The log likelihood tests agree with those reported above. The Chow test is insignificant for all other interest proxies for all deposit groups.

26. The regression results for the 1973-1988 period when using the other interest proxies are virtually identical to the above reported results for the small and medium deposit groups. The service charge variable is positively signed as before, but marginally significant for both of the two T-bill interest proxies for the small deposit group. The service charge variable is also positively signed for the medium deposit group which differs from the above reported results, although the variable is not statistically significant. The 1973-1988 period results for the large deposit group differ from the above reported results in that the other interest proxies are not significant, although still positively

related to net earnings. The service charge variable is negatively signed, but also not significant. These regressions are also not significant as the earlier one for the large deposit group is. Pre-1980 tests are not possible given data limitations. The post-1980 regression results are virtually identical to those results reported above for all deposit groups.

27. The Farley-Hinich test results for interest-bearing checkable deposits are uniformly insignificant as are the Gujarati tests except for three marginally significant Farley-Hinich tests for the medium deposit group. The log likelihood test does show that any shift in the regression generally occurred between 1982 and 1983 which would coincide with the introduction of money market demand accounts which were permitted by the Garn—St Germain Act of 1982. The results of the Chow tests are generally uniformly significant for the small and medium deposit groups and insignificant for the large deposit group. However, all results for these tests should be interpreted cautiously given the missing data for this deposit type.

28. The regression results for the 1973-1988 period when using the other interest proxies are virtually identical to the above reported results for the small and large deposit groups. The large deposit group's processing cost variable is no longer significant, but is still negatively related to net earnings. The processing cost variable changes from significantly negative to positive for the medium deposit group when the other interest proxies are used. The pre-1980 regression results for the large deposit group are virtually identical to the results reported above. The small deposit group's results for the pre-1980 period differ from those reported above in that the interest proxy is not significant, but still positively related to net earnings; the processing cost and service charge variables are both positively signed, but are not significant. The medium deposit group's pre-1980 results differ from those reported above in that both the service charge and the processing cost variables are significantly positively related to net earnings. In the results reported above, the processing cost variable is negatively related to net earnings, but not significantly so. The post-1980 results for the small and medium groups are virtually identical to the results reported above. The results for the large deposit group finds no variables significantly related to net earnings and the regressions have R^2s of 0.1643 or less.

29. The regression results for the large deposit group when using the other interest proxies for the commercial demand deposits are as with interest checking in that the pre-1980 period has significantly positive interest proxies while the post-1980 period's are not. In fact, they are generally negative (although not significant). Again, this result is consistent with CMT expectations as well as the phaseout of Regulation Q. The Farley-Hinich test is generally significant for the small and medium deposit groups, but always insignificant for the large deposit group for the other interest proxies. The Gujarati test is uniformly insignificant for all deposit groups for the other

interest proxies. The log likelihood tests continue to show any shifts to have occurred between 1978 and 1979 or 1980 and 1981. However, the Chow tests comparing pre- and post-1980 are generally uniformly insignificant.

30. The regression results for the 1973-1988 period using the other interest proxies are virtually identical to the one reported above for all deposit groups. The interest proxies are found to be significantly positive for the two larger deposit groups, but all variables are of the same signs as reported above. The pre-1980 period results are very similar, but the variables, while of the same sign as reported above, are generally much less significantly related to net earnings no matter the variable. The same pattern of results compared to those reported above holds for the post-1980 period.

31. The Farley-Hinich tests for personal checkable deposits for the other interest proxies are generally not significant. The Gujarati tests have significant differences only for the large deposit group with the changes from processing costs and service charges. The log likelihood results for each group are the same as those reported above. The Chow tests comparing pre- and post-1980 are only significant for the medium deposit group.

32. The pre-1980 regressions results when using the other interest rate proxies are very similar to the above reported results for all three deposit groups. The only difference is that the economic proxies are more likely to be of the expected sign, although still insignificantly related to net earnings for the small and large deposit groups. The pre- and post-1980 results are virtually identical to the results reported above for all deposit groups.

33. When the other interest proxies are used in the real estate net earnings regressions, the Farley-Hinich test is still uniformly insignificant for the large deposit group and generally significant for the medium deposit group. These results agree with those reported above. However, the small deposit group's results are generally not significant as reported above. Results from the Gujarati tests generally find any shift to be from the intercept and only for the small deposit group. The log likelihood test results generally agree with those reported above, but with a greater range of potential switch dates than found earlier with deposits. The Chow test results are just as likely to be significant for the small deposit group as not. The two larger deposit groups have only two variations in which the Chow test is found to be significant.

34. The 1973-1988 period regression results are virtually identical to the results reported above when the other interest proxies are used in the model for the medium deposit group. The results for the large deposit group have the same signs, although the interest proxies are more likely to be significantly related to net earnings. The small deposit group's results also have the same signs, but the unemployment variable is significantly negatively related to net earnings. The pre-1980 period results are virtually identical to the results reported above for the medium and large deposit groups. The small deposit group's variables have the same sign, but the interest proxy is generally

significant when unemployment is the economic proxy. The post-1980 period results are virtually identical to those reported above for the two larger deposit groups. Insufficient data do not allow tests for the small deposit group.

35. The Farley-Hinich test results are uniformly insignificant for the small deposit group and generally insignificant for the large deposit group no matter what combination of interest and economic activity proxies are used for credit cards. The results are significant for the medium deposit group for all combinations using unemployment as the economic activity proxy, but are generally not significant for the other economic activity proxies. The Gujarati test generally has the same results as reported above when unemployment is not used as the economic activity proxy and various interest proxies are tested. However, there is only significant change in the intercept (for the large deposit group) and processing cost (large and medium deposit groups) when other economic activity proxies are used. The log likelihood test results generally point to the same switch points as reported above, but with a greater range for the medium deposit group. The Chow tests are uniformly significant with unemployment as the economic activity proxy and generally insignificant with the other economic activity proxies. Lack of post-1980 data does not allow a Chow test for the small deposit group.

36. The regression results for the 1973-1988 period for all deposit groups are virtually identical to the results reported above when using other interest rate proxies. The only difference for the pre-1980 results for any of the deposit groups is that the economic proxies are no longer marginally significant for the small deposit group as compared to the above results, but the sign remains the same. The post-1980 results are virtually identical to those reported above for all deposit groups.

37. The Farley-Hinich test results are uniformly insignificant for the small deposit group no matter the combination of interest and economic activity proxies. However, the medium deposit group's results are generally only significant when unemployment is the economic activity proxy while the large deposit group's results are uniformly significant when unemployment is not the economic activity proxy and generally insignificant when unemployment is included. The Gujarati test results generally do not change. The log likelihood test results are generally as reported above, but with a wide range of possible switch dates. The Chow test results are generally significant for all three deposit groups when unemployment is not used as the economic activity proxy.

38. The results for the 1973-1988 and pre- and post-1980 periods are virtually identical to the results reported above for all deposit groups when the other interest rate proxies are used. The only slight difference is that the interest rate variable is generally less significant when the cost of money is used as the proxy. However, variables signs remain the same.

39. The Farley-Hinich tests for commercial loans are generally significant when the cost of money to the bank is used as the interest proxy, but otherwise generally insignificant. The Gujarati tests generally show the same pattern as reported above, except when unemployment is used as the economic activity proxy. The tests then show change only in the unemployment variable and only for the large deposit group. The log likelihood test show the same pattern for the switches, but find a wider range for the medium deposit group. The Chow tests are generally as reported above no matter the proxies used.

40. The OBHC category contains bank holding companies that are OBHCs and also those companies that are known to be BHCs, but could not be determined if they were OBHCs or MBHCs. For this reason, the test results are not expected to be as clear as they might have been otherwise.

41. Flannery and James (1984) report that common stock returns of depository institutions are correlated with interest rate changes. As the maturity gap of an institutions assets versus its liabilities increases, the greater the stock returns, on average. Therefore, some of the rise in the market valuation measures is potentially explained by generally rising interest rates (assuming that the average bank maintains a positive maturity gap) as well as the general rise in stock market values during the 1980s.

42. The BHC category includes OBHCs and those companies that are known to be BHCs, but not known specifically to be OBHCs or MBHCs.

43. The possibility of regulatory avoidance measures such as MBHCs, chain banking, et cetera is ignored when assuming that the banking organization in a unit banking state is limited to one office.

44. It is also possible that banking operations in states allowing some form of branching are better able to take advantage of potential scale economies and, thus, have higher EMVs.

V

Implications of Results and Future Research

This chapter is organized as follows: first, a short summary of the findings from Chapter 4 are presented followed by a discussion of the implications of those results and finally, future research questions to be examined are listed.

SUMMARY OF RESULTS

Chapter 4 presented detailed results from four different methodologies to test for CMT implications in the U.S. commercial banking industry: profitability measurement for individual products, a one factor market model, excess market value, and Tobin's q approximation. The general findings of the profitability measurement tests are that evidence of imperfect contestability is found for credit card and installment loans and for personal and interest-bearing checkable deposits. These results are as generally expected given the discussion of CMT and the regulatory environment during test period in Chapter 1.

CMT predicts lower prices (net earnings) in areas that are opened to potential competitors. DIDMCA and Garn—St Germain allowed thrifts and credit unions, which traditionally focus on individuals and not businesses, to compete directly with banks in new areas without eliminating competition in product areas already allowed. That evidence of imperfect contestability is found for credit card and installment loans and for personal and interest-bearing checkable deposits is as expected because these products are marketed to individuals—the domain of the new potential competitors, S&Ls and credit unions. No evidence of a newly contestable environment is found for the product areas in which competition already existed before DIDMCA and Garn—St Germain. Traditional savings accounts and CDs, for example, did not react in the same manner as the newly competitive areas. Finally, products that were not believed to be greatly affected by this new potential competition, such as real estate and commercial loans, also did not react in the manner of the products found to exhibit qualities of imperfect contestability.

It most be noted that the results are consistent with other economic conditions during the test period. Results consistent with CMT that show banks paying relatively higher rates to customers are also consistent with the phaseout of Regulation Q in many cases. The generally lower net earnings in products is also consistent with the higher operating costs of initiating automated services such as ATMs. Finally, the increase in loan losses, especially from oil and LDC loans, are consistent with lower commercial loan net earnings.

The results of the one factor market model provide some support for CMT in that MBHCs and BHCs are found to have generally greater betas than banks and MBHCs have greater betas than BHCs. Multistate operations are found to have significantly greater betas than one-state operations as CMT would predict. The comparison of statewide and limited branching states to unit banking states reveals that statewide branching has greater betas, as expected, while the limited branching comparison results did not support CMT. Comparing statewide with limited branching produced greater betas for the statewide branching group as CMT predicts. However, the results are not uniformly in support of CMT. While the difference between MBHCs and BHCs becomes significant after the 1970s as CMT would predict, the difference between the two bank holding company forms, MBHCs and BHCs, and banks lessens. This result is not as CMT would predict, but the evidence is not considered very strong given the limited number of observations in the bank category.[1] More worrisome is the general pattern for the betas for each year 1973 through 1988. CMT would predict greater betas as threats of entry increased, which should lead to a pattern of greater betas from 1973 through 1982 or possibly further. However, no such pattern is found.

The results from the excess market value (EMV) test should find lower EMV with greater threats of entry to agree with CMT implications. The general pattern of a switch from negative to positive EMVs around 1982 is not as CMT would predict, but is not totally unexpected given the confounding factors of generally rising stock market values, lower interest rate levels, the economic expansion, and the write down of the book value of LDC loans. Comparison of MBHCs and BHCs with banks finds results that do not support CMT, but are not statistically significant. Comparing MBHCs and BHCs provides some support for CMT with MBHCs having lower EMV after 1978. Stronger evidence in support of CMT is found in comparing multistate and one-state operations. The multistate operations are found to have lower EMVs after 1979. Comparing statewide and limited branching states with unit banking states finds lower EMVs for the unit banking subset after 1983. This pattern is generally not supportive of CMT. The comparison of statewide and limited branching subsets finds the statewide branching states to have higher EMVs, which is also not supportive of CMT.

The results from the Tobin's q approximation closely follow those of the EMV method and will not be discussed further. The similarity in the results of the two tests is not surprising since the market value of the liabilities and any preferred stock is proxied by their book values in the calculations and, therefore, the only source of difference between book and market value comes from common stock. Given the general rise in the stock market from 1982, the finding of greater EMV and q approximation values from 1982 is not surprising. However, these results are still generally not as CMT would predict, but not unexpected given the confounding factors affecting both EMV and q approximation measures.

IMPLICATIONS

Overall, the findings from the tests of the entire firms (as opposed to individual products) are not surprising given that only certain products are found to exhibit characteristics of contestability and appear imperfectly contestable at best. The implications of these tests are many. General implications for CMT are discussed first followed by discussion for the banking sector in particular.

The results continue the general pattern of less than conclusive findings for CMT from studies in other industries such as transportation. The nature of contestability requires that one keep records of prices (or earnings spreads) for given products, but it is quite normal that the required records are not kept until after a new threat of entry is perceived or actual entry has occurred. This system helps lead to less sensitive tests and, perhaps, poorer results.

The earlier conjecture of Bailey and Baumol (1984) that contestability may not hold immediately with deregulation is supported by the general findings of this paper. Of course, the question then becomes: how long does it take for contestability to take hold? Given that the theory is predicated on reactions to threatened entry, a delay in reacting to potential entry, even in a deregulatory framework, should be taken as evidence against CMT. This criticism of CMT must be tempered by remembering that the theory is based on a rational expectations framework that emphasizes information allocation efficiency. Even in a "slow" informational context, perfect results would not be expected. Therefore, the fact that results in this study are not ideal is not surprising given the tremendous amount of information in the test period that must be considered as less than normal.[2] [3]

Another implication for CMT studies is to reinforce the idea that focusing on competition at the firm level may preclude finding instances of contestability. The stronger evidence supporting contestability in the transportation industry has generally been found at the market and not firm level. This study shows the same is true in the banking industry. Another implication for CMT is that the relatively small potential competitors in this case may not have had the impact on the banking industry that a larger potential competitor may have. Theoretically, a perfectly contestable market would be affected by relatively small entrants. However, it seems that imperfectly contestable markets are not greatly affected when the potential new entrants are relatively small compared to the incumbents.

In the banking sector, the implications of the results are somewhat different for the three main groups of players in the industry: customers, bankers, and regulators. For the customers, the results show that a limited number of "banks" does not necessarily mean a limited amount of competition for banking products and services. Individual consumers are helped by the deregulation of the 1980s, as evidenced by the relatively lower net earnings margins for banks in areas in which new competition was both threatened and realized. It must be noted that this threat of entry has not worked uniformly well for consumers, as evidenced by the sustained profitability of the credit card industry even with the entry of traditionally non-finance companies such as Sears' Discover Card and AT&T's indirect entry via purchased credit card receivables. However, it is quite reasonable to argue that banks' earnings from credit cards would have been even greater if the additional competitors had not entered the market.[4] Overall, consumers should continue to hope for product innovations that blur traditional lines or for greater regulatory relaxation to allow more effective threats to incumbents which force lower earnings spreads.

The implications of the results to bankers is that they need to continue to make their production processes more efficient to enable them to keep earning margins at historical levels. They also should worry about their proposed entrances into the investment banking and insurance markets (to name the two most likely areas).[5] The evidence from this study suggests that the earnings level of the incumbents will decrease with new entry. Assuming that commercial bankers have no cost advantage or disadvantage in any proposed entry areas, they should include this likelihood of lower earnings spreads and not assume that present or historical earnings levels of the incumbents will be found. Such entry should help consumers, but may not provide the earnings desired by the bankers pushing for entry into the new product areas.

The most important implications of the results from the study are for regulators. First, focusing regulations on entry and exit at the firm level may be reducing competition (which is part of the desired results from the viewpoint of deposit insurance programs). The regulatory system that is now in place does almost as much to inhibit potential competition as to promote it. Many of the deregulatory actions of the 1980s were intended to allow regional product innovations that were created to circumscribe the then current regulatory environment to be legally offered nationwide. Any regulation that increases the barriers to entry, thus making circumscription of those regulations more difficult, potentially harms the consumer by decreasing the amount of potential competition.

Second, regulations that are aimed at disallowing certain mergers based on market share or market concentration indexes may not be appropriate, if effective competition can be had from other non-traditional sources or if new entry is possible from traditional competitors. The results of this study imply that consumers would be helped more if regulators allowed greater competition between the potential offerers of financial products.

FUTURE RESEARCH

The results of this study point to particular future research areas and raise the possibility of such studies in other areas. The most obvious area for future study is to obtain disaggregated FCA data from the Federal Reserve System to allow the current profitability tests to be run with greater accuracy. Another possible use for that data would be to then create a matched-pair sample based on asset size (and possibly other characteristics) with firms reported on the CRSP tapes. These data could be used to recalculate the one factor model, EMV, and Tobin's q approximations to see if results between the calculation methods are in closer agreement when more closely accounting for size of the institutions in the data sets.

Additional work to separate the current market data into money center and regional banks may provide additional insight based on the result of Black, Fields, and Schweitzer (1990) who found the reaction as measured by abnormal returns of money center and regional banks to differ with the passage of legislation that would allow interstate banking mergers. It is quite likely that knowing the timing of these abnormal returns may provide added insight to the studied firms in two such subsets.[6]

The increase in shareholder owned S&Ls during the test period lends the possibility of examining the market based measurements for these institutions as well. It is expected that great difficulty will arise in interpreting results given the problems in the S&L industry during the study period.

Two potential areas of competition for banks in the future are insurance companies and investment banks, as mentioned above. The threatened entry of the commercial banks into these areas provides two other possible areas to test CMT implications by examining the earnings spreads of the current incumbents. CMT would predict a lowering of the earnings of the incumbents given the greater potential of entry by bank holding company subsidiaries.

A very rich potential area for testing CMT implications inside the financial institutions arena and with almost all other industries is the European Economic Community's 1992 union. Almost every industry is now faced with greater potential competition with the union as national market lines are intended to blur. These threats of entry should bring reduced prices for consumers and/or reduced earnings margins for the incumbents.

NOTES

1. Another reason why the decreasing difference between banks and the bank holding companies is possibly not very strong is the argument contained in Chapter 4 that was made for banks in unit banking states. It was argued there that banks in unit banking states could possibly be affected more by the new potential competitors given their lesser ability to practice regulatory avoidance as compared to banks in limited or statewide branching states. The same argument applies here if banks had less ability to practice regulatory avoidance than BHCs and MBHCs to minimize the affects of the new potential competitors. If this argument were closer to the truth, then the results of the decreasing difference between banks and the bank holding companies could be supportive of CMT expectations.

2. Some of the unusual information set during the 1973-1988 period includes: the OPEC related inflation periods of 1973 and 1979, the long economic expansion in the 1980s, the default on many LDC loans, the S&L industry's woes, the increase in bank failures, and the regulatory changes to name just some of major stories.

3. CMT is put forth as to be both in the "short run" and the "long run" as Davies and Lee (1988) point out. However, there is very little distinction as to when the switch from short term to long term takes place in the theory. Therefore, changes in regulations would usually take place in the short term and a theoretically contestable market may be delayed in its reaction to additional threats of entry.

4. The aggressive marketing techniques, such as mass mailings with pre-approved credit lines, has led to greater default percentages in card issuers portfolios. To maintain earnings, more credit card processing operations are being combined to achieve economies of scale. (See Table 1.1 for a listing of recent credit card portfolio sales.) The new competition from Sears and AT&T has brought an opportunity cost to the traditional credit card issuers in the form of possibly lower profits than would have been earned otherwise.

5. The banking industry's efforts to enter the insurance field was given a boost when a federal appeals court overturned a Federal Reserve Bank ruling that would not have allowed state-chartered subsidiaries of bank holding companies to underwrite and sell insurance. (Lambert, W. and D.B. Hilder. Banks Cleared to Underwrite, Sell Insurance. *Wall Street Journal* June 11, 1991 p. 3.)

6. Black, Fields, and Schweitzer (1990) found significantly negative abnormal returns for money center banks and significantly positive abnormal returns for regional banks on the passage of the interstate banking legislation.

They argue that the restriction of the money center banks from the agreements was a major potential reason for the difference between the two groups.

BIBLIOGRAPHY

Amel, D.F. and D.G. Keane. State Laws Affecting Commercial Bank Branching, Multibank Holding Company Expansion, and Interstate Banking. *Issues in Bank Regulation* Autumn 1986, pp. 30-40.

Ausubel, L.M. The Failure of Competition in the Credit Card Market. *The American Economic Review* March 1991, pp. 50-81.

Bailey, E.E. and W.J. Baumol. Deregulation and the Theory of Contestable Markets. *Yale Journal on Regulation* Volume 1, 1984, pp. 111-137.

Bailey, E.E. and A.F. Friedlaender. Market Structure and Multiproduct Industries. *Journal of Economic Literature* September 1982, pp. 1024-1048.

Bain, J.S. *Barriers to New Competition.* Cambridge: Harvard University Press, 1956.

Baumol, W.J. Contestable Markets: An Uprising in the Theory of Industry Structure. *American Economic Review* March 1982, pp. 1-15.

Baumol, W.J., J.C. Panzar, and R.D. Willig. *Contestable Markets and the Theory of Industry Structure.* Harcourt Brace Jovanovich, 1982.

Baumol, W.J. and R.D. Willig. Contestability: Developments Since the Book. *Oxford Economic Papers* November 1986, pp. 9-36.

Benston, G.J. Economies of Scale of Financial Institutions. *Journal of Money, Credit, and Banking* May 1972, pp. 312-341.

Berger, A.N., G.A. Hanweck, and D.B. Humphrey. Competitive Viability in Banking (Scale, Scope, and Product Mix Economies). *Journal of Monetary Economics* Volume 20, 1987, pp. 501-520.

Black, H.A., M.A. Fields, and R.L. Schweitzer. Changes in Interstate Banking Laws: The Impact on Shareholder Wealth. *Journal of Finance* December 1990, pp. 1663-1671.

Boczar, G.E. Competition Between Banks and Finance Companies: A Cross-Section Study of Personal Loan Debtors. *Journal of Finance* March 1978, pp. 245-258.

Brewer, E., III. The Impact of Deregulation on the True Cost of Savings Deposits: Evidence from Illinois and Wisconsin Savings and Loan Associations. *Journal of Economics and Business* February 1988, pp. 79-95.

Brock, W.A. Contestable Markets and the Theory of Industry Structure: A Review. *Journal of Political Economy* 1983, pp. 1055-1068.

Brown, R.L., J. Durbin, and J.M. Evans. Techniques for Testing the Constancy of Regression Relationships over Time. *Journal of the Royal Statistical Society*, Series B Volume 37, Number 2 1975, pp. 149-192.

Bundt, T.P. and R. Schweitzer. Deregulation, Deposit Markets, and Banks' Costs of Funds. *The Financial Review* August 1989, pp. 417-430.

Butler, R.V. and J.H. Houston. How Contestable Are Airline Markets? *Atlantic Economic Journal* June 1989, pp. 27-35.

Caves, R.E. and M.E. Porter. From Entry Barriers to Mobility Barriers: Conjectural Decisions and Contrived Deterrence to New Competition. *Quarterly Journal of Economics* May 1977, pp. 241-261.

Cebenoyan, A.S. Scope Economies in Banking: The Hybrid Box-Cox Function. *The Financial Review* February 1990, pp. 115-125.

Chen, K.C., G.L. Hide, and D.C. Cheng. Barriers to Entry, Concentration, and Tobin's Q Ratio. *Quarterly Journal of Business and Economics* Spring 1989, pp. 32-49.

Chow, G.C. Tests of Equality Between Sets of Coefficients in Two Linear Regressions. *Econometrica* July 1960, pp. 591-605.

Clark, J.A. The Efficient Structure Hypothesis: More Evidence from Banking. *Quarterly Review of Economics and Business* Autumn 1987, pp. 25-39.

———. Market Structure, Risk, and Profitability: The Quiet Life Hypothesis Revisited. *Quarterly Review of Economics and Business* Spring 1986, pp. 45-56.

Clark, J.B. *The Control of Trusts* New York, MacMillan, 1912.

Cook, T. and L. D'Antonio. Credit Union Taxation: Competitive Effects. *Journal of Economics and Business* May 1984, pp. 251-262.

Cooperman, E.S., W.B. Lee, and J.P. Lesage. Commercial Bank and Thrift Interdependence and Local Market Competition for Retail Certificates of Deposit. *Journal of Financial Services Research* March 1990, pp. 37-52.

Davies, J.E. The Theory of Contestable Markets and its Application to the Linear Shipping Industry. Canadian Transport Commission, Ottawa-Hull, 1986.

Davies, J.E. and F.S. Lee. A Post Keynesian Appraisal of the Contestability Criterion. *Journal of Post Keynesian Economics* Fall 1988, pp. 3-24.

Dowling, W.A. and G.C. Philippatos. Economies of Scale in the U.S. Savings and Loan Industry: 1973-83. *Applied Economics* Number 21, 1989, pp. 1-12.

Dowling, W.A., G.C. Philippatos, and D. Choi. Economies of Scale Through Mergers in the S&L Industry. *Proceedings of a Conference on Bank Structure and Competition*, Federal Reserve Bank of Chicago, Chicago, Illinois, 1983 pp. 480-497.

Ederington, L.H. and S.L. Skogstad. Measurement of Banking Competition and Geographic Markets: The Market for Checking Account Services. *Journal of Money, Credit, and Banking* August 1977, pp. 469-482.

Elliehausen, G.E. and J.D. Wolken. Product Segmentation and Market Definition for Consumer Credit. *Working Paper in Banking, Finance, and Microeconomics* No. 86-2. Federal Reserve System, April 1986.

———. Market Definition and Product Segmentation for Household Credit. *Journal of Financial Services Research* Volume 4, 1990, pp. 21-35.

Farley, J.U. and M.J. Hinich. A Test for a Shifting Slope Coefficient in a Linear Model. *Journal of the American Statistical Association*. September 1970, Theory and Methods Section, pp. 1320-1329.

———. Detecting "Small" Mean Shifts in Time Series. *Management Science*. November 1970, pp. 189-199.

Farley, J.U., M. Hinich, and T.W. McGuire. Some Comparisons of Tests for a Shift in the Slopes of a Multivariate Linear Time Series Model. *Journal of Econometrics* August 1975, pp. 297-318.

Flannery, M.J. How Do Changes in Market Interest Rates Affect Bank Profits? *Business Review* Federal Reserve Bank of Philadelphia September/October 1980, pp. 13-22.

Flannery, M.J. and C.M. James. The Effect of Interest Rate Changes on the Common Stock Returns of Financial Institutions. *Journal of Finance* September 1984, pp. 1141-1153.

Gauger, J.A. and J.R. Schroeter. Measuring the Nearness of Modern Near-monies: Evidence from the 1980s. *Journal of Macroeconomics* Spring 1990, pp. 247-261.

Gilbert, R.A. Bank Market Structure and Competition: A Survey. *Journal of Money, Credit, and Banking* November 1984, pp. 617-645.

Gujarati, D. Use of Dummy Variables in Testing for Equality Between Sets of Coefficients in Two Linear Regressions: A Note. *The American Statistician* February 1970, pp. 50-52.

Hannan, T. Bank Profitability and the Threat of Entry. *Journal of Bank Research* Summer 1983, pp. 157-163.

Hanweck, G.A. and S.A. Rhoades. Dominant Firms, "Deep Pockets," and Local Market Competition. *Journal of Economics and Business* December 1984, pp. 391-402.

Heggestad, A.A. A Survey of Studies on Banking Competition and Performance. In *Issues in Financial Regulation*, F.R. Edwards (ed.) 1979.

———. Comment on Bank Market Structure and Competition: A Survey. *Journal of Money, Credit, and Banking* November 1984, pp. 645-650.

Heggestad, A.A. and J.J. Mingo. The Competitive Condition of U.S. Banking Markets and the Impacts of Structural Reform. *Journal of Finance* June 1977, pp. 649-661.

———. Prices, Nonprices, and Concentration in Commercial Banking. *Journal of Money, Credit, and Banking* February 1976, pp. 107-117.

Hirschey, M. Market Structure and Market Value. *Journal of Business* Volume 58, Number 1, 1985, pp. 89-98.

Hirschey, M. and D.W. Wichern. Accounting and Market Value Measures of Profitability: Consistency, Determinants, and Uses. *Journal of Business and Economic Statistics* October 1984, pp. 375-383.

Hunter, W.C. and S.G. Timme. Technical Change, Organizational Form, and the Structure of Bank Production. *Journal of Money, Credit, and Banking* May 1986, pp. 152-166.

Hunter, W.C., S.G. Timme, and W.K. Yang. An Examination of Cost Subadditivity and Multiproduct Production in Large U.S. Banks. *Journal of Money, Credit, and Banking* November 1990, pp. 504-525.

Kane, E.J. Technological and Regulatory Forces in the Developing Fusion of Financial-Services Competition. *Journal of Finance* July 1984, pp. 759-772.

Kidwell, D.S. Technological and Regulatory Forces in the Developing Fusion of Financial-Services Competition: Discussion. *Journal of Finance* July 1984, pp. 772-773.

Kidwell, D.S. and R.L. Peterson. *Financial Institutions, Markets, and Money*, Third Edition. Dryden, 1987.

Lambert, W. and D.B. Hilder. Banks Cleared to Underwrite, Sell Insurance. *Wall Street Journal* June 11, 1991 p.3.

Lapp, J.S. The Determination of Savings and Loan Association Deposit Rates in the Absence of Rate Ceilings: A Cross-Section Approach. *Journal of Finance* March 1978, pp. 215-230.

Lawrence, C. Banking Costs, Generalized Functional Forms, and Estimation of Economies of Scale and Scope. *Journal of Money, Credit, and Banking* August 1989, pp. 368-379.

Liang, N. and S.A. Rhoades. Geographic Diversification and Risk in Banking. *Journal of Economics and Business* Volume 40, 1988, pp. 271-284.

Lindenberg, E.B. and S.A. Ross. Tobin's q Ratio and Industrial Organization. *Journal of Business* January 1981, pp. 1-32.

Lindsey, D.E. Structural Disequilibrium and the Banking Act of 1980: Discussion. *Journal of Finance* May 1982, pp. 397-398.

Marlow, M.L. Bank Structure and Mortgage Rates: Implications for Interstate Banking. *Journal of Economics and Business* Volume 34, 1982, pp. 135-142.

————. Bank Structure and Mortgage Rates: Reply. *Journal of Economics and Business* Volume 36, 1984, pp. 289-290.

————. Entry and Performance in Financial Markets. *Journal of Bank Research* Autumn 1983, pp. 227-230.

Mester, L.J. A Multiproduct Cost Study of Savings and Loans. *Journal of Finance* June 1987, pp. 423-445.

Mitchell, D.W. Explicit and Implicit Demand Deposit Interest. *Journal of Money, Credit, and Banking* May 1979, pp. 182-191.

————. Explicit Interest and Demand Deposit Service Charges. *Journal of Money, Credit, and Banking* May 1988, pp. 270-274.

Morrison, S. A. and C. Winston. Empirical Implications and Tests of the Contestability Hypothesis. *Journal of Law and Economics* April 1987, pp. 53-66.

Mullineaux, D.J. Economies of Scale and Organizational Efficiency in Banking: A Profit-Function Approach. *Journal of Finance* March 1978, pp. 259-280.

Murray, J.D. and R.W. White. Economies of Scale and Economies of Scope in Multiproduct Financial Institutions: A Study of British Columbia Credit Unions. *Journal of Finance* June 1983, pp. 887-902.

Nathan, A. Contestability, Cost Efficiency, and Competitive Viability of the Canadian Banking System. FMA Finance Doctoral Consortium -1988.

Noulas, A.G., S.C. Ray, and S.M. Miller. Returns to Scale and Input Substitution for Large U.S. Banks. Unpublished Manuscript 1989.

Panzar, J.C. and R.D. Willig. Economies of Scope. *American Economic Review* May 1981, pp. 268-272.

Pyle, D.H. The Losses on Savings Deposits from Interest Rate Regulation. *Bell Journal of Economics and Management Science* Autumn 1974, pp. 614-622.

Quandt, R.E. The Estimation of the Parameters of a Linear Regression System Obeying Two Separate Regimes. *American Statistical Association Journal* December 1958, pp. 873-880.

———. Tests of the Hypothesis that a Linear Regression System Obeys Two Separate Regimes. *American Statistical Association Journal* June 1960, pp. 324-330.

Rhoades, S.A. Structure and Performance Studies in Banking: A Summary and Evaluation. *Staff Economic Studies* Board of Governors of the Federal Reserve System, Fall 1977.

———. Nonbank Thrift Institutions as Determinants of Performance in Banking Markets. *Journal of Economics and Business* Fall 1979, pp. 66-72.

Rose, J.T. Entry in Commercial Banking, 1962-78: A Comment. *Journal of Money, Credit, and Banking* May 1986, pp. 247-249.

Rose, P.S. Diversification of the Banking Firm. *The Financial Review* May 1989, pp. 251-280.

Schmidt, P.J. Comment on Bank Market Structure and Competition: A Survey. *Journal of Money, Credit, and Banking* November 1984, pp. 656-660.

Schwartz, M. The Nature and Scope of Contestability Theory. *Oxford Economic Papers* November 1986, pp. 37-57.

Sealey, C.W., Jr. Interest-Bearing Demand Deposits, Bank Costs, and Economic Efficiency. *Journal of Economics and Business* Winter 1979, pp. 134-137.

Shaffer, S. Cross-Subsidization in Checking Accounts. *Journal of Money, Credit, and Banking* February 1984, pp. 100-109.

Sharpe, W.F. A Simplified Model for Portfolio Analysis, *Management Science* January 1963, pp. 277-293.

———. Capital Asset Prices: A Theory of Market Equilibrium Under Conditions of Risk, *Journal of Finance* September 1964, pp. 425-442.

Shepherd, W.G. "Contestability" vs. Competition. *The American Economic Review* September 1984, pp. 572-587.

Slovin, M.B. and M.E. Sushka. A Note on the Evidence on Alternative Models of the Banking Firm: A Cross Section Study of Commercial Loan Rates. *Journal of Banking and Finance* March 1984, pp. 99-108.

Small, K.A. and H.S. Rosen. Applied Welfare Economics with Discrete Choice Models. *Econometrica* January 1981, pp. 105-130.

Smirlock, M. Evidence on the (Non)Relationship between Concentration and Profitability in Banking. *Journal of Money, Credit, and Banking* February 1985, pp. 69-83.

Smith, P.F. Structural Disequilibrium and the Banking Act of 1980. *Journal of Finance* May 1982, pp. 385-393.

Spence, M. *Contestable Markets and the Theory of Industry Structure*: A Review Article. *Journal of Economic Literature* September 1983, pp. 980-990.

Startz, R. Implicit Interest on Demand Deposits. *Journal of Monetary Economics* October 1979, pp. 515-534.

Teece, D.J. Economies of Scope and the Scope of the Enterprise. *Journal of Economic Behavior and Organization* September 1980, pp. 223-247.

Thomadakis, S.B. A Value-based Test of Profitability and Market Structure. *Review of Economics and Statistics* May 1977, pp. 179-185.

Thomas, C.R. and R.J. Rivard. Geographic Deregulation and New Bank Entry in Florida. *Atlantic Economic Journal* June 1990, pp. 57-65.

Tobin, J. A General Equilibrium Approach to Monetary Theory. *Journal of Money, Credit, and Banking* February 1969, pp. 15-29.

———. Monetary Policies and the Economy: The Transmission Mechanism. *Southern Economic Journal* April 1978, pp. 421-431.

Wolken, J.D. and F.W. Derrick. Advertising, Market Power, and Non-Price Competition: Evidence from Commercial Banking. Working Papers in Banking, Finance, & Microeconomics. Federal Reserve System, April 1986.

Banks & Branches Data Book. Published by the Federal Deposit Insurance Corporation for each year 1981-1988.

Economic Report of the President (1989). U.S. Government Printing Office, Washington, D.C. 1990.

Functional Cost Analysis. Published by the Federal Reserve System for each year 1973-1988.

Moody's Bank & Finance Manual. Published by Moody's Investor Services, Inc. New York for each year 1973-1990.

INDEX